General Reference Clauses in the Judicial Process

Lex et Res Publica

Polish Legal and Political Studies

Edited by Anna Jaroń

Volume 19

PETER LANG

Leszek Leszczyński

General Reference Clauses in the Judicial Process

Context of Legislative Intentions and Interpretative Discretion

PETER LANG

Bibliographic Information published by the Deutsche Nationalbibliothek
The Deutsche Nationalbibliothek lists this publication
in the Deutsche Nationalbibliografie; detailed bibliographic
data is available online at http://dnb.d-nb.de.

Library of Congress Cataloging-in-Publication Data
A CIP catalog record for this book has been applied for at the
Library of Congress.

Cover illustration: Courtesy of Benjamin Ben Chaim

This work contains the results of a study conducted as part of a research project funded by
the National Science Centre, project number 2016/21/B/HS5/00139,
entitled "Aksjologiczna dyskrecjonalność sędziowska. Między intencjami prawodawcy a
autonomią sądownictwa".

This work has been reviewed by Marko Novak
(New University in Nova Gorica, Slovenia).

ISSN 2191-3250
ISBN 978-3-631-85789-2 (Print)
E-ISBN 978-3-631-86337-4 (E-Book)
E-ISBN 978-3-631-86340-4 (EPUB)
DOI 10.3726/b18767

Peter Lang – Berlin · Bern · Bruxelles · New York ·
Oxford · Warszawa · Wien

www.peterlang.com

Table of contents

Introduction

1. The monograph,[1] containing an analysis of the functioning of axiological extra-legal references expressed in general clauses is based on two assumptions. The first of them is that this type of reference constitutes a common means of normative expression today, appearing as an instrument of legislative policy regardless of the type of political system in which the law is created, and regardless of the type of branch of law to which the said legislative activity relates. The second assumption, in turn, raises the frequency of the use of this normative structure by courts and administrative bodies in the processes of applying the law, not excluding taking the extra-legal criteria into account by the ordinary addressees when exercising their own subjective rights.

The presence of extra-legal references in contemporary legal systems, initiated by the so-called great European civil law codifications of the nineteenth century (which included, among others, references to the criteria of customs, equity, good faith, good manners or public order), altered the form and content of law. By changing the linguistic properties of legal texts, it opened the content of the law to social, political and economic norms and values. By saturating the processes of creating and implementing law with axiology, it significantly broadened the scope of judicial decision-making freedom. References thus become the most "informal" and sensitive component of legal discourse, both in the context of its ties with social discourse, and its susceptibility to the influence of political discourse.

The main objective of the present work is to define the relationship between the intentions of the legislator creating purposefully extra-legal references as part of statutory law order and the use of the axiological decision-making discretion by the organs applying the law. The way in which this freedom is exercised in judicial application of the law substantially affects not only the functioning of the extra-legal references themselves, but also the functioning of the entire legal order. Hence, so important for the shape of the model of this relationship is the real independence of judiciary, which, within the legal discourse, ultimately determines the effects of referring to extra-legal values and norms. Its lack or

---

1 The work was prepared in the result of the research project entitled "Axiological judicial discretion. Between the intentions of the legislator and the autonomy of the judiciary," financed by the National Science Centre on the basis of contract No. 2016/21/B/HS5/00139.

even a limited scope creates the advantage of political discourse over legal discourse, regardless of whether it is about the general dimension of the law or its specific elements.

The study has been prepared on the basis of the application of an analytical research method, leading to the development of appropriately generalized comparative conclusions and an attempt to outline an optimization model for the legal order of a democratic rule of law state. It is based on theoretical legal literature, both Polish and foreign. The purpose of analyses, however, was not polemics with individual approaches and doctrinal statements, quoting them merely in the context of emphasizing the presence of the issue in the theoretical discourse. This is because the statements formulated in the present work have been built on the base of author's own jurisdictional experience (as the judge of The Supreme Administrative Court in Poland) as well as on analysis of normative regulations and various courts' decisions (or actually – their justifications) in which references appear. Evidently, the majority of examples are taken from the Polish legal order (embracing judicial practice of both before and after 1989 periods), although legal orders of other countries (mainly European ones), as well as the jurisprudence of the European Court of Human Rights, were also referred to.

2. Extra-legal references have impact on all components of the law application process, shaping its autonomy in relation to legislative activities. They appear already in the process of establishing the facts of the case (where their influence is still relatively small), only to play a fundamental role in the various phases of operative interpretation of the law made in the decision-making process. By linking its participation in it with the determination of the basis for the application of the clause and with the determination of the content of the extra-legal criteria contained therein, the references are included in all interpretative activities leading to the construction of a normative basis for a decision, later reduced to the decision of application of the law itself.

The structure of the present work, consisting of six chapters, serves the purpose of defining the relationship between legislative intentions and axiological decision-making discretion in the processes of applying the law. The first one concerns the creation of references, the subsequent three – their application, while the last two are devoted to essential comparisons and generalizations, both descriptive and optimizing.

Chapter I presents the issue of creating extra-legal references in the form of general clauses, which are an example of an intentional normative structure forming an element of legislative policy, which, in turn, may assume various specific purposes of references. Its subject is the analysis of various linguistic forms of clauses, their localization within the regulatory system and the determination of the initial conditions for the functioning of references, which is to help determine the scale of the legislator's (acting in various political systems) influence on the use of references.

Chapter II analyses the grounds for including an extra-legal reference in a process of applying the law, assuming that the use of the clause is determined by the decision-making need. A reference may be used in various ways, among which its direct application from a legal provision regulating the respective facts of the case (specific provision) is admittedly the basic method, albeit only one of the few possible. It is also necessary to distinguish between indirect applications ("borrowing" references) from other applicable legal provisions (specific or general ones) and the use of references that are not grounded in the applicable provisions, which broadens the scope of the decisional freedom.

The broadest scope of discretion however is connected with, analysed in Chapter III of the study, determination of the content of extra-legal criteria expressed in the reference clause. This reasoning manifests itself primarily in linking the content of these criteria in various combinations of moral, political or economic axiology, largely regardless of the verbal form of the referring clause. What is not without significance for the final result of these content determinations is the possibility of combining these types of axiology (in various configurations, including collision relations) as well as its "juridization," "normativization" and "concretization" in the context of the properties of the established facts of the case, which constitutes a kind of verification of general axiological content.

Specifying the basis for the application of the clause and determining the content of the criteria leads to the inclusion of references in the operative interpretation of the law. The role of references in reasoning and interpretative activities is the subject of Chapter IV. It manifests itself first in the form of the participation of extra-legal criteria in the so-called interpretative orientation, then modification of the basis for the application of legal provisions (after all, they play the role of the basic carrier of law in the culture of statutory law) and modification of the process of reconstruction of the legal norms contained therein. The patterns of behaviour interpreted in this way, containing some element of extra-legal axiology, then participate in the construction of the final normative basis of the decision, which will ultimately be reduced to the content of the decision on the application of law with regard to the qualification of the facts of the case and the determination of its legal consequences.

The work ends with two chapters, which are in a way summarizing its detailed arrangements, relating both to the creation and application of extra-legal references.

The assumption of the analyses carried out in Chapter V is the need to capture not only universal relationships, but also to take a relativistic view that creates the comparative conclusions. The factors that structure this image are: the type of legal culture (which makes it possible to perceive the role of extra-legal references also in orders different than the order of statutory law), the type of social environment of law (indicating the differences in these roles in the democratic and autocratic political system and the specificity of the situation of deep social change), the location of references within the legal system (especially their place in the structure of the normative act and in the vertical and horizontal structure of the legal system) and the type of decision-making practice (indicating the distinct features of the administrative type of application of law and the differences in the application of references by different kinds of courts).

In Chapter VI, which concludes the work, there is room for generalizations regarding the functions performed by references in the order of statutory law. The three main effects of the clauses: of opening up and "deformalizing" the legal content, of broadening the decision-making discretion and of "axiologizing" the entire legal order, has been here emphasized. The result of these generalizations is an attempt to come with a draft of an optimization model relating both to the creation and application of extra-legal references in a democratic rule of law state, an element of which is an independent judiciary, undeniably playing the most fundamental role here.

Chapter I Extra-legal references and legislative intentions

1. The legal system and its opening

1.1. Methods for opening the legal system

The relations between formal and informal components of the legal order constitute an important element of development of law. It is also not unanimously settled in the history of law and legal thought. Within its framework attaching greater importance to formalistic elements is intertwined with periods, when greater importance was given to elements directly "detaching" from the form of law (the letter of the law). For example, the analysis of the way law is understood and its role in pre-state societies and societies that organize simpler organizational forms of the state clearly gives us the impression of the dominant role of customs and moral norms as the basis for making "legal decisions" in specific matters concerning the life of individuals and the functioning of the community.[1] On the other hand, early state codifications (e.g. the Code of Hammurabi), leave no doubts as to the then dominant casuistic way for regulating social reality at that time, which necessitated the attribution of decisive importance to the formal method of determining the behaviour of community members and their control.[2]

The primary form for opening legal regulations is the gradual departure from the casuistry of regulations and the use of abstract names (having no designates in the realm of real phenomena) or generalized specific names, which can be attributed to the feature of being inexplicit and vague. Especially the latter form for construction of legal language, due to the complexity of its semantic structure, may be associated with the concept of the legislator who, unable or unwilling to specify the content of these names, opens the linguistic dimension of the content of law. This may take place when the legislator creates a legal term[3] that does not coincide with the expression found in the common language, sometimes associating with it a specific general meaning (as developed by the doctrine and judicial practice), and not always fit for precise definition. The imposition of the

1 Cf. B. Malinowski, "Zwyczaj," esp. pp. 17–22, 35–45.

2 Cf. J. Klima, *Prawa*, esp. pp. 69 ff., M. Kuryłowicz, *Prawo*, pp. 14–21.

3 Cf. K. Ajdukiewicz, *Logika*, p. 30; Z. Ziembiński, *Logika*, p. 69; see also below: 1.2.

content of such a term for the purposes of the decision-making process requires reference to certain facts and events so that the elements of such a concept (e.g. attempt, necessity) can be precisely determined. The requirement to refer to elements that are not specified by the legal text in this case is related to the properties of both the common language and the legal language. This also applies to terms with axiological properties (e.g. pluralism, impartiality or independence).

(2) We can distinguish two basic trends within the history of law, as to the way in which extra-legal criteria may be included in the legal order. Both of them, without abandoning the emphasis on intra-legal values, assume that in order to achieve some satisfactory state of flexibility of law and its adequacy in relation to changing relations, assessments and social norms, it is necessary to apply such criteria in the process of creating, implementing and functioning of the law (in the context of the methods for determining behaviour and measures of its control), which are neither prescribed nor more precisely defined by applicable regulations.

The first method of "opening the law" consists in the establishment of special bodies reaching their decisions directly on the basis of extra-legal criteria. They function "alongside" the regular judicial bodies, creating a kind of "competitive" system for making legal decisions. It includes both the activity of the praetor in Roman law, who made decisions based on customary norms or the principles of equity (*ius aequitas*),[4] as well as the institution of *iudicium aequitas*, which was present in early feudal Europe, identified with, among other things, the judicial powers of the Frankish kings as the supreme guardians of justice.[5]

The practice of resolving disputes by Court of Chancery on the basis of informal rules of equity under the English legal order, and then adopting some of its solutions to the legal order of the American colonies and the USA, developed in the sixteenth century, was similar in its character.[6] To some extent, the continuation of this practice can be seen in contemporary mediation practices within the framework of alternative dispute resolution (ADR).[7]

---

4 Cf. Taubenschlag, *Rzymskie*, p. 28; Kupiszewski, *Prawo*, pp. 178 ff., pp. 227 ff., Kuryłowicz, *Prawo*, pp. 14–21.

5 Cf. W. M. Bartel, "Z dziejów," p. 340, K. Koranyi, *Powszechna*, pp. 108 ff. The reception of Roman private law fostered the popularization of these practices in Europe (more on reception of Roman law see F. Wiaecker, *Das Romische*, pp. 3–46, G. Strauss, *Law*, passim, H. Kupiszewski, W. Wołodkiewicz, *Le droit*, passim).

6 Cf. C.K. Allen, *Law*, pp. 366–371, 382 ff., H.E. Yntema, "Equity," passim, J.E. Martin, H.G. Hanbury, *Modern*, passim. W. Dziedziak, *O prawie*, pp. 41–78, On the reception of English law in the USA cf. R. Pound, *The Formative*, passim, G. L. Maskins, "A Problem," pp. 842 ff., E. G. Brown, *British*, passim.

7 Cf. L. Kanowitz, *Alternative*, pp. 3–33, A. Korybski, *Alternatywne*, esp. pp. 27 ff.

The second way for "opening the law" consists in the deliberate introduction, by the legislator, of appropriate words, terms, concepts, or entire phrases to the text of statutes and other normative acts, which authorize entities making decisions on the application of law to take into account the criteria expressed (formulated) in provision, albeit undefined and non-determined. It is a method characteristic of the continental legal culture (or the part of Anglo-Saxon law tradition that is regulated by statutes). These constructions include references to extra-legal criteria in the regulations, mainly in the form of general referring clauses (e.g. principles of equity, good manners, social interest) and estimated reference clauses (e.g. important reasons, due diligence). They are purposeful and related to a particular legislative policy.[8] Their first systematic use took place in the nineteenth-century codifications of civil law (Code Napoleon of 1804, Austrian ABGB of 1811, German BGB of 1896 or the Swiss ZGB of 1907).

1.2. Legislative instruments of opening the legal system

The above-mentioned extra-legal references appear in various legislative forms. The legislator does not create one universal and maximally broad authorization for the body exercising the right to base decisions on extra-legal criteria. It may, however, refer it either to the facts or to the values (or axiologically justified norms).

(1) References to facts are most often connected with the authorization of entities applying the law to refer to socially shaped customs. This form of reference does not prejudge whether the intention of the legislator was to take into account in the processes of applying the law the customary norms formed on the basis of sufficiently persistent facts. Even though the reference to standards assumes a stronger influence on the decision-making process, it is not a significant element differentiating the way the reference is used. Furthermore, at the level of judicial decision-making processes, there are no reliable instruments for distinguishing between the customs as facts, and the customary norms. In both cases, the essence of referral is not to direct the judge's attention to axiology, but to the shaping of customs (relationships, habits, traditions) within the life of the society, which in certain situations acquire normative force.

(2) References to values occur either in the form of an indication of a situational assessment or in the form of a reference to a generally defined system of

8 See below: 3, 4 and 5.

> values. The first form can be called estimating referral clauses (estimating references), while the latter – general referral clauses (general references).

Estimating references are expressed in the form of such normative phrases as: important reasons, due diligence, justified causes, special circumstances, typical consequences, permanent and complete breakdown of the marriage, appropriate remuneration, major contribution, average measure, appropriate age difference, gross loss, etc. They contain two clearly distinguishable elements: referring to facts (circumstances, causes, consequences, loss, remuneration, age difference, etc.), the occurrence of which should be established in the decision-making process, and reference to "estimate," which leads to the expression of a specific qualification (significant, specific, appropriate, permanent, etc.).

The evaluation element of such a phrase is not connected with the requirement to express typical approval or disapproval of given phenomena (assessment of the "basic type"[9]) or to refer directly to socially formed extra-legal values or norms. This is because the legislator does not indicate the direction of this estimate (e.g. moral or political axiology), although the use of certain norms, mainly moral ones, is not excluded, despite the general lack of legislative indication of criteria for assessing significance, durability, appropriateness, etc. Instead, it indicates the need to estimate the degree, size, gravity, intensity, etc. of the occurrence of a given condition described as a fact. Such an assessment is individual, one can say situational, because it is made on the basis of a comparison between the facts that occur in the respective case and the model state of affairs or imagined facts that could occur in such, or similar situations.[10] Sometimes it may be linked with the requirement of the assessing entity to refer to the analysis of cause-effect relationships (e.g. social purpose) or to "statistical" data that can be more precisely calculated (e.g. with the criterion of "average salary" or "appropriate age difference"). The situation-related nature of such an assessment is primarily related to its "gravity" for the specific case (there are no valid reasons at all, there are reasons whose importance in a given situation should be assessed).

In turn, the essence of the general reference clause should be perceived in the normative phrase indicating the "system" of values (evaluations) or extra-legal norms, defined in a generally directed manner by quoting the name of the extra-legal criterion.[11] It is also in this case, at least at the level of legislative referral, that

9 Cf. Z. Ziembiński, *Problemy*, p. 124.
10 Cf. K. Engisch, *Einführung*, p. 110.
11 Cf. Z. Ziembiński, "Stan dyskusji," passim, M. Pawełczyk, "Uwagi," passim, L. Leszczyński, *Klauzule*, pp. 22–27.

it cannot be determined whether, for example, considerations of equity belong to system of values or system of norms. Especially since the lawmakers are inconsistent and use the terms "considerations of equity," "principles of equity" or "equity" interchangeably. As in the case of reference to customs, the differences in this respect do not affect the essence of the legislative reference itself, which is apparent at the level of application of the law.

2. General reference clauses

2.1. Some examples

The analysis of the term and the definition of the content of the term "general reference clause" should be preceded by a review of the normative structures marked with this term. The reason for this is the extraordinary variety of normative forms of occurrence of this type of clauses.

The "first wave" clauses with their systemic appearance in legislative regulations in the field of civil (private) law assumed several "dominant" names, commonly used in the above-mentioned European civil law codifications.[12] The most common are "rightness,"[13] "good faith"[14] and "good customs."[15] However, the certain repetition of nomenclature did not prevent the occurrence of original and, in a sense, unique clauses in other regulations. These include "natural legal principles,"[16] "Regeln der ordnungmassigen Wirtschaft:[17] or "odertliche Betriebe der Wirtschaft."[18]

The first three of the above-mentioned names of extra-legal criteria become somehow classic, and frequently repeated in later laws of European countries. They are becoming so typical that they also appear in the authoritarian systems of the twentieth century, although here they clearly give way to new names. They use the very structure of opening the legal system to extra-legal values and norms, whereas their very name demonstrates the legislative intention to indicate different axiological preferences. Speaking in a generalizing manner, the names of criteria are

12 Cf. M. Stubenrauch, *Commentar,* passim, P. Tuor, *Das Schweizerische,* passim.

13 See: "*l'equite*" in Article 1135 of Code Napoleon (CN), "*Billigkeit*" in § 315 or § 660 of BGB or in Article 4 of Swiss ZGB).

14 See: "*bonne foi*" in Article 550 of CN, "*Treu und Glauben*" in § 157 and § 242 of BGB or Articles 2 and 3 of ZGB).

15 See: "*les bonnes moeurs*" in Article 6 of CN, "*gute Sitten*" in § 26 of ABGB or § 138 of BGB.

16 § 7 ABGB.

17 § 1036 and § 1135 of BGB.

18 § 230 of ABGB.

politicized already at the stage of creating the normative text. The clearest examples of this are the post-revolution Soviet clauses and the clauses in the laws of fascist Germany. The first of them include, for example, references to "revolutionary conscience and revolutionary legal awareness[19] or the "moral principles of the society building communism."[20] An example of the latter may be a reference to the criterion of "faithful service to the German Nation and State."[21] And, what is remarkable, references have been used here also in the Soviet[22] and German fascist[23] penal laws.

---

19 See Article 5 of the Decree of the Council of Peoples' Commisioners in Soviet Russia of 24.11.1917, being called "Decree No. 1 on the court," according to which courts' decisions might be based on the statutes of the overthrown governments only if these statutes are not contrary to the revolutionary conscience (*riewoljucionnoj sowiesti*) and revolutionary legal consciousness (*riewoljucionnomu prawosoznaniju*). According to this provision "*Местные суды решают дела именем Российской Республики и руководятся в своих решениях и приговорах законами свергнутых правительств лишь постольку, поскольку таковые не отменены революцией и не противоречат революционной совести и революционному правосознанию*"). See also: S.M. Dżorbenadze, "O kształtowaniu," pp. 23–28.

20 Art. 5 of the Law of the Union of Soviet Socialis Republics of 8.12.1961 on the Approval of the Fundamentals of Civil Legislation of the USSR and the Union Republics (gazette of the Supreme Soviet of the USSR No. 50, 1961, item 525). Cf. also *Fundamentals of Legislation of the USSR and the Union Republic, Moscow 1974*

21 For example Art. 2.1 of Reichsbürgergesetz of 15.09.1935 (Reichgesetzgeblatt 1935, p. 1146) according to which a German citizen is a one, who "*geeignet ist in Treu dem Deustchen Volk und Reich zu dienen*." On the features of the German law of that time see: L. Gruchmann, "Rechtssystem," pp. 83–103, D. Majer, *Grundlagen*, passim, B. Haftl, "Das nationalistische," pp. 137 ff.

22 See for example Articles 6 and 7 of the Criminal Code of the R.C.F.C.P. of 26.02.1926 (C3, 1926, No. 9, 71) according to which the concept of crime was connected with social danger of the act (*diejstwo obszczestwienno-opasnyje*) defined (Article 6) as "activity directed against Soviet political system or legal order established by worker-peasant authority leading to the communist system." The clause of "social danger of the act" has been repeated in later Soviet legislation, for example in Law of the USSR od 25.12.1958 on the Approval of the Fundamentals of Criminal Legislation of the USSR and the Union Republics, referring to this criterion in Article 1, 3 and 7 of Fundamentals (cf. *Fundamentals of the Legislation of the USSR and the Union Republics*, Moscow 1974). The presence of that criterion has continued in penal codes of socialist countries after World War II (for example in Art. 1 of KK of 1969 according to which "only the person who commits a socially dangerous act, forbidden under threat of punishment by law, is liable to criminal liability").

23 German example of Law of 28.06.1935 on Changing the Penal Code (*Gesetz zur Anderung des Strafgesetzbuch, Reichsgezetzblatt* 1935 I, p. 839) indicating in § 2 of the changed Code criterion "*gesundes Volksempfinden.*"

The emergence of authoritarianism after World War II in Central and Eastern Europe popularized and strengthened this tendency. However, such extremely politicized terms were not applied here, as was the case in both of the above-mentioned totalitarian systems, and replaced with references to the criteria of general social interest, public interest, the objectives or interests of the state (sometimes it concerns the objectives of a specific state – e.g. the Polish People's Republic), interest of the national economy, social and economic destination of law or, to the most "popular" clause of these orders – principles of social coexistence, instead. However, the presence of such references testifies to the continuation of the autocratic trend in a softer "verbal formulation."

This feature is not changed by the fact that it coexisted in some countries, with the maintenance, at least for some time after the autocratic change, of classic names of references[24] or politically neutral names ("good of child," "good of family"). Nevertheless, generally speaking, the clauses here created "channel" in that the political axiology enters the legal system and judicial processes,[25] especially when one takes into account the new names and the pressure on the new interpretation of the classic references.[26] This also applied to criminal law, where the trend of linking the criminal nature of an act and the basis of the penalty with the criterion of the social danger of the act[27] was developed.

The twentieth century (and this also applies to non-authoritarian states) brings yet another important and lasting trend. It involves the transfer of civil law clauses to the branches of public law (especially to the regulations of the constitutional and administrative law[28]). This leads to changes in the nomenclature of clauses, which more often refer to criteria of public interest, the interest of state security, public good, public order, principles of social justice, etc.

---

24 E.g. Art. 2 of POPC of 1946 referring to custom that, if is common in the state, might have a strength of the statute or Art. 5 of this act indicating a good faith as a criterion of the execution of the subjective rights.

25 What has been clearly underlined by J.W. Hedemann foreseeing the effects of the presence of the clauses (see *Die Flucht*, passim).

26 See for example art. 4 (derogated in 1990) of KC where the principles of the political order and the purposes of the Polish People's Republic occurred to be the criteria for application and interpretation of all code rules or art. 417 (derogated in 1996) of KPC where the violation of the interest of the Polish People's Republic was the criterion for the extraordinary revision of the court's sentence.

27 Cf. I. Andrejew, *Zarys*, pp. 63–70. In KK of 1969, the criterion of social danger of an act appears in Art. 1. Art. 26, Art. 27 and Art. 50.

28 Cf. E. Forsthoff, *Lehrbuch*, pp. 77–85.

The differentiation of nomenclature is also profound in international law. It is particularly visible in the field of human rights protection law, where there are clauses referring to the criteria of necessity in democratic society, supplemented by more specified criteria like: public order, interest of public safety or national security, economic well-being of the country, protection of morals[29] treated as criteria for the assessment of the actions of a member state by an international court. The criterion of good faith, on the other hand, appears as the universal criterion for interpreting international treaties.[30]

The deep social and legal changes that occur since 1989 in Central and Eastern Europe, bring about two, partly contradictory trends. The first maintains the nomenclature formulated in the autocratic system (e.g. principles of social coexistence), while the second returns to the classic names of extra-legal references, which is associated with a clear tendency to depoliticize the nomenclature of new references. Both tendencies were visible, for example, in amendments to the Polish Civil Code (KC), which included references to the criteria of equity or good customs,[31] but at the same time maintained a reference to the principles of social coexistence.[32]

2.2. The concept and its constituents

(1) The term "general reference clause" (or the more common name "general clause"[33]) was derived from doctrinal statements. Nevertheless it is also found in the language of legal (judicial) practice, but it was not and, in principle, is still not an element of the language of normative acts.[34]

---

29 The ECHR might be a good example of forming various open criteria, first of all in Articles 8, 9, 10 and 11 of the Convention.

30 Cf. Art. 31 sect. 1 of VCLT.

31 Cf. Art. 764^3 or Art. 72 of KC.

32 This criterion was not removed from any maintained in force provision of KC, which has become an object of doctrinal controversy, but it was associated with the already shaped jurisprudence, mitigating the ideological sounding of the name associated with this particular criterion (cf. e.g. A. Tomaszek, "Dobre," passim, L. Leszczyński, "Dobre," passim).

33 The name "general clause" need not, however, be linked exclusively with an extra-legal reference. It is also understood as a general, non-exhaustive list of the powers of a given authority (cf. H. Izdebski, *Historia*, p. 81).

34 In Polish law, the term: "general clause" ("*klauzula generalna*") appears exceptionally in the annex to the regulation of the Prime Minister of June 20, 2020 on the principles of legislative technique (Dz.U. 2020, item 283), which in par. 155 sec. 1 defines, *among*

The term "clause" (as a legal term) denotes a reservation or condition in a contract, treaty or legal document, and may have specific forms such as a derogation, delegation, or enforcement clause.[35] The part of the name indicating the "referring" nature of the clause means that the criteria indicated (named) in it are not defined or otherwise specified in the provisions of law and to require referral to extra-legal (not forming part of the legal system) values or norms in order to determine their content. On the other hand, the "general" nature of the reference means that the determination of its content is to be made on the basis of an extra-legal (e.g. moral or political) axiological or normative system that is, at least to some extent, directed generally through the name of the reference.

The relations between the three elements of the name "general reference clause," distinguished above, define several possible understandings of this term.

The broadest of them is to perceive the clause as any normative basis of decision-making discretion in the process of applying the law (a clause in functional terms[36]), that is not related to a separate normative structure. The second (narrower) approach emphasizes the presence of a referring clause in a normative regulation, linking the clauses either with a linguistically undefined phrase, or with a reference to external criteria, regardless of whether it refers to norms, values or facts, and regardless of their nature (and therefore also the principles of knowledge, science or technology).[37] The subsequent (third) approach limits the field of reference and includes in the clauses only those clauses that require reference to norms or extra-legal assessments, regardless of the nature of these assessments (i.e. not only to value systems but also to estimates).[38]

In the fourth approach we observe the substantial narrowing, as it is treating the clause as a normative phrase referring the decision-maker to a "system" of extra-legal values or norms, defined in a generally guided manner by the name of the extra-legal criterion, which separates general clauses from estimation clauses. In the fifth, even narrower approach, a clause would refer only to extra-legal norms, which would allow for the separation of clauses from value phrases. An additional narrowing of the fourth and fifth approach could link the essence

other things, these clauses as means for "ensuring flexibility of the text of a normative act."

35 Cf. *Słownik* (ed. W. Doroszewski), pp. 710–711, *Słownik* (ed. M. Szymczak), p. 927, W. Kopaliński, *Słownik*, p. 216, *Leksykon*, p. 524.

36 Cf. Z. Ziembiński, *Problemy*, pp. 472 ff.

37 Cf. J. Wróblewski, "Gloss," pp. 67–70, F. Studnicki, *Działanie*, p. 65 (here the clause is the referral to preexisting customs).

38 Cf. Z. Ziembiński, *Teoria*, pp. 144–145.

of the clause with references to extra-legal standards or indications of extra-legal values, falling within a sufficiently general part of the legal system or of a normative act, and could therefore be used in the application of various specific regulations in the respective normative act (which would make it possible to distinguish between general clauses and special clauses, understanding the latter as references or indications contained in specific provisions of a normative act[39]).

It seems that the fourth approach, connecting the essence of the general referring clause with the normative phrase indicating the "system" of extra-legal values or norms, defined in a generally directed manner by the name of the said extra-legal criterion, is the most useful for the purpose of analysing the clause as a normative (legislative) structure opening the process of applying the law to the use of extra-legal criteria. The context of the position of the clause, when we understand it in this approach, in the system of legal regulation would, however, be a factor differentiating the effects or scale of opening the grounds for judicial or administrative decisions.

Therefore, a general reference clause would be a normative phrase (legislative structure), forming an element of a legal provision, the content of which is an authorization, addressed to an organ applying the law, to use criteria (norms, values) expressed (named) in a legal text, but not incorporated (for various reasons) in the legal system, in order to establish the grounds for qualifying the behaviour of the addressee of the decision and the normative consequences of this qualification. From the viewpoint of an ordinary addressee, a reference would be a guideline to take into account the extra-legal criteria referred to therein, when determining one's own action.

(2) The names of the extra-legal criteria contained in the general reference clause usually include three optional components. The first one defines the form of values or norms (e.g. good, interest, goal, principles, considerations), the second – an axiological formula (e.g. justice, equity, coexistence, morality, custom), and the third – the sphere of social reality on the basis of which the interpreter has to identify the content of the phrase (e.g. social, public, state, civic). The determination of the realm of reality forms the main indication of identifying the type of value, focusing on the choice of moral, political or economic axiology. The linking of the name of the criterion with the type of axiology is indicative, however, as regardless of the clarity that sometimes occurs in this respect (e.g. the political nature of the criterion of revolutionary consciousness, the goals of the state or the principles of the political system), in most cases

39 Cf. A. Ohanowicz, "Gloss," p. 287

the actual identification of the type of value takes place "only" in the process of applying the law. Sometimes the value takes the form of an evaluation that refers to the category of good or rightness (e.g. good customs, just interest of the citizens).

Reference clauses usually contain two of the three elements listed above (e.g. principles of equity, public interest, social purpose, taxpayer's interest, best interests of the child). It happens, however, that all three elements are present (e.g. the principles of social justice, principles of social coexistence, just interest of citizens).

2.3. Extra-legal referencing and its direction

(1) As already indicated above, the name of a extra-legal criterion may refer to facts, norms and values.

References to facts (established or local customs, local relations[40]) occur relatively rarely and do not require reference to the value in determining their content. They can, nevertheless, obtain a normative dimension (established customs transform into customary norms), which usually strengthens their impact on the content of decisions on the application of the law.

Such criteria appear primarily in civil and commercial law. They take the form of a "simple" reference to, for example, established customs[41] of local relations[42] or trade customs.[43] The addressees of such regulations build patterns of behaviour on the basis of confirmation of the "existence" of a custom or the validity of a customary norm, without linking their content with axiology. The system of customary norms is usually associated with lack of an axiological justification for the validity of its behavioural patterns,[44] which causes references of this type to be classified as non-valuing ones.[45]

This happens regardless of the historical relationship between customs and the formation of law in general, regardless of the numerous cases of overlapping

40 Art. 1135 of CN in the form of "*l'usage*," Art. 65 and Art. 354 of KC in the form of established customs ("*ustalone zwyczaje*") or Article 144 of KC in the form of local relations ("*stosunki miejscowe*").

41 Cf. Art. 1 of ZGB, art. 56 of KC.

42 Cf. Art. 144 of KC.

43 Cf. Art. 1873 of CN or Art. 532 of KH.

44 Cf. Z. Ziembiński, *Teoria*, pp. 73 ff.

45 Cf. J. Wróblewski, "Gloss," p. 67. J. W. Hedemann also seems to attach some importance to the existence of references (clauses) that do not valuate (cf. J.W. Hedemann, *Einführung*, 414).

customary norms with moral, legal, religious, and other ones, and also regardless of the fact that the system of norms in force may also form an intrinsic value for this group (may be valuable due to its respect for tradition). The issue becomes slightly more complicated when we deal with the phrase "good customs"[46] as the legislator combines therein elements of customs and moral judgments with which the content of moral norms is usually associated.[47]

The remaining references have axiological provenance, regardless of whether it is possible to establish the normative layer of the reference (principles of equity, principles of social coexistence) or it is possible to "solely" identify the value, in determining the content of which one should find the norms indicating the order to protect this value (e.g. the child's welfare, social interest).

The assumption stating that an axiological reference may be directed towards a system of values (assessments) or extra-legal norms is based on the assumption that neither at the stage of legislative referral nor at the stage of determining the content of the reference itself, it is not possible to determine whether in a specific case we are dealing with a reference to assessments or to rules. This is attributable both to the nature of the assessments (values) and norms and to the mutual relations between them,[48] as well as to the wording of the referring phrase itself (e.g. as in the "child's welfare" clause, which indicates a value and not a normative system). In order to establish the function of references in the application of the law, it is sufficient to assume that the organs applying the law in the case of clauses directly refers to the value or to the axiological justification of the respective extra-legal norms. At the same time, it is not important whether the particular assessment by this organ will be derived from a previously formed extra-legal norm, or "only" from a value or rating system that has "not yet" been sanctioned. Verification would prove at least difficult, if not impossible, in the case of referring to social (moral) norms that do not take the shape of formalized rules. The aforesaid also applies to evaluative phrases[49] indicating a value in general (e.g. dignity, solidarity), because including them in the decision-making process and judicial interpretation, apart from determining their axiological content, requires (similarly to the criterion of "good of child") deriving a norm that protects this value, forming the measure for the assessment (qualification) of the behaviour, which is the subject of the decision-making process.

---

46 E.g. Art. 6 of CN, § 26 of ABGB, § 138 of BGB, Art. 55 of KZ).

47 Cf. Z. Ziembiński, *Teoria*, pp. 73–74.

48 Cf. Z. Ziembiński, *Logika*, pp. 102 ff.

49 M. Zirk-Sadowski, *Rozumienie*, pp. 62 ff.

The extra-legal nature of the criteria to which the legislator refers and the direction of this reference are related to the fact that, firstly, the legislator is aware of the existence of socially important values and the functioning of extra-legal norms, and secondly, it assumes the possibility of their identification and application in the decision-making process. By using the form of such a reference, the legislator neither explicitly declares its extra-legal evaluations, nor specifies the content of specific social norms that may be used in the processes of applying the law. These are valuable for the legislator (otherwise it would not point to them), but either not as valuable as those that are incorporated into the legal system or not yet fully elaborated and therefore unsuitable for such a "formal" incorporation.

(2) An extra-legal reference in the form of a general clause is a targeted reference (what differs a general clause from an estimation reference). The legislator does not decide to refer to a single extra-legal criterion in the entire legal system, the name of which would be a universal reference, which could be used in every act of implementation of law and which would create a decision-making freedom in the law application processes in a scope similar to the equity jurisdiction.[50]

Anticipating later analyses, it can already be stated at this point, that the general clauses refer to moral (which constitute their broadest direction, including some understanding of equity), political and economic criteria. This division is of course neither a disjoint nor an exhaustive one, since the clauses may readily combine various types of criteria even in their names (e.g. the socio-economic objective[51]).

Generally speaking, moral criteria (values) are connected with assigning given objects, phenomena, conditions, etc. the characteristics of good or rightness on the basis of either assumptions that are adopted *a priori*, or evaluations formed in the respective social environment. Some of them are incorporated into the law to become part of the legal axiology, while others, due to their diversity, variability, local character or difficulties in defining their content, remain outside the borders of the legal system, becoming precisely the criteria of reference.

The extra-legal moral criteria, the most diverse in this set, may have a universal dimension (universal or human values,[52] Christian value system[53]), a

50 Cf. above: 1.1.

51 Cf. Art. 5 or Art. 140 of KC.

52 See Preamble to the RP Constitution.

53 See Art. 18 of the Polish Broadcasting Act of 29.12.1992.

universal dimension in the respective legal culture (criteria of equity,[54] good faith[55] or good customs,[56] acquiring this dimension due to "repeatability" of their occurrence in the European culture of statutory law) and a more specific dimension, referring to current social assessments and various aspects of the broadly understood social reality. The last of these groups may reflect the general social context (the common good,[57] the good of the community, or the general good,[58] principles of social justice,[59] principles of social coexistence[60]), but it may also have an individualized context, indicating the axiology of a subjective category, either rather broadly (the interests of citizens[61]) or narrowly (the good of the child) and even the axiology of a specific addressee (e.g. professed moral principles[62]).

Political criteria are values related to a specific set of (more permanent or more temporary) interests in an organized (in various manners) community that influence the exercise of power. They may be of basic value (e.g. systemic principles)

54 E.g. Art. 1135 of CN ("*l'equite*"), § 315 of BGB (indicating "*Billigkeit*") or § 660 of BGB (indicating "*billige Ermessen*") and Art. 4 of ZGB ("*Billigkeit*").

55 Cf. e.g. Art. 550 of CN ("*bonne foi*" in the context of determining the holder's position), § 157 and § 242 BGB ("*Treu und Glauben*" in the context of determining the scope of the debtor's obligations) or Art. 2 ZGB ("Treus und Glauben" as a criterion for the behaviour of participants in civil law transactions). This criterion also appears in the pre-war Polish civil law codifications – e.g. in Art. 107, 135, 470 of KZ (1933) or e.g. Art. 10, 24, 503 of KH (1934). Also significant is the function of the principles of good faith as a criterion for interpreting treaties under Art. 31 of VCLT.

56 Art. 6 of CN ("*les bonnes moeurs*"), § 26 of ABGB ("*gute Sitten*") or § 138 of BGB ("*gute Sitten*"), or the above-mentioned Polish pre-war codifications – e.g. Art. 55, 56, 132 of KZ or Art. 240, 414 of KH.

57 Art. 1 of the RP Constitution of 2.04.1997 ("The Republic of Poland is the common good of all citizens" ("*Rzeczpospolita Polska jest dobrem wspólnym wszystkich obywateli*")).

58 See for example § 364 of ABGB ("*allgemeinen Wohles*") or § 365 of ABGB ("*allgemeine Beste*")

59 In a sense, the *jori* criterion, as formulated in Art. 3 of the decree of the Japanese State Council of 1875 on the application of law as the basis for making judicial decisions in the absence of written rules and customs (*kanshun*) also has such a character, interpreted as a social understanding of justice but also as general principles of law, equity, natural law, natural reason or even legal logic (cf. M.K. Young, "The Japanese," pp. 21, 28, K. Takanayagi, "Contact," pp. 1–11, H. Itoh, "How Judges," pp. 775–804.

60 Cf. Art. 5, 58, 65 and many other regulations of KC.

61 Cf. Art. 7 of KPA.

62 Cf. Art. 85 sec. 3 of the RP Constitution (as a criterion for exemption from military service).

or instrumental one (e.g. state objectives). They may or may not have a content relationship with moral values. Due to their institutionalization, they are usually expressed more directly than moral values in the legal regulations, which are created with the active participation of representatives of these organized social groups and political structures. Since it is usually not necessary to include all political values into the legal system, there are numerous, even those having the character of more permanent values, that become criteria for extra-legal references, sometimes "competing" with the most common moral values.

The extra-legal political criteria, no longer as diverse as moral values, always express a public or general social perspective in their name. Their relationship with moral values is complex. Certain moral criteria may, under favourable conditions, be combined with the intention to indicate political content (e.g. the criterion of a social interest or social goals, public interest or public good[63]). The very content of the criteria indicating political axiology may be either more pragmatic (e.g. the interest of public security[64]) or biased towards ideology. The latter may either appear in a strong version, characteristic for the totalitarian systems (revolutionary conscience[65] or the moral principles of a society building communism[66]) or in a "milder" version (e.g. state objectives, state interests).

Political values may interfere with economic values (especially in the system of centrally planned economy), although the latter are relatively the most distinguished in their essence. Value in economics is a "measurable" category and means, generally speaking, rationality or profitability of this activity.

Economic criteria appear in legal regulations in their "pure" form, referring to economic rationality both on a general scale (e.g. ordinary management principles,[67]

63 § 26 of ABGB.

64 Cf. Art. 9 sec. 2, 10 sec. 2 or 11 sec. 2 of ECHR.

65 Cf. above: 1.2.

66 Art. 5 of the Law of the Union of Soviet Socialist Republics of 8.12.1961 on the Approval of the Fundamentals of Civil Legislation of the USSR and the Union Republics (gazette of the Supreme Soviet of the USSR, No. 50, 1961, item 525). The Constitution of the Union of Soviet Socialist Republics of Dec. 5, 1936 introduces the criterion of the rules of socialist intercourse ("It is the duty of every citizen of the U.S.R.R. to abide by the Constitution of the Union of Soviet Socialist Republics, to observe the laws, to maintain labour discipline, honestly to perform public duties and to respect the rules of socialist intercourse"). That clause appeared in the softer form of "rules of social coexistence" in similar regulations of citizens' duties in other socials constitutions (see for example Art. 90 of the PRL Constitution).

67 § 230 of ABGB ("*ordentliche Betriebe der Wirtschaft*").

principles of proper economy[68]) and on the scale of individual economic interest (interest of the taxpayer, interest of the company[69]). They may also be related to moral criteria, usually related – within the market economy system – to the axiology of distinct category of subjects (e.g. mercantile customs,[70] principles of fair trading), but they may also be related, which is characteristic for the autocratic systems, to political criteria (e.g. the principles of a planned economy[71] or the interest of the national economy[72]).

(3) At the level of normative regulation, there are also references linking different types of criteria. This linking may take place in the form of referring to various aspects of single-type values (e.g. combining political axiology in the criteria of revolutionary conscience and revolutionary consciousness of the masses[73] or the principle of the system and state objectives[74]) and of referring to values of various types in single regulation (e.g. combining good customs with criterion of public order[75]) or in in a single clause (e.g. to the socio-economic purpose of law, binding moral and economic criteria, without specifying model relations[76]).

Combining two or more separate criteria in one legal provision may include, in addition to linking the extra-legal criteria, also linking them with intra-legal criteria, some of which in the form of legal principles. The intention of both forms of opening is to make it possible to weigh various axiological contents within the framework of both mutually supporting and confrontational (collision) relations.

2.4. Reference clauses and legal principles

The relation observed in the last part of previous paragraph requires further elaboration because principles and reference clauses are axiological constructs, albeit directed to various axiological orders.

68 § 1036 or § 1135 of BGB (indicating criterion of "*Regeln einer ordnungsmassigen Wirtschaft*")
69 Cf. e.g. Art. 22 of OP and Art. 56 § 1, Art. 249 § 1 or Art. 422 § 1 of KSH.
70 E.g. Art. 240 and Art. 414 of KH.
71 The political content of this criterion was alleviated in Art. 386 (repealed in 2003) of KC through the criterion of "economical production and marketing."
72 Cf. Art. 826 and 827 of KC.
73 Art. 5 of the Decree of the Council of Peoples' Commisioners of November 24, 1917 ("decree No. 1 on the court").
74 Art. 4 (repealed in 1990) of KC.
75 E.g. § 26 of ABGB combining decency criteria of good customs (*gute Sitten)* with public order (*öffentliche Ordnung*).
76 Cf. e.g. Art. 5 of K.

Among the views on the essence of principles, the most suitable seems the assumption that the principle of law is a legal norm protecting a value (ordering the protection of value) that is of particular importance from the point of view of the legal order. It therefore forms a fundamental norm belonging to the legal system, one that is momentous and axiologically superior to other, "ordinary" rules of the system.[77] By protecting the good defined in this way, the principle of law creates a fundamental intra-legal axiology, having a significant impact on the entire process of law interpretation.

The term of legal principle may also include various points of the currently leading concepts of legal principles. The principle there can be understood as a kind of directive (legal norm) or as a descriptive structure (stating the way the respective legal sphere is shaped).[78] It can also be treated as a binding norm (principle of the legal system, principle-norm) or as a principle-postulate.[79] While the second type of rules "only" affects axiological changes in law, the position and role of the first type of rules (principles-norms) results from their axiological importance (caused by determining the basic values for the whole system or entire branch of law) and functional significance (influence on legal reasoning or the process of interpretation of law), possibly supported by hierarchical location (in legal acts of the highest legal position in the legal system).

The characteristics of the construction of principles of law may see their essence in the binding standards according to the scheme "more or less" instead of the definite conclusion that deals with the rules connecting additionally the concept of principles with policies.[80] Other approaches may see essence of principles in their defeasibility[81] as well as in their optimizing (defining the highest level of realization of the desired state of affairs)[82] or finalistic (purposeful) character.[83] The concepts may show also the openness of principles in shaping a generic

---

77 Such a "definition" can be derived from the most important approaches in Polish theory of law (cf. S. Wronkowska, M. Zieliński, Z. Ziembiński, *Zasady*, pp. 28, 54 ff., J. Wróblewski, "Prawo," pp. 24–28, J. Stanosciak, *Studia*, pp. 95, 102–107). The formula that the principle of law is a norm ordering the protection of value expressed by the principle has been proposed directly by M. Kordela (cf. *Zasady*, pp. 113 ff).

78 Cf. S. Wronkowska, M. Zieliński, Z. Ziembiński, *Zasady*, pp. 28–48.

79 Cf. J. Wróblewski, "Prawo," pp. 18 ff., J. Wróblewski, *Zagadnienia*, pp. 255 ff.

80 Cf. R. Dworkin, *Law's*, p. 209 ff.

81 Cf. C. Bäcker, "Rules," pp. 77 ff.

82 Cf. R. Alexy, *A Theory*, pp. 47, 58.

83 Cf. H. Avila, *Theory*, p. 40.

situation with a closed scope of normalization[84] and the role of "principles-maxims."[85] The important point of characteristics of the principle deals with the role of mechanism of balancing (weighing), solving the conflicts between various principles of law.[86]

From the viewpoint of the relationship of principles and clauses, it is important to recognize the fact that legal principles are not solely legislative constructions, although such a provenance prevails. Principles of law may be also created through the doctrine and judicial practice on the basis of the cultural tradition of the respective legal order (understood more broadly than the legal system of the particular state) and define the axiology of a given legal order, linking it with e.g. the so-called Western legal culture or, more narrowly, the continental (European) culture of statutory law. What we observe in some of the orders (e.g. EU law), a direct "principle-shaping" may occur in particularly important judgments of the CJEU.[87]

Linking the principles with legislative activity does not introduce a uniform method for creating them. Since the principles are usually not clearly named as such by the legislator, who, in addition, does not distinguish sets of legal principles in the normative acts[88] the status of principle in the case of the regular norm is determined by the doctrine and judicial practice. This practice may be associated with granting the status of a principle to "ordinary" norms expressing, for example, stable specific preferences of the legislator. In each of the above-mentioned types of legal principles, the search for their content takes place within the legal system, and its "discovery" then creates a value that becomes the intrinsic value of the legal system (regardless of whether it concerns substantive or procedural law).

The relationship between the principles of law (especially the "legislative" principles) and extra-legal references (and proportioning the role of intra-legal and extra-legal axiology[89]) is marked by three basic situations.

---

84 Cf. M. Atienza, J.R. Manero, *A Theory*, pp. 28 ff. esp. p. 40, M. Atienza, *Curso*, pp. 48, 151–153.

85 Cf. C. Perelmann, *Logika*, pp. 128 ff., 133 ff.

86 Cf. R. Dworkin, "The Model," p. 27, R. Alexy, "On the Structure," pp. 295 ff.

87 Cf. e.g. L.N. Brown, T. Kennedy, *The Court*, pp. 347 ff., J. Shaw, *Law*, pp. 331 ff.

88 In Polish law, apart from the RP Constitution (Chapter One), such an indication is found only in KPA (Articles 6–16) and in KP (Articles 10–18).

89 On complex relations between these two constructs cf. M. van Hoecke, *Law*, pp., A. Bröstl, "Jigsaw," pp. 13 ff, M. Kordela, "Inter," pp. 29 ff. As for the criterion of "good of child," cf. K. Hanas, "Interpretative," pp. 89–92.

In the first, simplest situation it denotes the formulation of a legal principle in a provision that does not refer to any extra-legal criteria (e.g. the principle of an adversarial proceeding), determining the intra-legal nature of the value expressed in this manner, which was recognized by the legislator as important for the legal order. The remaining situations introduce some degree of relativization.

In the second situation this means deriving the principle of law from a regulation containing an extra-legal reference. It takes place when a reference is a leading one, appearing in many specific regulations, some of which are recognized by the doctrine and practice as norms so important for e.g. a given branch of law that they are assigned the status of a principle of law. This is so in particular when they are placed in the most general part of the act, which usually gathers rules.[90] Such a way of "axiological opening" of the principles of the legal system may mean (depending on the type of criteria) either a declaration of "socialization" of the process of shaping basic legal values, or an attempt to "designate" leading ideas to be fulfilled by the present, but also the future (in the sense of evolving) legal system (which would bring such principles closer to the principles-postulates) or the direction of the content of the principles towards political axiology (e.g. if the criterion of the purpose or interest of the state would appear in such a reference).

And finally, the third situation means that the legislator formulates clauses referring to the "border" criteria, which lie at the so-called "axiological edge" and thus enabling their treatment as components of both legal and extra-legal axiology. This is the case when reference is made to, for example, the natural principles of law, the principles of the political system or the fundamental principles of the legal order.[91] Blurring the boundary between intra-legal and extra-legal criteria[92] it may potentially politicize the axiology of such references.

---

90 E.g. Art. 1, 3 and 4 of ZGB or art. 5 of KC and art. of 7 KPA, Cf. A. Wolter, *Prawo*, pp. 160 ff. (treating reference to the rules of social coexistence especially in art. 5 of KC as a kind of legal principle in civil law)

91 Cf. § 7 ABGB (indicating the principles of natural law) or Art. 4 (repealed in 1990) of KC (indicating the system principles and objectives of the Polish People's Republic) or Art. 6 of the PPM (referring to the criterion of basic principles of the legal order).

92 Referring to, for example, the systemic principles creates freedom in two dimensions: first, in the dimension of including a given norm among the principles of the system (such a reference does not always mean referring to specific principles of the Constitution, but it is also a reference to systemic values, to systemic foundations), and secondly, in terms of interpreting the meaning of such a principle, even if such a principle will be clearly formulated in constitutional provisions. The need to establish such meaning, which is by no means a simple operation, is evidenced by the content of e.g. Art. 3, 5 or 8 of the

3. Extra-legal reference as a component of legislative policy

3.1. References and rationality of legislation

(1) The creation of extra-legal references in the form of general reference clauses (as in the case of estimation clauses or legal principles) forms an element of legislative policy, which in this case is understood as setting the assumptions, objectives and basic components of the content of a normative regulation by entities of political authority, entities preparing the draft or drafts of the normative act and, finally, the legislative authorities, which in the appropriate procedure terminate the law-making process in terms of determining the specific content of the normative act and render it binding.[93]

The actual, specific relationships between the decisions of these entities depend on various factors, among which the type of political system is of fundamental importance. The more features it has, generally speaking, of an authoritarian regime, the more legal content is decided already at the stage of determining a political decision and the more it is associated with the implementation of the current ideology and political line of the monolithic centre of political power in the state. Conversely, the more it is democratic, the more important a content correction may appear in the phases following the initiation of the legislative process. Moreover, the *strictly* political decisions themselves then become the result of a pluralistic influence of various centres of power and various centres of influence on the power, having the character of proposals ("legislative offers") rather than "ready" decisions on the basic assumptions of the new legislation. The phase of the legislative procedure then becomes not only the phase "controlling" the implementation of political and legal arrangements in the prepared

---

PRL Constitution of 1952 (from the period before the 1989 amendment), which additionally contain references to extra-legal criteria. It is therefore a triple reference – to the principles of the political system (e.g. on the basis of former Art. 4 of KC), which by itself creates a gap, can be "found" in the Constitution, within the framework of the legal system. However, in this Constitution, they are included in norms which indicate the need to refer to other extra-legal criteria. Nonetheless it does not always have to be this way, especially when the constitutional interpretation resigns from "ideologizing" the text of the constitution in favour of its juridization. The latter, in turn, does not have to resign from references altogether, however, it usually allows avoiding excessive "axiological entanglement" in the regulations themselves.

93 Cf. L. Petrażycki, *Wstęp do nauki prawa*, pp. 13–14, L. Petrażycki, *Wstęp do nauki polityki*, pp. 25 ff. On different concepts of legal policy, cf. T. Biernat, M. Zirk-Sadowski, "Politics," pp. 11 ff.

and submitted draft, but an independent phase of law-making, bringing new content to it.

The requirement of rational legislative actions, assuming the existence of correlation between the identification of the need for a new regulation, the setting its goals and appropriately selected measures for its implementation,[94] includes the axiological grounding of all these components. It also includes the formulation of extra-legal references as legislative means of achieving the pursued goals, which are a manifestation of the legislator's "axiological responsibility." For the references, being a construction consciously designed by the legislator, fit into the axiological dimension of legislative activities. Therefore, it is not a construction that could appear accidentally or result from the legislator's error. The legislator, although it cannot predict all the effects of introducing these structures into the law, should base its concept on a relatively precise image of how these references should actually function. It is required to qualify its actions from the point of view of rationality or predicting the effectiveness of the law being created.[95]

The use of reference clauses as a legislative instrument may bring the achievement of the goal of creating a rational system of norms that would constitute the basis for the behaviour of ordinary addressees and the basis for decision-making by state organs. From the viewpoint of the requirement of flexibility of law and its application, in many cases it will be more convenient to leave the entities applying the law free to decide than to assume the possibility of stipulating the strictest criteria for the content of decisions on the application of law in the regulations, which would still remain an unrealistic assumption. In such cases, the value of flexibility harmonizes with the value of the rationality of the legal order, functionally supporting the accomplishment of legal effectiveness.

(2) The requirement for the legislator to strive for rationality of the legal regulations retains a certain universal dimension throughout the entire legal system. However, it must also be imposed on the properties of individual branches of law and, more specifically, on the properties of the subject of regulation. It is not without reason that the references first appeared in private law, where traditionally shaped and precise juridical constructions need to be supplemented by extra-legal values and norms, and this axiological opening, even if it turns out to be wrong, usually does not cause irreversible legal effects. However, it is also in private law,

94 Cf. L. Nowak, *Interpretacja*, pp. 39–53, G.L. Seidler, *Z zagadnień*, pp. 41–49, T. Kotarbiński, *Traktat*, pp. 123–124.

95 Cf. S. Wronkowska, *Problemy*, passim, J. Wróblewski, *Teoria*, pp. 132 ff., A. Podgórecki, *Założenia*, passim.

that the usefulness of references can be graded, starting from their broadest scale in the law of obligations through family law, and ending with elements of *ius cogens* or the property law an inheritance law, which require greater degree of precaution. It is not without reason that the relatively greatest limitation in the creation of extra-legal references is related to criminal legislation, where the linguistic and juridical precision of the regulation is the most desirable requirement for its application, and certainly where such reference cannot form the basis for classifying an act as a crime. It is finally not without reason that serious precautionary measures in the field of referral are also put forward in relation to the creation of public law, and administrative law (broadly understood, also including tax law or public economic law) in particular. Here each such reference is in some sense an authorization for the executive authority to extend the basis for detailed regulations or specific executive actions, consisting in the administrative determination (interference in) of the legal situation of the addressee. From this point of view, the properties of constitutional law, which, on the one hand, constitutes (also through the extra-legal references) a component giving the state bodies (including the legislature) the authority to act, but on the other hand, may also constitute an element of determining the content of norms protecting human rights and shaping the content of the constitutional principles of law (e.g. the principle of a democratic and rule of law state that implements the principles of social justice), prove to be the most complex.[96]

3.2. Purposes of referencing to the extra-legal criteria

(1) Based on observations of contemporary law-making processes, we should assume that each and every actual process of creating norms assumes the use of some form of extra-legal references. It is therefore an essential element of any law-making policy. Only the scope of use of extra-legal references and the role assigned to them may differ, or to put it otherwise, the proportions of the participation of these structures in the resulting legal texts may be different.[97]

As long as one of the requirements for legal order is the flexibility of application the law, the creation of grounds for making this process more flexible in the form of extra-legal references is one of the most important general objectives of the legislator, meeting the requirements of axiological rationality at the same time. Depending on the adopted concept of the application of law, the assumed scope of the impact of references may be either slightly limited (with the concept

96 Cf. Art. 2 of RP Constitution.

97 Cf. S. Wronkowska, M. Zieliński, *Problemy*, pp. 104–114.

of free decision to apply the law) or subject to legislative "control" (with the concept of a rational and lawful decision).[98]

The general objective behind making the law more flexible is "convenient" for the legislator, as it limits its responsibility for the shape of the legal order, and especially for the results of the law application processes. It shifts the main responsibility for the use of referrals to entities applying the law (mainly courts) and is loosely related to the ways in which referrals are created. Only a complete "dysfunction" of the legal order resulting from uncontrolled and too broad, and therefore unreasonable, creation of reference clauses could potentially directly link the effects of extra-legal referral to the legislator's "liability."

(2) Nevertheless, the legislative structure of extra-legal references still fails to explain the potential specific purposes of the referral. The latter remain somewhat hidden at the time of regulation, since their "discovery" takes place (assuming, of course, that the legislator has correctly linked the means with the objectives, and its operation is effective) only at the level of the effects of formulating references, i.e. in the processes of applying the law. However, a general definition of these goals is possible already at the norm-creating stage, at least on the basis of observation of the functioning of already functioning references, which the legislator must take into account when creating references. If we exclude a situation, in which the legislator would use references to obscure the processes of applying the law as much as possible or in order to create a state of a specific legal anarchy, we should assume that the legislator may link the construction of extra-legal references with two specific objectives.

The first one is the desire of actual and direct "opening" of the legal system to autonomously shaped social values and norms, to "saturate" the content of law with those values that are considered important by the legislator, yet – for different reasons – at the same time unsuitable for their expression in legal text (e.g. due to their lack of definite shape). Consequently, the result of such intentions will be a kind of "soft axiological control" and a more socialized process of the emergence of new components of legal axiology, which may become legal principles over time, even without the need to change specific provisions of law. This corresponds to the tactic of cautious legislative interference, where autonomous assessments and norms are effective enough, and in relation to which a detailed legal regulation could weaken these properties (e.g. family relations or economic processes and relations).

The second specific purpose of extra-legal referral may, however, be completely different. The intention to make the application of law more flexible may be associated with the intention to make the content of the law and the processes of its

98 Cf. J. Wróblewski, *Sądowe*, pp. 383–396.

application dependent on current trends, arrangements or political objectives, creating a climate of a kind of "manual" axiological management of the processes of applying the law, conducted with the use of ad hoc political directives. For this purpose, first of all, political criteria would be used, because these are the most strongly influencing for the method of instrumental use of extra-legal references consistent with this purpose. In an autocratic system, however, such an intention may also be carried out when the name of the reference does not directly indicate political values. The effects of such an influence in the centrally planned economy, with the additional reference to the rigid assumptions of the official political ideology, lead in turn to the weakening or even annihilation of the operation of market economy mechanisms.

The above-mentioned specific objectives are opposing goals. They cannot be adopted in their pure form at the same time. However, a specific compromise is possible, especially in a "soft authoritarian" system, allowing for the fragmented use of both in relation to, for example, various spheres of social relations, or the activities of various entities applying the law. Additionally, these activities may be subject to modification in terms of the intensity of the presence of authoritarian or democratic elements in different time periods.

3.3. Initial conditions for legislative "reference policy"

The most general determinant of extra-legal referral in the form of general clauses is law-making in the form of its enactment (legislative activity). The making of law through judicial decisions allows the use of social values and norms, but does not involve the formulation of reference clauses. The use of a social value or norm in a judgment, which becomes a precedent, and thus constitutes the basis for subsequent decisions, fulfils *common law* functions analogous to the formulation of such a reference in a legal provision, but it differs from the latter practice in terms of the manner, form and scope of the said reference and the durability of the construction of referring to extra-legal criteria.[99]

(1) Certain initial conditions have to be met in order for the legislator to be able to use extra-legal references as an element of its law-making policy.

The prerequisite for extra-legal references and for the correct "perception" of this structure by decision-makers are the characteristics of the law-making process. This can be associated with the gradual rationalization of the law in the

99 Cf. D.N. MacCormick, R.S. Summers, "Introduction," pp. 1–15, L. Leszczyński, "Precedent," pp. 11 ff., L. Leszczyński, J.M. Marshall, *Precedens*, pp. 67–72, 166–171.

course of its historical development, regardless of the fact that such rationalization is, in consequence, more conducive not only to the efficient use of this structure, but also conditioning the creation of references in general. It can also be associated with a departure from the casuistic method of forming the rules,[100] which excludes not only extra-legal referencing, but also the creation of norms in a general form. Therefore, the legislator may decide to use the construction of references, if it is favoured by the dominant method of legal regulation of social relations, meeting the conditions of rationality adequate for the respective legal culture and corresponding to the properties of the regulated legislative matters (individual branches of law).

The condition of judicial practice and its perception by the legislator is also an important condition for the correct extra-legal referencing. A rational legislator does not decide to create references if, in the legislator's opinion, the executive apparatus is in some sense ineffective or if the performance of the entire legal practice (especially judicial) does not favour increasing the freedom of its operation.

The maturity of the legal practice (mainly – judicial) is the precondition for the referral policy, because it is the actions of law enforcement agencies that determine the effects of referral. An important element of the legislative policy in this context is the awareness of the effect of such actions in the form of a discretion in applying the law. However, taking into account the fact that this discretion has natural (independent of the legislator) sources, the extra-legal referencing, which is a deliberate source for its creation, effectively opens it additionally. This applies in particular to the extension of the scope of discretion that occurs naturally as a result of, for example, the vagueness of legal language, the variety of rules of interpretation and differences in interpretative practice and the passage of time from the moment of establishing the provision (in relation to its application). All these sources acquire a new dimension following the inclusion of extra-legal references, and in particular general reference clauses, as the broadest reference structures.

The factors that link the processes of creating and applying law in this respect include the required degree of the legislator's trust in the executive apparatus. In a sense, the axiological "compatibility," understood differently in various political regimes, forms an element of such trust.

100 On the juxtaposition of the casuistic method and referral in the form of general clauses, cf. K. Engisch, *Einführung*, pp. 119, 121.

Speaking generally, broader referral in the form of general clauses is favoured by characteristics such as an extended structure (when it comes to instances and the subjective scope) of judiciary, effective judicial procedures, real independence of judiciary in making decisions, good organization of work, substantive preparation of judges, the ability to develop permanent decision-making principles, essentially uniform interpretation practices, diligence and correctness of justification of decisions, achievement of the necessary uniformity of practice and certainty in the application of the law, or the reasonable exercise of the freedom granted.[101]

In the case of the uniformity of the legislator's axiology and judicial practice, the degree of "political" trust of the legislator increases, which in turn enables an even wider application of the construction of references at the legislative level. The lack of such trust may not foster the wider formulation of clauses in the texts, even if the organizational and substantive conditions on the part of the practice do not raise any doubts (e.g. in a situation of authoritarian change of law, when the "still independent" courts, despite the "new" nomenclature of references, continue to manifest attachment to "old" content, established in the jurisprudence of the previously functioning democratic system).

Regardless of the above factors that determine the very use of referrals in legislative activity, the legislator must take into account the characteristics of the social environment (cultural, political and economic) of the legal system, even though they affect less the legitimacy of the referral and more the way the referrals are applied in the context of their assumed objectives.

(2) The aspect of the relationship between the method of regulation and the creation of reference clauses are the features of the branches of law in which references are created. Some of these branches "invite" the clauses (private law), other almost exclude the use of clauses (penal law) or affect their form and scope of applicability (public law).[102]

These features should be additionally relativized in respect of the type of law application. The legislator's awareness of the different properties of the administrative application of the law may, in turn, result in a more careful use of general clauses (especially those referring to political criteria) in the broadly understood administrative law, especially in a democratic legal order. This type of application of law is more "exposed" to the influence of centres of political power than the judicial one. Caution may consist in the reduced frequency of occurrence of

---

101 Cf. Z. Ziembiński, "Moralność," p. 95, Z. Ziembiński, *Teoria*, p. 100.

102 Cf. below: 4.3.

various references, the narrowing of the scope of their application, and in departure from the use of political criteria ("proximity" to which it is always sensed in this type), but also – in constructing a stronger system of judicial control, e.g. in relation to discretionary administrative decisions. Such limitations are usually not important in authoritarian systems, where the legislator's trust in administrative practice, determined primarily by the compliance of the political line in the assumptions and actions of legislature and administration, rather prompts the wider use of references.

(3) In model terms, general reference clauses, forming of an element of legislative policy, are intentional (neither are they created by chance, nor are they the result of an oversight or error), overt (they are "visible" in the text of a normative act as structures creating freedom), controlled (their use is essentially subject to instance control) and targeted (opening the legal order based on criteria that are appropriately named and located in the regulatory system) source of judicial discretion.

All the above features of the judicial discretion determine the relationship between the effects of legislative activity and the practice of applying the law, but while the quality of the first two (purposefulness and openness of the reference) is determined by the legislator itself, while the implementation of the third feature (controllability) and the essence of the fourth feature (targeting of the reference) is a kind of juridical "joint-venture" – at the starting point it depends on the legislator, and at the point of reaching (issuing the decision on the application of the law) – on the judicature.

A court practice which would be unable to use referrals, taking into account the above features of the decision-making discretion created by referrals, would not be conducive to the forming the extra-legal references as part of the legislation. It is therefore of utmost importance to analyse the means, which the legislator can use to influence (or try to influence) the way references are applied in the law enforcement processes.

4. Measures for legislative influence on the use of extra-legal references

The element forming the link between the initial conditions for extra-legal references and legislative policy are the measures for legislative influence on the use of referrals by courts. The legislator, if it has decided to formulate a general reference clause, may only to some extent influence the way in which the entities applying the law use the references. It focuses on the above-mentioned element of directing the way of reading the content of the reference and the way of its application in the decision-making process by (1), the appropriate name of the criterion, which is included in the clause, (2) the location of the reference clause within the system of normative regulation, and (3) the indication in the regulation of the preconditions for applying the clause.[103] While the names of the criteria are intended by the legislator to influence the interpretation of the general reference clause (determining the content of the criteria indicated here), the location of the clause within the regulatory system and indication of the conditions for its application primarily affects the basis for the use of the clause in the judicial decision-making process.

4.1. Selecting the name of the extra-legal criterion

(1) The differentiation of the names of extra-legal references forms an expression of such a legislative concept, in which it is not assumed to open the legal system to any extra-legal criteria, named as generally as possible and referring to values and norms that are completely undefined (undifferentiated) in content and in "names." The names of the criteria vary and, regardless of their precision and the legislator's expectations related to it, they are intended to act as a means for guiding the process and the results of determining the content of these criteria (i.e. interpretation of the general reference clause). Thus, it forms an instrument of legislative control of this process or an element of anticipating its course and results (assuming that the actions of judicial practice can be predicted at the level of legislative activity). The subsequent chapters of this work will analyse how to determine the content of the criteria and their role in judicial interpretation.[104] The most important thing at this point is to define the manner in which the legislator names the criteria (differentiates their names) to which it refers.

The model method of legislative influence on the manner of determining the content of a given extra-legal criterion would be to name it in such a way, that the name evokes a relatively narrow scope of decision-making freedom. The activities of the legislator, however, have a limited effect here, mainly due to the characteristics of the names of such criteria. There are also no grounds for formulating a classic statutory definition (legal definition) relating to the meaning of the name of a extra-legal criterion. Such actions could not be effective in the sense of unifying its meaning (this applies not only to general clauses but to estimation clauses as well). Although the names of extra-legal criteria are somewhat indefinite (vague) in their nature by using fuzzy and indistinct abstract names,

103 See more precise analysis of these factors: L. Leszczyński, "Extra-legal," pp. 1075 ff.
104 Cf. III and IV, where both aspects are analysed more precisely.

the process of determining their content is not oriented towards the linguistic properties of the name or the normative phrase, but towards its axiological content, for which the linguistic content is in fact of only secondary significance. Hence the limited (i.e. auxiliary a most) usefulness of semantics in determining the content of the criteria of "rightness," "good customs" or "social interest."

The legislator formulating the name of the criterion may, however, attach some importance to the anticipation of the scope of axiological openness related to this name. It not only can, but also should, attach this importance depending on the maturity of judicial practice or the type of political system that influence the determination of the content of the criteria in the process of applying the law. This is because wide openings (e.g. with the criterion of equity) are possible, where the reference to social axiology may overlap with the judge's axiology (own or "corporate" sense of the judge's righteousness). But there are also narrower openings in which determining the content enables (although it is not always implemented) to refer to formed assessments or social norms (e.g. rules of social coexistence), not to mention establishing certain facts (e.g. local customs). Between these opening scales there is a whole range of criteria that may approach the wider or narrower opening range. However, no name of an extra-legal criterion "guarantees" the reading of the legislator's intentions, especially since this is not what the creation of extra-legal references is about. From the legislator's point of view, the point is that the scope of axiological choices should not "invalidate" the intra-legal axiology, the emanation of which is the set of legal principles contained in the system of regulations.

As regards the naming of the reference clause criterion, the legislator cannot be attributed with strong influence on the practice of applying clauses. Some signs of it deal however with three factors: with the differentiation of names in the context of the type of value (direction of reference), with a certain diligence with regard to the choice of a name within the respective direction of reference, and with a tendency to limit the scope of the created gap by binding clauses with legal principles.

(2) The names of the criterion indicate, however, certain directions of extra-legal axiological choices, linking the determined values, more or less precisely, with moral, political or economic axiology. This is because the reference to the criterion of equity includes an indication of moral values, reference to the purpose or interest of the state – of political values, and reference to the interests of the company – of economic values. The fact that these directions are not always reliable is further evidenced not only by the expectation in the authoritarian system of assigning political content to the moral or economic criteria indicated in a clause, but also in the method of combining different types of criteria in a single reference, enabling manoeuvring between, for example, economic and moral criteria under

the "socio-economic objective" criterion depending on the political demand, which is frequently applied in law-making practice. Such a combination, linking e.g. political and moral values, also applies to some names indicating a single criterion (e.g. social or public interest).

The relatively narrowest range of gap in determining the content of an extra-legal criterion takes place in the case of legislative references to customs (which adopt various detailed forms). In fact, it is a legislative reference to facts, the existence of which can be empirically proved. This also applies to the potential reference to customary norms, although in this case, translating the describing theorem into a deontic one would slightly change the nature of this reference.

One cannot have such expectations with regard to the axiological criteria. Nevertheless it is also the case that we sometimes can find a reference, among the general clauses, in that the intention to limit the scope of judicial freedom becomes clearly visible. This is the case, first of all, when the criteria are named in such a way, which indicates the need for a compromise use of "border values" – located both outside and within the legal system (e.g. with the criteria of natural principles of law,[105] principles of the political system,[106] and fundamental principles of the legal order[107]). Such a reference, literally indicating a reference to the principles of the legal system (but with a certain element broadening the field of their interpretation by the word "natural" or the phrase "legal order" being a broader category than "legal system"), may functionally approach a typical extra-legal reference using (under favourable conditions) political assessments. However, it may also constitute an expression of attaching importance to the relationship between references and values incorporated into the system of legal norms[108] in the context of the values of the rule of law and the application of law.

The combination of extra-legal and *stricti iuris* criteria then depends on the form of the latter. For if there are ordinary legal provisions in this role,[109] clauses are created to correct their content. However, if there are legal principles acting as

105 § 7 of ABGB.
106 Art. 1 of POPC of 1950.
107 Art. 6 of PPM.
108 Cf. J. Nowacki, "Niektóre," pp. 102–103; A. Łopatka, Z. Ziembiński, "Próba," p. 805.
109 On the basis of Art. 5 of KC, the examination of the manner of exercising a subjective right was based on its compliance with the law, the principles of social coexistence and the socio-economic purpose of the law (the same criteria are the basis for assessing the effects of a legal action under Art. 56 and the assessment of the debtor's performance under Art. 354 of KC).

legal criteria, then, especially if they are principles formulated in a normative text[110] (unwritten legal principles based on legal tradition and culture do not have to have such an impact), they are to become the framework for determining the content of the extra-legal criteria.

(3) It is also the case that on some occasions the legislator decides to use a different linkage by indicating more than one extra-legal criterion in a single reference clause. These can be both references to single-type values (e.g. combining political axiology in the criteria of revolutionary conscience and revolutionary awareness of the masses[111] or principles of the political system and the objectives of the Polish People's Republic[112]) or to values of various types (e.g. principles of social coexistence and the socio-economic purpose of law[113]). In both of the aforesaid situations, such a combination is supposed to strengthen the reference itself and its direction, but in the latter situation, the legislator actually cedes the determination of the relationship (e.g. balancing the scale of influence) between different types of values to the applying organ.

As part of the practice of combining the names of extra-legal criteria, we should also notice the category of axiological legislative graded references, "measuring" the general axiological criterion indicated in the reference, which to some extent approximates general referring clauses to estimation clauses. In this case, however, the estimation of the scale does not concern the occurrence of facts (e.g. as it is the case for "important reasons"), but the determination of the weight of the indicated value (e.g. the legitimate interest of citizens,[114] important public interest[115]), requiring additional qualification of the basic criterion. However, it is actually more an attempt to "force" the diligence of the law applying organ in the application of this criterion than a limitation of its discretionary freedom.

110 For example, the constitutional systemic principle of a democratic state ruled by law cooperating with the criterion of social justice under Art. 2 of the RP Constitution.

111 Cf. Art. 5 of the Decree of the Council of Peoples' Commisioners of November 24, 1917.

112 Art. 4 (repealed in 1990) of KC.

113 Cf. discussion dealing with the necessity of replacing the reference to the rules of social coexistence by the classic criterion of good customs (A. Tomaszek, "Dobre," passim, L. Leszczyński, "Dobre," passim).

114 Cf. Art. 7 of the KPA.

115 Art. 22 of the RP Constitution.

4.2. Locating the reference clause in the system of legal regulations

An important component of the legislative policy with regard to the construction of model functions of general reference clauses in the application of law processes is the appropriate placement of clauses within the regulatory system. From the point of view of the scope of the influence on the legal order and the processes of applying the law, as expected by the legislator, this factor is probably even more important than the formulation of such and not another name for the respective extra-legal criterion. It affects both the specific properties of the legal system (in its horizontal and vertical structure) and the possibility of using a clause in the respective process of law application, which in turn affects the role of open criteria in the construction of the normative basis for decisions on the application of law.[116]

The legislative localization of extra-legal references concerns three main structural aspects of the legal system: its horizontal and vertical structure and the systematics of a normative act.

4.2.1. Horizontal structure of the legal system

(1) The basic determinant of the horizontal structure of the legal system is its division into branches of law. It leads to an assumption that branch localization of the extra-legal reference appears to be an essential element of the rationality of legislative activity and it, to some extent, also determines specific legislative objectives (regarding the inclusion of social or political axiology in the processes of law application). It results from the very history of formulating general clauses in the nineteenth century, although the development of this practice indicates a gradual shift of this activity from the branch of civil (private) law to the public law, including, already in the twentieth century, criminal and international law (especially in regulations concerning human rights[117]). This is reflected not only in the changing nomenclature of the criteria for reference clauses, but also in extending the scope of application of clauses to the actions of the legislative authority (whenever clauses appear in constitutional regulations interpreted by ordinary legislation) and the executive authority (which extends the processes of applying the clauses to actions of public administration). Even if, at present, references in private law still prevail, these proportions, at least with regard to public law (with the exception of criminal law), are gradually levelling out.

116 Cf. II.

117 See above: 1.1.

Several basic variables have the strongest effect on the scope and manner of using this normative structure. These include the features of the regulated sphere of social reality and the type of disposition of the created legal norms.

(2) Whenever the nature of the regulation requires careful legislative interference, either because of the autonomy and a certain closure of relations existing there to external influences (family relations), or because of the recognition of a certain degree of spontaneous efficiency of the internal mechanisms of operation of the participants (economic relations). The extra-legal references here may simply limit the negative impact of direct legislative interference. Therefore it applies to relations regulated by civil, family and commercial law, which rely primarily on the autonomous behaviours of participants, for which the law only creates a formal framework.[118]

The historical relationship of referrals with private law[119] leads to the conclusion that it is in this branch of law that reference to extra-legal criteria is also the most natural. It is also least dangerous from the point of view of possible "breaking" of intra-legal values. It results from the way this branch of law is regulated, which is based on the formation of various forms of subjective rights[120] or rules defining the way the rights are to be exercised. The system of private law norms enables the existence of legal relations "unforeseen" by the regulations (e.g. the so-called unnamed contracts) and the subjects of private-law relations are largely independent of the act in determining their legal position (especially within the *ius dispositivum*). The political and legal acceptance for the pluralistic interests of private law participants is, to some extent, a rule also in authoritarian political systems, political involvement in this branch is limited even if the very perception of civil law as private law is questioned.[121] The extent to which this pluralism is recognized obviously depends on the particularities of the political and social system. This is of crucial importance for the method for citing references and naming extra-legal criteria in the light of proportions in taking into account the general and individual interests in law. The relativeness of these

118 Cf. A. Stelmachowski, *Wstęp*, pp. 18, 295, 384; E. Łętowska, "Funkcjonowanie," pp. 12–15.

119 On the features of private law, cf. J. Nowacki, *Prawo*, passim, A. Stelmachowski, *Wstęp*, pp. 18, 50, 481–482; E. Łętowska, "Funkcjonowanie," pp. 8–10, C. Perelman, *Logika*, p. 120 (on the criteria adopted, e.g. by the Belgian Court of Cassation). On the place and role of clauses in civil law regulations, cf. M. Safjan, "Klauzule," pp. 48 ff.

120 On the issue of subjective rights see: W. Lang, J. Wróblewski, S. Zawadzki, *Teoria*, pp. 324 ff., esp. 343–345, Z. Ziembiński, *Problemy*, pp. 364–373.

121 Cf. J. B. Paszukanis, *Ogólna*, pp. 137 ff.

interests means that the need for flexibility and adaptability of regulations are the proprieties of this branch of law. Hence, it is primarily in private law that we find references to customary norms, which are relatively least "exposed" to political interference.

The features of some branches of private law influence the practice of formulating the extra-legal references in yet another way. The content of relations regulated by the provisions of family law depends, to a large extent, on autonomous, group (family) norms and moral judgments. The legislator, who implements its policy here, must be aware of the barriers resulting from the possible "closing" of this sphere to the effective interference of "imposed" legal norms. The effectiveness of regulations requires limiting the scope of regulation with norms, which is to be performed with moderation and caution, especially when the legislator would like to perform some "didactic" tasks in doing so.[122] The political and legal manifestation of such an approach may be, on the one hand, the incorporation of dominant and fully formed moral norms, and, on the other hand, just referring the court to moral evaluations and norms that are not incorporated into the legal system.

The impact of the properties of private-legal regulation on the formulation of references is also visible in the commercial law, especially in the part of it that concerns economic transactions in the market system. Overall, similar features are characteristic for regulation of labour law, which, being a resultant of private law and public law regulations, usually follows the basic regulation methods of law regulating economic activities. In this area, however, it is not the adopted scope of state interference in economic processes (although it is important for determining the initial scale) that has an impact, but the assumed and implemented scale of the implementation of the social function of the state in relation to employees (including private workplaces) instead.

(3) On the other hand, the spheres of social relations of a public-legal nature, regulated in the form of prescribing and prohibiting norms (e.g. criminal law, tax law, and generally speaking – administrative law), are much less suitable for referrals. Here they extend the grounds for authoritative decision making by administrative bodies. These, in turn, not only are not characterized by the feature of independence, but also implement a specific policy of decision-making, which, as a model, connects extra-legal referral with political axiology.

---

122 Cf. J. Winiarz, *Prawo*, pp. 10–11, K. Pałecki, "Społeczne," pp. 209 ff., K. Pałecki, "Warianty," pp. 361 ff.

The separate path for applying administrative law, demonstrating numerous features of a managerial type[123] and a different legal relationship, consisting in subordination to competence,[124] "determine" the juridical aspects of the nature of the regulation, confronted with the scope of tasks of the state administration (within its organizational function). The general requirement to bind the administration by law, correcting the natural "closeness" to the implementation of administrative law and "political activities," concerns the legal side of the nature of this regulation in a soft manner. With regard to the policy of extra-legal referencing, both these "determinants" find expression in the fundamental meaning of the construction of administrative discretion and the creation of such references that express, first of all, values in general social, public or state perspective. Indication in regulations of the necessity to take into account, in decision-making, values containing an individual or group perspective (e.g. the legitimate interest of citizens[125]) is usually treated here as creating a counterbalance, preventing a single-way evaluation underlying the decision, and finally as a correction of the natural advantage of public arguments, protected by this right. Submitting administrative decisions to judicial review should be subject to the very same treatment. As can be seen, what is of crucial importance here, are the provisions of procedural law by which this correction can be achieved. These steps demonstrate the intentions of the legislator, the effectiveness of which in the context of the assumed specific objectives[126] can be determined only on the basis of observation of the decision-making practice.

The public nature of legal regulation manifests itself, in yet another manner, in the case of criminal law and extra-legal referencing in this branch. Requirements regarding certainty, elementary uniformity or "objectivity" of the application and interpretation here, as well as the postulate of a closed system are at the fore of the desired features of regulation.[127] They find even a deeper ideological justification than it is the case in other branches of law. It is not conducive to the shaping of a policy of referral when creating this law, even though the relationship between criminal law and moral norms remains irreconcilable. It would be hard to argue that this relationship is even stronger in criminal law than, for example, in civil

---

123 Cf. W. Lang, J. Wróblewski, S. Zawadzki, *Teoria*, pp. 412–413; W. Dawidowicz, "O stosowaniu," pp. 74–76.

124 Cf. S. Wronkowska, Z. Ziembiński, *Zarys*, pp. 117 ff.

125 In accordance with Art. 7 KPA.

126 See above: 1.2.

127 Cf. e.g. W. Wolter, "W sprawie," pp. 75 ff.

law, where it can only be revealed at the stage of applying the law,[128] while in criminal law the provisions themselves "positivize morality"[129] from the point of view of the legislator's axiology. Penal regulations incorporate certain socially significant moral rules, according to the assumptions of the legislator. Hence, the characteristics of certainty of criminal law, which I have indicated above, by obviously "authorizing" this rationing, push to the background, or even – provided that they are formulated in their strong versions – "prohibit" the referring to non-incorporated evaluations and norms, that need to be established in the process of deciding on the criminal character of the respective acts. In practice, however, such a legislative policy model is subject to various modifications. References in the form of evaluation clauses formulated in detailed provisions and systemic references (general reference clauses) are sometimes treated as criteria for the sanctioning (they are related to a specific "measuring" of a criminal sanction). It is unimaginable, however, to have such a political and legal assumption that would make the criminal nature of an act dependent solely on compliance with legally unspecified and socially diverse moral standards. However, this does not prevent the indication of lack of social danger or harmfulness of an act from becoming one of the criteria determining the lack of the criminal nature of behaviour.[130]

(4) The constitutional law occupies a special place with regard to extra-legal reference. Forming part of the public law, it also penetrates various aspects of private law regulations. If it is applied directly, it may influence the use of references in law application processes.[131] In each case, however, it is also a certain determinant of the creation of references in ordinary legislation, regardless of the branch of the law they are to be enacted.

A good example of such a regulation is the Polish Constitution of 1997, which contains a large number of references. Some of them are already located in the Preamble (justice, common good, good, beauty, universal values, human values), others in chapter I ("The Republic") containing a set of legal principles and in chapter II regulating human and civil rights. These include. among

128 Cf. A. Stelmachowski, *Wstęp*, p. 87, A. Wąsek, "Prawo," pp. 47 ff.

129 Cf. Z. Ziembiński, "Moralność," pp. 104–105, Z. Ziembiński, *Teoria*, p. 136.

130 Art. 1 of KK of 1997 and Art. 1 of KK of 1969.

131 This applies, for example, to the reference to the principles of social justice in Art. 2 of RP Constitution, which under the rule of direct application of this Constitution (Art. 8 sec. 2) may be used in the judicial application of the law without reference to other statutory criteria (Cf. II).

others: common good, principles of social justice, human good, public interest, public good, good of family, good of the state, economic interest of the state, public order, public objectives, professed moral principles, human dignity, public morality, morality, necessity in a democratic state, unfair market practices). On the other hand, in the chapters regulating the system of state authorities, there are clauses that refer to several additional criteria: the good of the state, the interest of the State Treasury and state security. They all emphasize the public (general) and sometimes even universal (human) dimension of the axiology being invoked (apart from the criteria of professed moral principles and unfair market practices), but they do not politicize this axiology. They become an element of not only legal principles but also axiological declarations and program norms and moreover, not only substantial but also procedural and competence legal norms.

(5) Taking into account the horizontal structure of the legal system in the context of the policy of extra-legal referral cannot ignore the differences with regard to substantive and procedural law. While references in substantive law are directed both to the ordinary addressees and to decision-making bodies, references in procedural law are directed to a special addressee, i.e. to the authority applying the law, with intention to indicate the criteria for making partial or the final decisions in the process. So they are an element for "steering" the axiology of these entities but they are also of significance for ordinary addressees. This is because they may, for example, constitute a criterion for appealing against a decision of an authority. They may also, which is perhaps even more important, constitute an element of predicting the content of a decision on the application of law, which, especially in legal relations involving the implementation of their own subjective rights, allows them for a conscious choice of a specific behaviour.

(6) The implementation of the assumptions of the legislative policy in the entire legal system is a complex matter. Usually, it is easier to find these assumptions in relation to individual parts of the system (a branch of law, a group of acts related in content, a given act, individual legal institutions). However, it can be assumed that the legislator (of course treated in an idealizing manner[132]) refers both in the perspective of individual institutions, normative acts, groups of these acts, branches, but also in the perspective of the entire legal system. One could find references to the type of legal culture modified by the type of political regime within that culture. However, without going that far in comparisons, one can

132 Cf. L. Nowak, *Interpretacja*, pp. 39–53, Z. Ziembiński, *Problemy*, pp. 374 ff.

certainly see the "intersection" of references and their crossing of the boundaries of legal branches.

As it seems, from the legislator's point of view, as important as the direction of the reference is the mere indication of the requirement to take into account extra-legal criteria in general. Therefore, in addition to the references that are present in individual branches, there are also system-wide references that reach beyond the normative field of one or several related branches. For example, in the law of European countries, this scope can be attributed to references to equity (principles of equity), good customs, good faith and social interest. In Polish law, this is the most important clause of the principles of social coexistence, established in almost every part of law. References to the socio-economic purpose of law, social interest, state interest, public interest, etc., and the clauses of good customs, principles of equity and good faith "returning" to legislation after 1989 have slightly lower "range" in respect of frequency. And there are the "single-branch" references that include the clauses of: good of the child, good of the family, good of the workplace, social danger (harmfulness) of an act, interest of the taxpayer, interests of the national economy or the interest of the company.[133]

In each case of referring, the entire "system" of clauses is, from the point of view of legal policy assumptions, an axiological orientation of the discretion accepted by the legislator, and it must be correlated with the criteria set by the basic principles of the legal system, defining the framework of specific axiological choices both at the level of legislation and at the level of law application.

4.2.2. Vertical structure of the legal system

When it comes to place of extra-legal references in the vertical structure of the legal system, the most important role is played by the features of normative acts, depending on their legal force (their place in the hierarchy).

The location of general reference clauses in the statute does not raise doubts in the context of its features. This is because it is the type of act that is not only the most general, but also modelled in terms of the most careful legislative policy and the most careful preparation and procedure. This applies in particular to statutes in the form of codes, which constitute the basic and unifying normative act for the entire branch of law, and such an objective may accompany locating references in these acts.

---

133 The latter criterion appears e.g. in Art. 249 and Art. 422 of KSH.

Doubts as to the location of the references may not include constitutional regulations, the norms of which have not only the most open structure in terms of their content, but also the broadest application. Their impact on the legal order, apart from the use of clauses as part of the direct application of the constitution by courts, also consists in an indirect impact, taking place by opening the determinants of the policy for making statutory and understatutory norms, which may contain further references. Thus, it can be said that this location is an element of the most general linking of the content of law and the processes of its application with extra-legal axiology, balancing the relations between social (moral) and political axiology in the relatively broadest scope there is.

These characteristics are further magnified in the case of localization of references in the general part of constitutional regulation, affecting the processes of their creation and application to the greatest possible extent.

The most doubts arise in connection with the formulation of clauses in substatutory acts, having an executive character and thus, the most susceptible to direct influence on the part of the centre of political power. The application of these acts is carried out by administrative bodies, which not only makes them more sensitive to such influence, but also not subjecting these actions to complete judicial control (e.g. with regard to judicial control of the administration in the European continental model, limited to the control of the legality of the activities of the administration[134]). It can therefore be assumed that the more references appear in such acts, the more it is related to the will to legislatively and politically "direct" the use of references.

4.2.3. Systematics of a normative act

(1) An extremely important determinant of legislative policy in terms of the location of clauses is their placement in the systematics of a normative act. There are three main options for the legislator in this regard. The first is the location of the reference in the provisions of the specific parts of a normative act, the second is its placement in the general provisions of such an act, while the third is the combination of the two aforesaid.

When a clause is included in specific provisions related to the regulation of a specific legal situation (e.g. ownership) or a given type of legal relationship (e.g. a lease agreement), what is articulated is the will to limit its application mainly to this situation or relationship. In the event of a need to "borrow" a

134 Cf. V.4.1.

clause to a similar institution or legal relationship, such a location requires more complex arguments (*per analogiam legis*), if they are at all possible. The intention to extend the basis for the application of clauses appears, however, if it is included in a provision where its scope of application covers several institutions and relations[135] (e.g. provisions that are common to easements), especially since such an operation often involves overlapping the scopes of application of the references.[136]

The broadest basis for the use of clauses is the location of clauses in the general provisions of a normative act (and sometimes even in its preamble[137]), which is functionally close to opening the system in the model of equity judgments,[138] in terms of creating the possibility of basing court decisions on extra-legal criteria. This is especially important when the clause is included in the initial provisions of the code forming the basic act for the entire branch of law. This practice, regardless of the fact that it determines the addressees of the most general patterns of behaviour,[139] leaves the courts free to use the reference that can actually cover any situation or relationship regulated in such an act, also when the extra-legal reference does not appear with its detailed regulation.[140] The general nature of a provision can be graded, because apart from the perspective of the entire act, it may also include general provisions of its separate part (e.g. contract law forming part of the framework of civil law).

---

135 For example, clauses of Art. 353[1] and Art. 354 of KC, which define relationships between a creditor and a debtor, or clauses of Art. 65 of the said Code, specifying the criteria for the interpretation of each declaration of will in civil law transactions.

136 For example, the creditor's behaviour may be assessed under the KC in the context of violation of the principles of social coexistence under both Art. 5 (abuse of the subjective right) and Art. 354 (obligation to cooperate in the performance of the obligation by the debtor).

137 Cf. e.g. references to universal values and general human values in the Preamble to RP Constitution. Such a location of references may be of importance for the interpretation of other provisions of this act, and if it is a constitutional regulation – other provisions of the entire legal system

138 Cf. above: 1.1.

139 See for example Art. 2 of ZGB imposing the duty of acting in good faith ("*Jedermann hat in der Ausübung seiner Rechte und in der Erfüllung seiner Pflichten nach Treu und Glauben zu handeln*") or Art. 5 of KC, according to which, among others, an action contradicting the principles of social coexistence is treated as an abuse of subjective right.

140 E.g. Art. 6 of CN, setting the criteria of public order ("*l "ordre public*") and good customs ("*les bonnes moeurs*") as the basis for decisions on any private contract, § 7 of

The graduality noticed above indicates the third option for placing clauses in a normative act. In its broadest form, it means formulating references (often called the same) in general provisions for the entire regulation, in general provisions of its part and in specific provisions. Such a practice is not uncommon, especially in the codifications of civil (or more broadly – private) law. To sum it up, it further limits the (already limited) "control" of the legislator over the use of references due to the mere possibility of combining individual clauses and criteria contained in various parts of the normative act.

Summing up the three aspects of locating references – in various branches of law, in acts of different legal force and in various places of a normative act, although forming a manifestation of a specific legislative policy, in fact extends the freedom of decision-making in the processes of applying the law, enabling entities operating within their frameworks (mainly courts) their application in such a manner that is related to the characteristics of a specific case (actual condition).

4.2.4. Type of normative regulation

All the above-analysed aspects of placing the extra-legal references within the legal system are related to locating the reference in various legal provisions containing specific types of legal norm. This indicates the legislative intention to open the law in the width resulting from this location and to relate it to a specific form of action by the subject applying the law.

The broadest scope of openness is associated with placing open criteria within a normatively separated or universally recognized principle of law. Even when we consider the fact that it is connected with the linking of extra-legal and intra-legal axiology, it is the extra-legal criterion that determines the content of the principle, obtaining from the latter the "normative force" associated with the principle of law. It is not only about the direct normativization of such a criterion, but also about a wider field of application thereof. It may mean not only any act of applying such a principle within a branch of law (e.g. the principle determining the abuse of subjective right on the grounds of violating the principles of social coexistence in civil law[141]) but also within the entire legal order (e.g. the

ABGB setting the criteria of natural legal principles ("*natürliche Rechtsgrunsatzen*") as the basis for adjudication in a situation of ambiguity or impossibility to apply analogies) or Art. 4 ZGB designating the criterion of equity ("*Billigkeit*") as the basis for the action of the court in the so-called decision gap).

141 Art. 5 of KC.

principle of a democratic state of law taking into account the principles of social justice based on the constitutional regulation[142]).

To sum it up if the extra-legal criterion is included in the text containing the system-axiological declaration, the effects of its presents are similar. This can take place either in a preamble (e.g. an indication of the relationship between regulation and humane or universal values[143]) or in some systematically significant provision (e.g. defining the state as the common good of all citizens[144]). Regardless of whether such structures fulfil or not fulfil the independent role of the rule of law, their influence on the axiology of the respective regulation and even (if it is part of the content of constitution) on the entire legal order, cannot be overlooked.

The inclusion of an extra-legal criterion in the programic norm,[145] which can be treated as a kind of legal principle,[146] is of a slightly different nature (and legislative purpose). It means the intention to direct the actions of the state or the entity (state authority) designated in such regulation to implement a given program in such a way that the value indicated therein is met (e.g. with regard to the shaping of relations between the state and churches in the light of the criterion of common good[147] or the scope of consumer protection against the unfair commercial practices[148]). Despite the lack of direct sanctioning of such a norm, it may influence (as long it is a constitutional norm) the legislative activity taking into account the criterion indicated therein.

The provisions containing competence norms are practically devoid of formulation of extra-legal references. This applies in particular to the classic norms of competence that require greater normative precision, especially if they relate to actions taken by courts. To act contrary to this rule would mean increasing the scope of the authorization to act, which may be associated with different legislative intentions, depending, to some extent, on the type of political system.

The formulation of a reference in a procedural provision may have a twofold intention. If it is a provision containing a legal principle, it means that every action of the entity applying the law is generally dependent on taking into account

142 Art. 2 of RP Constitution.
143 Preamble to RP Constitution.
144 Art. 2 of RP Constitution.
145 Cf. T. Gizbert-Studnicki, A. Grabowski, "Normy," pp. 95 ff.
146 R. Dworkin, "The Model," passim.
147 Art. 25 sec. 3 of RP Constitution.
148 Art. 76 of RP Constitution.

the said extra-legal criterion. This can act either as an extension of the basis for action (in the case of indicating a criterion related to the state or public axiology) or as a definition of the criterion of the legitimacy and correctness of the authority's operation (in the case of indicating the criterion of social interest and the legitimate interest of citizens[149]). If, on the other hand, a procedural provision containing a reference is a provision regulating some part of the decision-making process (e.g. discontinuation of proceedings[150]) or a particular activity forming part of this process (e.g. participation of a prosecutor in civil proceedings[151]), its axiological impact is limited to such a precisely defined sphere of activity.

The most common locations, where extra-legal references are included are the norms of material law. They then constitute the basis for either the qualification of the respective behaviour, which, taking into account the *ignorantia iuris nocet* principle, should take into account the indicated open criteria (e.g. as part of the exercise of its own subjective right,[152] formulation of the content of the concluded contract,[153] manner of performance of the obligation,[154] etc.) or normative consequences (e.g. as a criterion for imposing a penalty[155] or determining the amount of compensation[156]).

4.3. Determining the conditions for the use of extra-legal criteria

The legislator may also influence the use of extra-legal references by specifying, within the normative act, additional conditions on the fulfilment of which depends the possibility of using and, to some extent, the manner of using extra-legal references in the application of law. In a sense, they are such conditions, regardless of the location of the reference within the normative act or the definition of the relationship between extra-legal and intra-legal criteria (both *stricti iuris* norms and legal principles).

If we assume that the legislative wording of the reference implies an obligation not so much to use, but to consider the use of an extra-legal criterion, then the determination of the conditions under which this consideration should

149 Art. 7 of KPA.
150 Cf. Art. 105 of KPA.
151 Cf. Art. 7 of KPC.
152 Cf. Art. 5 of KC.
153 Cf. Art. 353 of KC.
154 Cf. Art. 354 of KC.
155 Cf. Art. 53 of KK.
156 Cf. Art. 417^2 of KC.

take place determines the scope of such use. Legislators take advantage of this, treating this possibility as a means for implementing a targeted opening of the legal system, and thus as an element of influence on the range of the decision-making discretion, which is significantly extended in the model by such reference clauses.

Conditions for the use of extra-legal criteria may be related either to the condition or the properties of the normative regulation. A condition related to the state of the regulation may refer to the lack of legal provisions regulating the respective situation[157] or the insufficient precision of the normative text.[158] On the other hand, the condition related to the properties of a given type of normative regulation may make the use of clauses dependent on the criteria specified in the provision for extending the decision-making freedom of courts.[159] It may also involve limiting the scope of the clause's application to the indicated legal reasoning (e.g. the interpretation of legal provisions[160]), to a specific element of the decision-making process (e.g. the interpretation of a declaration of will[161]) or to the assessment of a specific legal situation (e.g. the validity of a legal act[162]). The scope of application of the reference may further be limited to specific activities in the decision-making process (e.g. to the option of applying provisions taken over from the previous legal system[163]).

The conditions determined in this way by the legislator primarily affect the basis and scope of application of extra-legal references, and only as an alternative, they affect the way they are applied or determine the content of individual criteria indicated in reference clauses.

5. Basic factors differentiating the legislative policy and its effects

The policy of extra-legal referral and the ways of its implementation in legislative activity depend on many factors. Some of them were already mentioned (e.g.

157 Cf. Art. 1 of ZGB.

158 Cf. § 7 of ABGB.

159 See Art. 4 of ZGB ("*Wo das Gesetz das Gericht auf sein Ermessen oder auf die Würdigung der Umstände oder auf wichtige Gründe verweist, hat es seine Entscheidung nach Recht und Billigkeit zu treffen*").

160 E.g. Art. 4 (derogated in 1990) of KC.

161 E.g. Art. 65 of KC.

162 E.g. Art. 58 of KC.

163 See Art. 4 of KC or Art. 5 of the Soviet decree on the court of 1917.

the type of branch of law or the type of normative act). Undoubtedly the type of legal culture also constitutes such a factor, because the very creation of clauses is related to the legislative form of creating law, which is a feature of the continental culture of statutory law. The referral policy may apply to the Anglo-Saxon legal order only insofar as its content is determined by the enactment of legal provisions containing references.

The strongest impact on the referencing policy and the creation of general clauses itself results from the type of political system and the situation of profound legal change.

(1) The influence of the type of political system concerns the statutory law orders in that they are implemented both in democratic systems (liberal constitutional democracy, a component which is the principle of the rule of law and civic society, which do not limit their activity to an election act), and in various autocratic systems, covering a whole spectrum of specific subtypes falling between totalitarian systems (e.g. Nazi fascism, Stalinist communism) and soft authoritarian systems (e.g. some of the so-called people's democracies in Central and Eastern Europe following World War II).[164]

It is characteristic that while the legislative policy concerning the creation of clauses in various democratic systems of the statutory law culture is based on uniform foundations and principles, and does not differ to any significant extent, such uniformity cannot be observed in various authoritarian systems. They create more detailed variants, and the main distinguishing feature here is the variety of versions of authoritarianism and its depth, which directly affect the link between the referral and the current, often changing, political situation.

Taking the above-analysed components of the legislative policy of creating clauses (names, location and conditioning of use) into account, it should be stated that the more totalitarian the political system is, the more the names of extra-legal clause criteria will refer to political axiology (and this applies not only to public law, but also to private one). This occurs either openly (e.g. revolutionary awareness of the masses, principles of the political system, goals or interests of the state) or in the form of an indication of criteria of a general social dimension, seemingly referring to moral axiology, which may even give the impression of trying to read social assessments (e.g. public interest). The authoritarian legislator, preferring what is more susceptible to politicization, i.e. the general social dimension of axiology, avoids indicating criteria referring to morality in

164 On the classifications of authoritarian systems, cf. e.g. A. Alvares, J.A. Cheibub, F. Limongi, A. Przeworski, "Classifying," pp. 3–36.

the group dimension, and especially in the individual dimension (because this does not match the authoritarian ideology). It is also less keen to refer to empirically verifiable criteria (e.g. established habits). In the latter two cases, this could make it difficult (although not completely impossible, especially in a totalitarian system) to ideologize the content of such a criterion. This is because it is facilitated in the situation of the frequent combination of various criteria (usually with the participation of political criteria), creating an example of a specific "axiological entanglement" of a given fragment of the regulation. The autocratic legislator will also avoid direct linking of extra-legal content with basic legal principles (especially those which are not the result of legislative activity, but refer to the tradition of legal culture), at best adjusting the legal principles formulated in the provisions to the content of politically involved open criteria. Certain aspects of the legislator's "axiological hypersensitivity" may be associated, in these systems, with a specific "emotionalization" of the terminology used in the above-mentioned examples of the law of fascist Germany or Soviet Russia.[165]

When it comes to the policy of placing clauses in the legal system, autocratic lawmakers transfer the construction of clauses more broadly to the branches of public and criminal law and to executive acts, thus "promoting" the use of clauses in the administrative law application, which, in principle, is not a subject to judicial review. The type of political system does not, however, decisively influence the location of clauses in the systematics of a legal act, although their location in the most general provisions of a regulation enables a broader political influence on the judicial use of the extra-legal references in an autocratic order (this type of localization can also be observed in democratic systems,[166] where it is usually a non-politicized form for widening the decision-making gap).

The authoritarian legislator is not interested in determining the conditions for the use of extra-legal criteria, as this could limit the scope of political influence on the judicature, which itself does not meet the condition of independence. The exception here is granting extra-legal criteria the function of criteria limiting the application or defining the politically accepted direction of interpretation of the regulations adopted from the previous system[167]).

---

165 Cf. above: 2.1.

166 Cf. § 7 of ABGB or Art. 1, 2 and 4 of ZGB.

167 Whether it was democratic, as was the case, for example, in the case of the application of pre-war regulations in Poland after 1945 or a less (after all) autocratic a system, as was the case with the application of pre-revolutionary laws in Soviet Russia after 1917.

In all the above aspects and manifestations of the authoritarian policy of referrals, the (largely justified) belief in the effectiveness of political control of the practice of using referrals is decisive. This, in turn, includes forms that fall within the broad range between direct imposition and the creation of normative foundations for a more sublime influence on the way in which references are applied by the courts.[168] This is especially true for the most sensitive method of determining the content of these criteria in this set.

In a sense, a factor analogous to the type of political system is the type of economic system in which the clauses are established. Tendencies are additionally strengthened, because usually the system of centrally managed (and thus politicized) economy corresponds to the authoritarian political type, and the system of market economy – to the democratic system. The subject matter of this practice is the politicization of economic criteria, mainly through appropriate names that generalize their material context (socio-economic objective) or directly indicate the "state dimension" of the economy (interests of the national economy[169]).

Completely opposite tendencies and expectations characterize the legislative policy of the legislator in a democratic order, of course, taking into account certain features characterizing various versions of democracy or market systems (especially in connection with the contemporary indication of its social character and acceptance of greater state intervention). The essential features of such a policy and the expectations related to it, however, go hand in hand with independent judicial practice and this is what constitutes an effective measure to limit the "political activism" of the centre of power. Generally speaking, it can be said that the more democratic (and to some extent liberal) the political system in which clauses are created, the fewer elements politicizing the moral and economic extra-legal axiology are found in their content. This also strengthens the link between the content of extra-legal criteria and the basic principles of law resulting from the cultural and legal tradition, and the conditions for using these criteria are more clearly formulated.

(2) The above differences are visible not only in the already formed political systems, but also in a situation of profound social change leading to a change of the system, either from democratic to an authoritarian or from authoritarian to a democratic one. This is even more so, since the very features of the social and

---

168 For example, by authorizing the politically controlled Supreme Court to issue general legal interpretations (and thus also to determine the content and use of extra-legal criteria) in the form of instructions, binding all courts (cf. V.4.2.).

169 Cf. Art. 826 or 827 of KC.

legal change, especially a profound one, inherently encourage lawmakers to leave certain normative content open, for which reference clauses are most suitable. However, depending on the direction of the change, the intentions behind this opening will differ. It is not only about the gradual reflection by the legislator of the features of the functioning of clauses in the "target" system, but also the perception of clauses and the criteria contained therein as a "constructing measure" for this new legal order.

The actions of the legislator creating the foundations of an authoritarian system are usually much stronger, ideologizing and "totalizing" the new axiology, an element of which is the inclusion of extra-legal political criteria in the regulations defining the conditions for the application and interpretation of provisions taken over from the previous system. This is well illustrated by the examples of the reaction of the Polish legislator after 1945 to the change of the democratic system to an authoritarian one.[170] Certain elements of such practice are visible in the situation of introducing changes in the legislation of an already relatively shaped democratic system, which limit not only the

170 These features are reflected in the evolution of extra-legal references in civil law in Poland after World War II. In the first legal act in this field (POPC of 1946), they did not contain any directly politicized content, referring to a custom that has the force of law as long as it is common (art. 2), social interest and legitimate interests of the parties, constituting the basis for judicial decisions in the absence of statutory grounds for settlement (art. 3) and the social purpose and the requirements of good faith, as criteria for the exercise of private rights (art. 5). The next regulation of the same type (POPC of 1950) changed the formula of extra-legal reference, setting the principles of the political system and the objectives of the People's State as a criterion for interpreting and applying legal provisions (Art. 1) and the principles of social coexistence in the People's State as the criterion for making use of one's rights (Art. 3). This nomenclature, more in line with communist ideology, was used in Polish KC by repeating the content of Art. 1 of the act of 1950 in Art. 4 of the Code and modifying of the formula of abuse of law under Art. 3 of POPC of 1950 by adding the criterion of the socio-economic purpose of law in Art. 5 of the Code. After 1989, Art. 4 was removed from the code, yet Art. 5 was retained, without linking the content of the principles of social coexistence with the Polish People's Republic. Thus, the legislator did not decide to replace the old clauses and names of criteria with new ones (e.g. the principles of social coexistence remained a criterion in over 20 provisions of the said code and many other normative acts), nevertheless, in the case of the amendments of the provisions of the Civil Code, the legislator, after 1989, refers to the classic criterion of "considerations of equity" in Art. 761^2 and "good customs" in Art. 72 § 2 or Art. 385^2 of KC.

scope of judicial independence but also the role of culturally shaped extra-legal axiology.[171]

Therefore, when the very essence is considered, the mere legislative nomenclature of the criteria, their location in the regulatory system and the determination of the conditions for their use would mean much less in terms of the impact on the processes of using references, if they were not imposed on the objectives of the legislative policy related to the characteristics of the social, political and economic legal environment. Compared to them (and especially to the type of political system), all other differentiating factors are either complementary or secondary.

171 For example, this applies to the references to the criterion of "social interest" introduced in Art. 137 § 2 of Polish Law of 28 I 2016 on Prosecutor Office (*Prawo o prokuraturze*) as a criterion excluding the disciplinary liability of a prosecutor acting exclusively in social interest.

Chapter II The basis for the use of extra-legal reference in the judicial decision-making process

The analyses and findings carried out in the subsequent three chapters (II–IV) are based on the model of the judicial (operative) interpretation process, in which we distinguish (1) the preliminary (indicative) phase, resulting from the interpreter's initial contact with the case materials, leading to further interpretation phases, (2) the phase of validation findings, the subject of which is to select the law carriers as sources for the reconstruction of the applied norms (3) the reconstruction phase, including determining the meaning of expressions and the reconstruction of behaviour patterns from the previously determined sources, (4) the construction phase, which combines the reconstructed patterns into the final normative basis for the decision and (5) the decision phase, the essence of which is the reduction of the normative basis to the content of the particular decision of the application of law.

At each of these stages of interpretation, the participation of extra-legal references is possible, which will be subject of our detailed analysis in Chapter IV of the present work. Nevertheless, the precondition for "measuring" the impact of references on individual interpretative reasoning is to decide on the use (application) of the reference itself in the decision-making process (which is the subject of the present Chapter II) and to determine the content of the criteria contained in the reference clause (which will be the subject of Chapter III).

1. Extra-legal reference as a validation argument for an operative interpretation of the law

(1) The issue of using the extra-legal criterion in the decision-making process of the judicial application of the law is determined in the statutory legal order by the application of the general reference clause (extra-legal reference). Even if certain specific situations of referring to such a criterion are noticeable, it does not change the fundamental dependence linking judicial decisions with legislative activity in this context.

The decision to use an extra-legal reference has the character of a validation decision. The reasoning and actions at this stage of the operative interpretation determine the choice of the carriers of the law, i.e. the sources from which the single, basic behavioural patterns will be reconstructed in the subsequent stage.

In other words, as a result of this decision, extra-legal criteria are included (along with legal provisions and other judicial decisions) to the set of carriers on the basis of which, after determining their content, the particular norms of conduct are reconstructed and the normative basis for other decision to apply the law is constructed. This, in turn, means that the validation phase of a judicial interpretation concerns both the application of the references themselves and their role in making decisions on the application of legal provisions and other decisions on the application of law.

These two aspects of the validation findings are however separated in the sense that this chapter will present the basics for using the reference itself, while chapter IV will focus on analysis of the role of references in the entire process of operative interpretation, including their impact on the application of the legal provisions.

(2) Generally speaking, the choice of validation arguments presupposes the possibility of applying provisions of law, open criteria and other decisions on the application of law (precedents), in the framework of the specific decision-making process.

The general arrangement of sources and their role in specific decision-making processes are, in turn, determined by the properties of the legal order (legal culture) in which these take place. They allow for assigning the dominant role of the legal provisions in the statutory legal order (the so-called continental legal culture), to precedents (case law, judge-made law)[1] in the common law order (Anglo-Saxon culture) and to open criteria (predominantly norms and moral values) in the order of equity law (*ius aequitas*, equity law,[2] but also the contemporary forms of ADR).[3]

The dominant role of legal provisions as the source for reconstruction of the rule (behaviour pattern) and the construction of the comprehensive normative basis for the judicial decision in the statutory law order[4] means that it is only possible to build such a basis solely on the ground of the legal provisions applicable in the respective process, regardless of their nature, and where they are located in the hierarchy of normative regulations. However, the observation of the decision-making processes in this order as well as of the decisions themselves

1 Cf. R. Cross, *Precedent*, pp. 25 ff., R.J. Aldisert, *The Judicial*, pp. 50 ff., J. Levin, *How Judges*, pp. 158–174.

2 Cf. R. Taubenschlag, *Rzymskie*, pp. 28 ff., W.M. Bartel, "Z dziejów," pp. 340 ff.

3 Cf. A. Korybski, *Alternatywne*, passim. A. Kalisz, A. Zienkiewicz, *Mediacja*, pp. 15 ff., Z. Kmieciak, *Mediacja*, passim, M. Myślińska, *Mediator*, esp. pp. 71 ff.

4 Cf. J. Wróblewski, "Concepts," passim.

and their justifications, especially in the judicial type of law application, leads us to the conclusion that, under actual conditions, apart from legal provisions, also other decisions on the application of law and open criteria, albeit to a differing extent, are also used as validation arguments. This is undoubtedly an optimal and rational practice from the point of view of the quality of the legal order. In this context we should also stress that the more such a legal order deviates from autocratic patterns, the more strongly, broader and deeper are the "non-regulatory" sources of reconstructing behaviour patterns and constructing a normative basis for decisions applied in judicial practice. This is certainly facilitated by the enhancement of the features of judicial independence that makes it possible, among others, to shape individual, autonomous to some extent, decision-making practices.

The inclusion of general referring clauses in the set of validation arguments of the respective law application process therefore has axiological grounding. The use of the authorization to refer to extra-legal axiology, which does not mean an order to perform such an operation, means that the subject applying the law notices such a need already at this initial stage of the decision-making process. It follows from the preliminary recognition of the characteristics of the decision-making situation, the features of the facts or the components of a legal relationship, leading to the conviction that normative regulations (*stricti iuris* standards) will not suffice for their legal qualification (determining the consequences of this qualification is usually considered at later stages of the process).

(3) The presence of open criteria in the set of sources in a given decision-making process within the statutory law order is characterized by several essential features, resulting from the court perception of referrals as validation arguments complementary to legal provisions.

Firstly, the intention to refer to extra-legal criteria in the application of the law is above-mentioned in various ways in the applicable legal provisions, contained in acts of different legal force (when assigning the essential role to statutory references).

Secondly, the above dependence on the legal provisions prevailing in this order means that the use of references in the decision-making process takes place, in a way, "in the second sequence," i.e. already after naming the legal provisions applicable in this process.

Thirdly, the complementary nature of the references, when compared to the legal provisions, means that, in principle, the references cannot constitute independent and only validation arguments.

Fourthly, the presence of extra-legal references does not exclude their co-occurrence also with earlier court decisions (precedents), which, although they themselves have a complementary role to legal provisions, may shape, also in the statutory law order, permanent ways of using extra-legal references in application of the law.

Fifthly, as a consequence of distinguishing both features indicated directly above, it is possible to combine the use of extra-legal references with all other legal carriers – i.e. with provisions of law and other decisions on the application of law.

Sixthly, the very presence of extra-legal references does not exclude their coexistence also with legal principles (regardless of whether they are principles formulated in provisions of law or appearing in jurisprudence on the base of cultural and legal tradition), which in later stages of operative interpretation leads to complex relations between extra-legal and intra-legal axiology within the specific decision-making process.

Seventhly, the use of extra-legal references in the decision-making process may take place as the inclusion of one or more extra-legal criteria, regardless of whether they are indicated in one or more reference clauses, leading to different relationships at later stages of interpretation within the framework of extra-legal axiology.

Eighthly, the relationship between the application of the reference clauses and their presence in the applicable legal provisions does not exclude specific situations, which include "borrowing" references from legal provisions other than those applied in this decision-making process, applying references contained in formally non-binding provisions or in past court judgments, as well as a specific "drafting" of a referral by the court applying the law.

2. Direct application of the general reference clause

The direct application of the general reference clause in the statutory law order takes place when the subject applying the law uses the reference contained in the applicable provision (on the basis of the formal justification of its validity with regard to *ratione loci, personae* and *temporis*), the content of which corresponds to the subject of the decision-making process, as determined by its facts (*ratione materiae*). Nevertheless we should supplement this general observation by relativization with regard to the type of a normative act in which such a provision is contained, to the type of legal provision as an element of that act, and distinguishing the situation of applying a clause from provisions of international and supranational law. The basis for the application of the clause is therefore, in these cases, transferred from the basis for application of the legal provision, also subject to a certain extent to the test of applicability of such provisions.

2.1. The use of references and the type of legal act containing the clause

The relationship between reference clauses and legal provisions in the context of the basis for their application (use) in the decision-making process does not predetermine the type of normative act within which the provision containing the clause should be sought for.

(1) A model situation for the use of clauses in the processes of applying the law, is the reference to clauses formulated in provisions with the rank of a statute. This dependence results not only from its superior legal force in the vertical structure of the legal system, but also from the careful drafting of its content, and thus also the referring clauses formulated in its text, and from the potentially democratic (i.e. correct reading of social axiology) grounding of the process for establishing it. This is particularly important in those branches of law, where the content of statutes is developed by executive acts.

Codes play a special role among the statutes, especially in the context of the separation of the branches of law. This is related to the legislative policy of creating references,[5] within which code references define the framework for the extra-legal axiology applied in the decision-making processes. In branches where there are no codes, such a role may be played by basic laws for the given area of regulation, the comprehensive nature of which is emphasized, for example, by their title that contains the word "law" (e.g. "Construction Law").

In those branches of law, which are regulated by many acts with various mutual relations, the entities applying the law "gain" an additional option to select the reference clauses contained therein, depending on the characteristics of the particular decision-making process. Although the detailed effects of these choices and possible summaries are revealed mainly when determining the content of these references, they may also affect the very fact of applying a particular reference.

(2) References may also become part of the decision-making process also when they are formulated in generally applicable sub-statutory provisions, issued on the basis of a statutory authorization (e.g. an ordinance of a minister). There are four potential situations there. The first, where the clause in an implementing rule is a repetition of a clause in an act, which usually leads to the application of both references. The second, when there is no clause in the executive act, and therefore the statutory clause applies. The third, when a clause appears in the

5 Cf. L. Leszczyński, *Tworzenie*, pp. 117 ff., pp. 142–144.

executive act without its prior wording in the statute, which "forces" the application of a reference solely from the executive act. The fourth situation, on the other hand, occurs when a clause referring to the statutory clause appears in the implementing act, but it is referring to a criterion different from that indicated in the statutory clause, necessitating the definition of the relationship between the criteria indicated in both clauses.

The use of reference clauses from the sub-statutory provisions in the first and fourth situations usually also means the reference to a statutory reference. The purpose of linking both references is to concretize their content in a more specific and precisely defined subject context. This is done by specifying the situation for the application of the reference. This limits the primary (statutory) decision-making discretion in applying the law.[6] As a consequence, however, such a combination of references leads to the strengthening of the axiological argumentation resulting from the extra-legal references expressed in both types of provisions.

The third situation, i.e. that of the decision-maker only has a clause in the implementing act at its disposal a reference formulated exclusively in a sub-statutory act, is rare in the practice of application of law.[7] Such a practice, although it cannot be accused of anything from the point of view of the law application model, seems to be a manifestation of an incorrect legislative policy. It violates the proper relations between the legislative and executive acts. It may also lead to the expansion of the discretion as to the content of the decision beyond the scope set by the legislator.

The model situation is the second one, where the statutory clause is "sufficient" to use the extra-legal criteria also in the application of a sub-statutory act. This situation does not lead to unnecessary repetitions or to the creation of potential content collisions between the criteria of different clauses.

(3) The above-mentioned relations between the use of references contained in statutes and sub-statutory acts can be transferred to other relations within the vertical and territorial structure of the legal system, denoting various situations of using references formulated in acts with a limited scope of application only.

---

6 Cf. e.g. SN Judgment of 16 IV 1967, III CR 429/66, OSNCP, item 181, SN Judgment of 5 I 1967, III PRN 81/66, OSNCP 1967, item 116. In GKA Decision of 18 V 1970, BO-3874/70, OSPiKA 1971, item 20 only the executive act is referred to, even though these reference criteria are similar to statutory ones.

7 Cf. e.g. SN Judgment of 9 II 1977, I CR 3/77, OSNCP 1977, item 218.

The first one is the application of clauses contained in acts of local law, referring in their content to national acts (e.g. resolutions of local government bodies). The second – the use of clauses contained in the files of internal management (internally binding), such as instructions, circulars, guidelines, etc. Whereas the third one – the use of clauses contained in the acts of professional self-government (e.g. statutes, regulations), in which a special role is played by the application of references contained in codes of professional ethics by various types of disciplinary committees or courts. In this latter situation, open criteria constitute an independent basis for a decision ending such proceedings, which in a sense brings them closer to the essence of the equity law practices.[8]

2.2. The use of references and the type of legal regulation containing the clause

(1) The assumption that a reference, before it is used by a court in the process of applying the law, appears in a normative regulation is an important starting point for determining the effects of different ways of referring in legal provisions. The essential role regarding the basis for the use of a clause is played not by the name of the criterion itself, but by two other factors of the legislative referral policy – the legislative location of clauses in the appropriate systematic unit of a normative act and the formulation of conditions for its applicability.[9]

Regardless of whether the reference is formulated in a statutory provision or a sub-statutory act, it may be included in different parts of such an act. This is related to the implementation of the concept of its systematics. In particular, the effects on the basis of the reference are different depending on whether the reference is included in provisions directly regulating the behaviour or legal relations in question (specific provisions, usually found in the specific part of a normative act), or it is included in the "complementary" provisions, i.e. those defining terms, constructing competences, rules of interpretation or validation for individual provisions of the act, etc. (provisions of the general part of the act).[10]

(2) The effects of the practice of locating references in a normative act are relatively most defined (also in the context of the effectiveness of the legislator's

8 Cf. G. Ławnikowicz, S. Pilipiec, "Nieskazitelność," pp. 233 ff.

9 Cf. L. Leszczyński, *Tworzenie*, pp. 132 ff.

10 Cf. Z. Ziembiński, *Logiczne*, pp. 129–130, 132 ff., 140 ff., S. Grzybowski, "Wypowiedź," passim, J. Wróblewski, *Sądowe*, pp. 265–268. See also the distinction formulated by H. L. A. Hart, *The Concept*, pp. 78–79, 80–84 (the *rules of adjudication* highlighted there seem to have a similar function, although they are also formulated in judicial practice).

influence) in the case of direct use of a reference contained in a specific provision regulating a given situation or legal relationship. It is then that the basis for the use of reference is a specific, subjectively defined authorization, confronted, of course, with the characteristics of a specific factual condition, which necessitates the use of an extra-legal criterion. Since the presence of the reference clause does not imply an obligation but an authorization to apply it, the decision on the actual use of the extra-legal criterion by the entity applying the right of decision is based on the statement of a "decision-making requirement" (including the characteristics of the facts) and in relation to this specific decision-making process. The application of such a criterion is therefore closely related to the qualification of the relevant elements of the established facts. Often, the application of these criteria, of course together with the *stricti iuris* criteria, no longer requires the search for other extra-legal criteria (e.g. those contained in the general provisions of a given act). The will of the legislator is thus, even in this relatively most strictly defined type of authorization, functionally "filtered" by the decision of the entity applying the law.

(3) The application of a clause contained in a general provision, which complements in some aspect the content of a specific provision, poses a more complex task. The criteria included in the clauses of the general provisions may either coincide with the clauses of the specific provisions, or be named differently in relation to them. It may also be the case, that the clause is formulated solely in general (supplementary) provisions and it does not appear in specific provisions. In both cases, the nature of the application depends on the relationship between the content of the general and specific provisions on the basis of factual findings in the decision-making process. If the link is direct, so will be the nature of the reference in the additional provision. In the absence of such a relationship, which is usually the case when going beyond a given normative act, we are dealing with a specific "borrowing" of a clause from a general provision within a given branch of law or even the entire legal system.[11] In both cases of application of clauses of general provisions, the same or differently named clauses overlap, which affects the determination of combined content of the criteria contained therein.

Such joint application is determined by the features of the facts of the case, for the qualification of which both types of criteria are combined. It means a reconstruction of more complete base norms, which in turn has an impact on the construction of a more complete normative basis for the decisions on the

11 Cf. (as for application of the clauses of Art. 5 of KC): SN Resolution of 20 VI 2013, III CZP 2/13, LEX 1425316 or SN Resolution of 18 XII 2013, III CZP 82/13, LEX 1523411.

application of the law. The systematics of a normative act may facilitate this type of application of criteria, especially if the references, appearing both in the detailed and general parts, contain substantial links.[12] "Fitting" within the limits of a normative act with these references to extra-legal criteria is characterized by greater content convergence and specificity in relation to the actual state of affairs. However, it is not excluded to refer in such cases to general parts of the branch of law (defined by the code) or of the entire legal system (defined by constitutional or international regulation). It seems that the more distant the general provision containing the extra-legal reference is, the more the use of the extra-legal criterion aims to strengthen the role of the extra-legal axiology as validation argument from axiology and means in fact "borrowing" the extra-legal criterion *per analogiam clausulae*.[13]

(4) The use of references may also apply to other types of provisions. It is also possible to resort to the extra-legal criteria contained in transitional or final provisions, even when these parts of a normative act are generally not the place for their formulation. Besides, references may be present in interpretative provisions.[14] This is important because the use of such references is possible both in relation to the essential findings of the validation in the operational interpretation (e.g. the application of legal provisions taken over from the previous formation) and to the reconstruction of norms contained in legal provisions.[15]

2.3. Application of references of international and supranational law

(1) The use of references may also involve direct reference to applicable provisions of international law. The referring clauses contained in these provisions can be used by both international courts and national courts. The use of references contained in international treaties by international courts (common or regional) does not differ from the analogous applications discussed above. This applies both to certain types of agreement (covenant, convention, multilateral or

12 C.F. the reference to the rules of social coexistence appearing in KC in many variants making their join use possible – in Art. 5 (as a criterion of exercising the right) art. 58 (criterion of the validity of the legal action), Art. 65 (as a criterion of interpretation of party/s will) and Art. 153 and 154 (as a criterion shaping the relations between the creditor and debtor) of this Code.

13 Cf. below: 3.1.

14 Established not only in the authoritarian systems (cf. Art. 1 of POPC of 1950 or, in derogated in 1990, art. 4 of KC) but also in the regulations of international law (cf. Art. 31 of VCLT or Art. 17 of ECHR).

15 Cf. III.

bilateral agreement, etc.) and to the types of provisions in which the references are included.

The practice of applying extra-legal references of international law by national courts takes place when the rule for the applicability of international law in the domestic legal order is established and so are also the procedural steps leading to the application of this law by domestic courts.[16] Therefore, it will depend on the type of political system in which international law is applied as well as the general attitude of legal practice towards taking into account the solutions of international law. Evidently, an autocratic political order, meaning at most a shaky conception of the validity and grounds for applying the norms of international law, strengthened by political involvement, will lead to a selective application of this law. Both variants of the limited operation of international law do not favour the references contained in its regulations, which to some extent limits the process of universalization of extra-legal axiology, taking place in the case of the functioning of acts of international law.

The features of the use of extra-legal references under international law by both types of courts do not differ from the analogous (as indicated above) actions of domestic courts in relation to references under state law if the use of references contained in the specific and general provisions and their possible combinations is concerned.

The possibility of using references contained in interpretative provisions, which are used particularly in relation to the interpretation of treaties, forms another constituent of these actions. This applies to relying on the criteria of good faith or custom by international courts[17] as well as domestic courts, making decisions within various branches of law.

The use of substantive criteria of international law must also assume a different structure of general sources of this law, which include generally recognized principles of international law and custom. The former create the internal axiology of international law. However, since they are usually more open and less juridically specified than the principles of domestic law, they play a similar role in relation to the use of references. Customs, on the other hand, form a separate and in a sense independent (but not having an axiological content) validation

16 Cf. referring to the ECHR in the case of the criterion of "good of child" by ECtHR (Judgment of 16 XII 1999, V. v. UK (24888/94) and by domestic courts (NSA Resolution of 2 XII 2019, II OPS 1/19, Legalis 2256199).

17 Cf. the criteria indicated in art. 31–33 of VCLT (cf. M.S. McDougal, H.D. Lasswell, J.C. Miller, *The Interpretation*, esp. pp. 154–156, 193–194, 260–261, 433–442).

argument, finding more frequent and wider application in the international legal order in relation to national orders.

The division of international law has an influence on the scale of the universal use of extra-legal criteria. For example, the specific axiological entanglement (also without the presence of extra-legal references) in the field of Human Rights prompts entities applying such law to use the references formulated therein. This is favoured, for example, by the references contained in the European Convention for the Protection of Human Rights and Fundamental Freedoms (ECHR), which are applied by the European Court of Human Rights (ECtHR) and national courts of the member states of the Council of Europe with regard to the qualification of the activities of the organs of the State being party to the Convention. References to criteria such as necessity in a democratic society, public order, economic welfare or the interests of state security are applied directly by the ECtHR in a way in that references from specific provisions in domestic law are applied by the national courts. At the same time, they may be linked with references to the law of the state concerned by the subject of proceedings before the ECtHR.[18] On the other hand, the courts of the member states of the Council of Europe also apply them in their decision-making processes, either as self-contained criteria or jointly with references contained in their national laws.[19]

(2) One should formulate certain remarks, largely analogous to those expressed above, with regard to the application of open criteria contained in the provisions of European Union law. Of course, this also directly applies to the use of international law, which is part of EU law, including agreements concluded with the participation of EU institutions. It is related to the application of provisions classified both as primary law and as secondary law, regardless of whether the latter manifests itself in the form of directly applicable provisions (e.g. regulations), provisions applicable "with effect" (directives[20]) or provisions of "soft law"(recommendations or opinions). Also in the case of this law,

---

18 Cf. e.g. ECtHR Judgments: of 7 XII 1976 Handyside v. UK (A.24) and of 20 VIII 1994 Otto Preminger v. Austria (A.295).

19 For example, the criterion of "necessity in a democratic society" and other open criteria formulated in Art. 8, 9, 10 and 11 of the ECHR and Art. 2 of the Fourth Additional Protocol (of 16 September 1963) to this Convention will be of direct relevance to the qualification of actions by national authorities by national courts, including a similar reference in Art. 31 of the RP Constitution ("necessity in a democratic state").

20 Their references might however be applied jointly with the references of the domestic laws that implement directives, what create analogous situation to the relations between statutory and sub-statutory references within the domestic legal order.

references may come within the jurisdiction of the CJEU and national courts of the Member States implementing EU law directly or as a result of a preliminary ruling. The latter may also apply to the interpretation of EU law in the context of participation of extra-legal referral in this process.

Even though the EU legislator sparingly resorts to extra-legal references, there are no grounds to state any particular aversion to the use of such references by the CJEU (notwithstanding also the fewer instances of application of extra-legal references than in case of national courts). This applies to the use of both "classic" reference criteria, such as: public interest, public order or public morality, as well as criteria linking the extra-legal criterion to the European Union itself (e.g. general interest of the Union or the financial interests of the Union).[21] On the other hand, it is characteristic to combine the use of such references with legal principles[22] that play a crucial role under EU law in determining the grounds for judicial decisions.

Still other characteristics should be linked with the application of the EU Charter of Fundamental Rights. The Charter itself, despite the fact that it regulates an axiologically well-grounded field, there are no regulations that would be similar to that of Art. 8, 9, 10 and 11 of the European Convention on Human Rights, i.e. the so-called restrictive clauses that would use extra-legal criteria. The text of the Charter only features a limited number of such criteria.[23] Importantly, however, the use of references in the jurisprudence of the CJEU may also involve the application of criteria indicated in the ECHR[24] or in national law.[25]

What, at least to some extent, forms a separate issue is the application of EU law references by national courts of its member states. Most often this is done by combining these references with references from domestic law, and the jurisprudence of such activities may be either a judgment of a national court[26] or a question referred to the CJEU for a preliminary ruling.[27]

21 Cf. A. Kalisz, "Klauzule," pp. 225–243.

22 Cf. A. Kalisz-Prakopik, L. Leszczyński, "Zasady," pp. 23 ff.

23 E.g. Charter refers to the criterion of "general interest" among others in Art. 52 (specifying its scope as an interest "recognized by the Union") and in Art. 17 as a criterion defining limitations in the exercise of rights and freedoms as a criterion for statutory regulation of the use of property.

24 Cf. e.g. CJEU Judgment of 5 IV 2016, C-404/15 and C-659/15.PPU (Pal Aranyosi) EU:C:2016:198) regarding the use of the criterion of "dignity."

25 Cf. CJEU Judgments: of 4 XII 1974, 41/74 (Van Duyn), EU:C:1974:133 and of 29 IV 2004 C-456/01 (Henkel) EU:C:2004:258.

26 Cf. e.g. A. Sołtys, "Wykładnia," pp. 539, A. Szot, "Wykładnia," pp. 551 ff., A. Kalisz, "Klauzule," pp. 217 ff.

27 Cf. e.g. I. Rzucidło-Grochowska, "Argumenty," pp. 565 ff.

3. "Borrowing" a reference *per analogiam clausulae*

The application of an extra-legal reference, in addition to the above-mentioned direct reference to the applicable legal provision for this end, may also be based on the use of a reference contained in a binding legal provision other than the currently applicable provision.

Such an operation, which can be called an indirect application, meaning in essence the "borrowing" of the reference *per analogiam clausulae* (whenever the semantic scope of the term *per analogiam legis* can be extended in this way), is carried out in several variants. The first, and most prominent division, is the borrowing of a reference from a specific provision (directly regulating a "similar" fact) or from a general provision (complementing the content of a norm reconstructed from a specific provision). Secondly, a reference may be borrowed in a given decision-making process from one of the above types of provisions or from a combination of both. Thirdly, the borrowing may cover a single reference or more than one reference (extra-legal criterion) contained in specific or general provisions. Fourthly, borrowing in each of the above cases of a reference contained in a general provision may either occur in the absence of such reference in the provisions regulating the respective type of facts being the subject of the actual decision-making process, or in a situation where the reference contained in the applicable provision is found to be insufficient (what results in the joint application of both types of references). Fifthly and finally, a provision containing borrowed references may be also found in the same normative act, in another act of the same branch of law, in an act of another branch of law (with appropriate location on the vertical structure of the legal system) or in an act of international or supranational (EU) law.

Each of these variants significantly extends the scope of the court's discretion in this aspect of the validation phase of the operative interpretation of law, which relates to the use of the extra-legal reference. The filtering determining the applicability of this reasoning is performed not only on the basis of the features of the decision situation, but also the legitimacy of the very borrowing of the reference from another fragment of the normative regulation.

3.1. Borrowing the clause from specific provisions (*per analogiam legis*)

The borrowing of a reference from a specific provision is based on the practice of reasoning *per analogiam legis* both as regards the possibility of its application, the determination of the condition of similarity and the "measurement of the distance" between the locations that both detailed provisions occupy in the normative regulation.

The context of the characteristics of the branches of law limits the use of references in this way, e.g. in criminal law or public law, opening it up more broadly under private law, especially in those layers that are based on the norms of *ius dispositivum*. This takes place to the extent to which the mere reasoning *per analogiam legis* is accepted in the respective branch of law.

(1) The condition of similarity may apply to both the factual situations regulated in both legal provisions and the legal institutions in which both provisions are contained.

In the first of the above-mentioned, we are dealing with a classic *analogia legis* in the application of law, but involving the reference itself and not the *stricti iuris* criterion. Basing the borrowing of a reference on the finding of the similarity of facts must take into account (as is the case in the classical reasoning *per analogiam legis*) the differences in the precision of defining the components of both factual conditions. The regulated facts in the provision can only be identified in a general (abstract, model) form, while the facts of the current decision-making process are determined precisely.

The similarity between the objects (legal institutions) or the methods of regulation may form the basis for borrowing a clause from another specific provision, regardless of whether the specific facts determined in the decision-making process are similar or not. Needless to say, the objective similarity presupposes a certain model similarity between the hypothetical factual conditions, but it somehow goes to the background in a specific dimension of the decision-making process. In such a case, borrowing a reference creates a wide range of decisions in applying the law, because the axiology resulting from the content of the references is transferred to the application of another fragment of the legal system on the basis of their existing objective relations. If these constructions are actually similar, borrowing is more appropriate. This applies, for example, to the relationship of similarity between personal easement and land easement, lease and tenancy agreement, sale and exchange agreement or the institution of ownership and of perpetual usufruct.[28]

(2) What proves the most complex an issue is the location relationship of both regulations. The matter is easier if it is related to the types of similarity. Any borrowing must be exercised with caution, but it is relatively smaller if borrowing

---

28 E.g. Art. 140 and Art. 144 KC. Cf. SN Judgment 1 IV1966, III CR 32/66, RPEiS 1967 No. 1, p. 329 and SN Judgment of 12 V 1972, II CR 95/72, OSNCP 1973, item 28.

concerns the extra-legal references from the provisions of the same part (systematic unit) of the same normative act (what frequently operates here is the similarity between the subject of regulation).[29] The "closer" this unit is located, the easier it is to borrow a reference and also to demonstrate it on the basis of similarity. Nevertheless this caution should be greater if it concerns references from the provisions of different normative acts of the same branch or sub-branch of law (e.g. under different types of tax law), and even greater if it concerns references from the provisions of various branches of law (although in the case of borrowing references from civil law, there will be fewer objections to the processes of applying them to family law or labour law than in the case of borrowing references, of e.g. civil law, to the application in administrative law or vice versa, which would require exercising special caution). The case is further complicated by the use (mainly by domestic courts) of references indicated by the specific provisions of international or supranational law (e.g. of the EU). A completely exceptional place in this list is occupied by criminal law, where the very extra-legal references are of a different nature and *analogia legis* is excluded from the scope of determining the criminal nature of an act.

However, the translation of all the above-mentioned conditions of reasoning *per analogiam legis* into this kind of borrowing references must be extremely careful. This is so because this type of borrowing is not based on a juridical structure that was shaped and "proven" in judicial doctrine and practice, often over the centuries (which is the case with the classic analogy connected with legal provisions), but it includes an extra-legal reference, the content of which is not only variable, but also unstable and additionally difficult to unequivocally determine in the process of applying the law.

3.2. Borrowing a clause from general ("supplementary") provisions

The use of references located in a binding legal provision other than the applicable specific legal provision may include borrowing a reference contained in a general provision, in a sense complementing the content of the specific provision, in which the reference does not appear or such a reference, although appearing, is not sufficient to construct a normative basis for a decision. Therefore, in a

29 The criterion of "good of child," being formulated in may regulations of KRiO might be "borrowed" for implementation of various specific regulations, as a kind of "leading thought," "general directive" or "spirit of the statute" (cf. 2,31-34-TK Judgment of 17 IV 2007, SK 20/05, LEX 270207). Cf. also NSA Judgment of 30 X 2018 r., II OSK 1868/16, Legalis 1860297 or TK Judgment of 17 IV 2007, SK 20/05, LEX 270207.

sense, any use of a extra-legal reference located in a general provision constitutes a borrowing of a reference, insofar as such use forms kind of the complement, by the general provision, of a norm reconstructed from a specific provision.

(1) The general provisions in which references are formulated may be located at different levels of generality, both in the perspective of the systematics of a normative act and the structure of the entire legal system.[30] From the point of view of the application of the reference clause, this broadens the spectrum of the court's choice of referrals according to its decision-making requirements, without excluding recourse to more than one such references. Even if the differentiation of the effects of possible variants mainly affects the content relations between individual references, it cannot be irrelevant to the determination of the set of carriers that become the basis for the reconstruction of the underlying behaviour patterns. There is no condition of similarity, typical for a *per analogia legis* reasoning, because the differences in the levels of generality of a regulation between a specific applicable provision and a general provision creates a relation between the scope of regulation of a general provision and the particular situation regulated by specific provision. This is somewhat reminiscent of *per analogiam iuris*, except that the point of reference here are not the principles of law (legal values), but the reference clauses, formulated in the main (usually in the initial provisions)[31] part of the normative act or the essential part of the entire legal system (e.g. in the constitution).

The most important, however, is the relation connected with the location of the general provision in relation to the specific provision, affecting the degree of caution exercised when applying the reference from the general provision.

This caution need to be less stringent if there is a reference from a general provision of a given part of the same normative act in the process of applying a

30 Cf. SN Judgment of 14 I 2015, I CSK 19/14, LEX 1648688, SN Judgment of 24 I 2017, V CSK 207/16, LEX 2255336 (on the relations in the frames of KC) or SN Judgment of 21 X 2010, IV CSK 236/10, LEX 943484 (including regulations of Art. 2 of RP Constitution). Cf also for the criterion of "good of child" implemented in connection to constitutional standards TK Judgment of 11 X 2011, K 16/10, LEX 992832 or NSA Judgment of 12 VII 2017, II GSK 3611/15, LEX 2356400. Such practice concerns as well application of the criteria of Art. 7 of KPA ("social interest" and "legitimate interest in citizens") in the jurisdiction of administrative courts (cf. NSA Judgment of 29 IV 2021, I OSK 208/21, CBOSA and NSA Judgment of 22 X 2019, I OSK 586/19, CBOSA).

31 Cf. e.g. SN Resolution of 20 VI 2013, III CZP 2/13, LEX 1425316, SN Resolution of 20 VI 2013, III CZP 2/13, LEX 1425316, SN Judgment of 16 I 2014, IV CSK 196/13, LEX 1436078 and SN Resolution of 18 XII 2013, III CZP 82/13, LEX 1523411.

specific provision of that part (e.g. general part of law of obligations applied in the rental contract).[32] This also applies (to a lesser degree) to borrowing a reference from a general provision of the entire normative act, if the act in question is a code (e.g. the use of a reference to the principles of social coexistence within the framework of the construction of abuse of any subjective right regulated in civil law or the use of a reference to the criterion of "social harmfulness of an act" when determining the criminal nature of each act or the size of each penalty on the basis of criminal law regulations).

Greater caution is usually exercised in the use of references to general provisions of other (not codified) normative acts of the respective branch (e.g. in a particularly extensive branch of administrative law) or in a sub-branch (tax law), even if such an act has a higher legal force than the act, in for which the specific rule applied, which is devoid of extra-legal reference, is contained.

Even greater caution should accompany all three of the above-mentioned types of use of references from general provisions, if the latter exceed the limits of a given branch of law, and especially if they concern objectively and methodologically separate branches. If, on the other hand, these are "related" branches (civil and commercial law) or branches that can be said to remain in a "sub-branch" relationship (civil law and family law), the lack of explicit authorization should not prevent a careful application of references so localized.

Branch divisions cannot constitute an obstacle to the use of constitutional references, both in provisions relating to matters connected with a given "specific" branch (e.g. constitutional regulation of ownership) and in general provisions of the constitution, constituting a general part of the entire legal system (e.g. determining the nature of the state or the rules of operation of state authorities).[33] This

32 Cf. SN Provision of 12 I 2018, II CSK 160/17, LEX 2483679 or SN Judgment of 22 VI 2018 r, II CSK 539/17, LEX 2521685.

33 The complementary nature of norms containing non-legal references may reach even further. It can also cover the "general part of the entire legal system," i.e. the constitutional regulation. In Polish law, this applies to Art. 90 of the PRL Constitution, which obliges citizens to observe the principles of social coexistence. The question arises whether this provision could become an independent basis for issuing a decision or whether the criteria of the rules of coexistence could complement the patterns of behaviour formulated without referring to any extra-legal references. In the practice of applying this provision, the prevailing view was that referring to Art. 90 of the Constitution could take place through the provisions of ordinary statutes containing the same reference. It seems, however, that the prevailing views on the impossibility of direct application of this reference could be related to the lack of conviction as to the direct applicability of constitutional norms in general.

also applies to the use of references contained in the related general provisions of international law (a special place here is occupied by universal or regional human rights regulations, which contain numerous references of this type[34]) or supranational law (e.g. references contained in the general provisions of the CJEU[35]). The last two cases relate both to the use of references by international or supranational courts (e.g. ECtHR,[36] CJEU[37]) and the courts of the Member States of such supranational structures.

As we can see, the scale of completing the formula from a specific provision by borrowing a reference from the general provision differs in the above cases. However, it should be clearly emphasized that in relation to each of the above-mentioned cases, it is only about caution (and the various degrees thereof) and not about the inability to apply such a reference from a general provision, which clearly falls within the scope of the system rules used in the validation phase of judicial interpretation. The presence of a clause in the supplementary provision presupposes the possibility of its application in each decision-making process on the basis of the provisions of the special part, if only there are reasons to refer to such axiological argumentation when applying the said specific legal provisions.

Even under the assumptions of the previous system we can still find an example of a broader approach than the dominant position would suggest. This is because the Supreme Court in 1966 clearly indicated: "As we know, respecting the principles of social coexistence is the fundamental duty of citizens (...). These principles must always be taken into account in the application of the law, and not only when it comes to provisions that expressly refer to them" (SN Judgment of 13 I 1966 III CO 306/63, OSPiKA 1967, item 108, pp. 193–194) The above declaration, although it did not become the basis for the widespread use of the structure contained in Art. 90 of the Constitution, nevertheless expressed the possibility of a broad supplementation of more specific patterns of behaviour formulated in the entire legal system. By comparison, there is no such reference in the RP Constitution. In a sense, a similar role may be exercised by the references contained in its Chapter I (e.g. public purposes and just compensation under Art. 21, important public interest under Art. 22, the good of man and the common good under Art. 25), and in particular the reference to the principles of social justice (Art. 2).

34 In particular, this applies to the open criteria under Art. 8, 9, 10 and 11 of ECHR (e.g.: necessity in democratic society, interest of national security, morals, public safety, public order).

35 E.g. criterion of "public morality" or "public order" – cf. e.g. CJEU Judgment of 28 X 1975, 36/75 Rutili, C:1975:137.

36 Cf. e.g. ECtHR Judgment of 7 XII 1976 Handyside v. UK (A.24).

37 Cf. e.g. CJEU Judgment of 10 V 1995 C-275/92 (Alpine Investments), RCR I-II41.

(2) The most specific links exist when references are applied from the general provisions of a normative act, especially a code. The above-mentioned scale of complementation decreases here. This applies in particular to such structures as abuse of law in the context of the exercise of every subjective right in civil[38] and labour law,[39] grounds for liability for every act prohibited in criminal law,[40] or grounds for making decisions in every administrative case,[41] as well as what is the "supplement" on the broadest scale, general grounds for applying the law.[42] References may also appear in code regulations concerning the definition of terms or indication of interpretation rules for other provisions (which contain, or do not contain a reference[43]) or determination of the grounds for instance control.[44] In any event, the use of a reference may reveal the complementary nature of the very norms in which they are placed.

---

38 For example, the lack of references in the provisions governing the contract of sale may not exclude the use of references under Art. 5 of KC, since the performance of the contract may be related to the exercise of one's own right. Moreover, the lack of the above-mentioned cannot exclude the application of not only references from Art. 5 of KC, but also references under Art. 56 and 58 of KC and also under Art. 353 and 354 of KC. It is related to the above-mentioned gradual completeness of basic patterns of behaviour.

39 Art. 8 of KP.

40 Art. 1 of KK of 1997.

41 Art. 7 of KPA (as a criterion of discretionary administrative decision), cf. A. Szot, *Judicial*, esp. pp. 13–35.

42 Referral to natural principles of law (§ 7 of ABGB) or principles of equity (Art. 4 of ZGB), if the normative basis of the code is missing or remains unclear (cf. L. Leszczyński, *Tworzenie*, pp. 52–54, 56–57).

43 A separate issue was the application of the meta-norms contained in the no longer binding Art. 1 POPC of 1950 and Art. 4 of KC, which functionally exceeded the application of the provisions of the Civil Code and civil law in general. The way in which this principle of application and interpretation of the provisions was formulated made it possible to base various decisions on the criteria of the principles of the political system and the objectives of Polish Peoples Republic (PRL), regardless of whether or not references were made in the respective provision. Of course, it would be difficult to assume that the content of each decision, e.g. in civil matters, was made on the basis of the compatibility of the manner of taking it from the point of view of the principles of the system or state objectives, or, which would be even more paradoxical, that the addressees of civil law norms account for these principles and objectives by entering into appropriate legal relationships. These criteria may have a possible meaning "only" in the control phase, but usually as a "final" criterion (as a kind of "meta-clause").

44 In total, a similar role was played by Art. 417 and 421 (derogated in 1996) of KPC ("state interest"), as well as Art. 7 of KPC and Art. 50 of KPK ("social interest"). All of them

The widest possible use of various scopes of completion is related to the code of civil law and the scope of generality of provisions contained therein. Thus, apart from borrowing the most general references from the initial provisions of the Code (e.g. those specifying the abuse of subjective rights), it is also possible to use the same clause when applying specific provisions to references from other provisions of the general part of the Code (e.g. specifying the interpretation of a civil law transaction[45]) from the provisions of the general part of a given part of the code (e.g. the law of obligations[46]) or from the general provisions of a given legal institution (e.g. property rights[47]). Considering, for example, the application of a specific provision relating to the exercise of the right of ownership by way of a legal transaction, it can be assumed that the borrowing of references from each of the above-mentioned general provisions of a different scope of generality is not excluded.

(3) The above cases of the use of references "borrowed" from the provisions supplementing the patterns of behaviour of particular norms may occur either in

---

were related to the basis for the control of decisions made by other authorities, the first two – control of court decisions in the form of extraordinary appeals against final sentences, and the last two – control of the grounds of the prosecutor's decisions. From the point of view of the pattern of behaviour formulated for these decision-making bodies, it can be stated that in each decision these bodies should take into account the references contained in these provisions, which could, in consequence, "protect" decisions made by them from a negative review decision.

45 It also may however be connected with the use of a reference from the general part of the act as a whole (Art. 56 or 58 of KC).

46 Completion may also involve the use of a reference from the general part of a given section of a normative act (as was the case in Art. 353 or 354 of KC, included in the general part of the third book of the Code, in relation to the sale contract).

47 This will take place where the extra-legal reference is formulated in a provision specifying the content of the legal institution concerned, and therefore may affect the application of any provision governing that institution, whether or not it contains this reference. Such a situation occurs, for example, when regulating the property rights, the content of which and the manner of exercising the right are defined using references to the principles of social coexistence and to the socio-economic purpose of law (Art. 140 of KC). The wording of Art. 144 of KC (exercise of the ownership right) or Art. 145 of KC (exercise of easement of access) contains other references (local customs, socio-economic interest), which, in the process of applying the law, must be synchronized with those basic references for the institution of property law. References from Art. 140 of KC will also play a "complementary" role for the regulation of, for example, land demarcation (Art. 152 and following of KC), even if the latter do not refer directly to any extra-legal references.

the absence of a reference in this specific provision, or in the case of an overlapping reference in the specific provision. The first case is unambiguous – the sole reference will be the reference from the complementary norm. The second case, i.e. when the use of references from specific provisions and general provisions requires the determination of priority of application (it seems that in a situation where both references could not be applied, priority should be given to the reference from specific provisions) and the scope and meaning relations between such different references (especially when these referrals are named differently), which is already related to the interpretation of the referral and establishing (usually) some content compromise.[48]

All the different instances for borrowing a reference from a differently located general provision may relate to the application of one or more clauses and one or more extra-legal criteria (in the latter case – present in one or larger number of clauses). It may, therefore, lead to a specific "axiological entanglement," which in the validation phase means the strengthening of the role of external axiology as the consequence of collecting numerous references (criteria), which, when determining their content, reconstructing the norm or building a normative basis for decisions, may lead to the domination of this axiology in determining the final content of the decision to apply the law.

4. Special situations for applying extra-legal references

The above-mentioned practice of direct application of an extra-legal reference and its borrowing were related to the applicability of the legal provision in which the reference is made. Therefore, what forms the decisive factor here is the construction of the formal validity of the provision that is transferred to the validity of the reference itself. This will also apply to the consequences of refusing to apply a clause contained in a formally binding provision. As a rule, for example, breaking the principle of non-retroaction when creating such a provision, or the provision containing the reference falling out of use (*desuetudo*), or finding it non-compliant with a higher-order norm (especially with a constitutional norm), usually results in a refusal to apply the provision that is in such a situation. This effect may also include an extra-legal reference contained in such

48 Similar dependencies took place under the former Art. 386 of the KC in which, despite different names used for the clauses, all these references were defined as a common category of "interests of the national economy" that appeared separately in Art. 826 and Art. 827 of KC (cf. GKA decision of 3 I 1966, BO-13043/65, RPEiS 1967 No. 1, item 340 and GKA decision 3 X 1978, OT-6546/78, OSPiKA 1980, item 10).

a provision, despite the fact that the axiological content of the latter, by model, "loosens" the formal grounds for its application, insofar as the axiological content of the reference may turn out to be useful in the respective decision-making process (e.g. as a supplement to the axiological content of other extra-legal criteria) despite the non-application of the provision in this process. It is possible because the justification for the application of open criteria is based not on the formal validity but on axiological arguments, which in this context may "break away," at least to a certain extent, from the formal (thetic) argument.

Therefore, the above-mentioned fundamental relationship does not mean that, in each case, the basis for applying a reference is related to the basis for applying the provision containing it. Situations where the justifications of the applicability of references and provisions break away from each other can be observed in particular in several cases that will be subject to our discussion below. They include the non-application of the formally applicable clause, the application of a clause that is "not yet in force," the use of the clause formally "repealed" and the use of an extra-legal reference contained in the provisions that are "non-binding" but operating in the same cultural and legal tradition of foreign law (the law of another country or non-binding international law).

In each of these cases, the qualification of applicability of an extra-legal reference is determined not in the process of law-making but in the process of implementation the law and is associated with the use of judicial discretion.

4.1. The issue of non-application of a "binding" reference clause

(1) The "detachment" of the basis for the application of a extra-legal reference and a legal provision is particularly evident and important in the event of failure to apply a reference, even though the applicable (and therefore binding) legal provision contains such a reference (that is also "binding"). This situation may be caused by two different reasons.

The first of them, which is general in nature, results from the assumption that the reference does not create a "compulsion" to use the extra-legal reference in each case of applying the provision containing it, but "solely" demanding consideration of such using, authorizes the organ applying the law to use the extra-legal criteria in the event of an appropriate "decision requirement." Therefore, the judge's perception of the circumstances of the decision-making process, which indicates the adequacy of the use of *stricti iuris* criteria, determines the non-applicability of reference.

The second reason is of a different nature. It is related to a special authorization to consider the validity of the use of a reference on the basis of whether or not the additional conditions are met by this reference. The court's decision in this respect will be the result of at least a preliminary determination of the content of the extra-legal criterion, leading to a belief that the axiology indicated by this reference is inconsistent with the legal principles or the content indicated by the general clauses playing leading role in the indication of an extra-legal axiology (what plays important role in a situation of the deep social change) .

(2) The court may refuse to use a clause either on the result of application of a special normative regulation enabling the use of a "validation filter" or on its own interpretative initiative.

The situation linking the legislative and jurisprudence sides of the potential restriction of the use of clauses contained in the applicable legal provisions, results from the formulation of a special interpretative directive in a separate provision, allowing for refusal to apply not only the provision itself but also a reference that fails to meet the specified criteria. This regulation may appear in a situation of profound social change, but actually only when it tends towards authoritarianism. In such a case, it mainly concerns the provisions taken over (not repealed) from the previous political formation, but may also be related to the references contained in them.[49] What is characteristic here is that the components of the directive resulting in the refusal to use the old references are extra-legal criteria, is usually both different from the "old" criteria and closely related to the official political axiology of the new authoritarian regime. The scope of application of such a directive is moderated, among others, by depth of autocracy and the scale of the relative autonomy of the judiciary.[50]

Another situation, leading to the same consequences, links the refusal to apply a referral solely with the opinion of the court. Also in this case, it should be noted that such a practice is connected to a profound social and legal change. It may also refer to a pro-democratic change, in which the court itself (i.e. without the above-mentioned normative structure), usually on the basis of new legal principles, may refuse to apply the "old" referring clause. It seems though, that in the case of such a change, instead of refusing to apply, we witness a modification of the content of the extra-legal criterion, shifting towards the new legal axiology

---

49 E.G. on the base of (derogated in 1990) Art. 4 of KC (cf. SN Resolution of 28 V 1968, III CZP 49/68, OSPiKA 1970, item 118 247-SN Judgment of 14 XII 1973, II CR 692/73, OSPiKA 1975, item 94).

50 It seems that these factors contributed to the relatively mild effects of applying the provisions of Art. 1 of POPC of 1950 and later of Art. 4 of KC in Polish judicial practice.

and a new understanding of socio-political values.[51] The practice of independent decisions not to apply the "binding" reference clause is on the one hand weaker (because it is not based on the interpretative directive discussed above), but on the other hand – stronger, as it results from judicial autonomy, especially when it is confirmed in the course of control by the higher instance. Although it is not always listed in the justifications of individual court decisions, it becomes particularly powerful in the case of an autonomous formation of an appropriate line of jurisdiction, which allows for noticing certain elements of precedential practice.

Failure to apply the referral clause in the formally applicable provision may also be connected with necessity to establish the content of conflicting criteria.[52] It originates in the result of application of conflict-solution rules with regard to two extra-legal criteria (e.g. the legitimate interest of a party and the public interest) or two conflicting norms reconstructed from provisions containing a reference. The result of the resolution of both collisions may be the refusal to apply one of the criteria listed in the provision, which in this particular situation is considered "weaker" axiologically (in the event of a conflict of extra-legal criteria) or normatively (in the event of a conflict of norms).

4.2. The problem of the application of a "non-binding" reference clause

The problem of applying a "non-binding" clause, even though it also indirectly links the very construction with the status of a provision containing the reference, albeit in a different way, but at the same time stronger than in the case of non-application of a binding clause, departs from the formal justification of the validity of such a provision. Thus, it is a manifestation of the exercise of judicial discretion, which means the judicial correction of the legislative policy through independent drawing the reference from sources other than the applicable legal provisions. As already mentioned above, the situations include: (a) the use of clauses that are "not yet in force," (b) the application of clauses that are "no longer in force" and (c) the use of references, which are formally located outside the

51 E.g. forming classic criterion of good customs in Poland after 1989 (instead of old criterion of the principles of social coexistence) both in KC (e.g. Art. 72 § 2 of KC) and in the judicial practice (Warsaw Court of Appeal Judgment of 18 IV 2013, VI ACa 1395/12, LEX 1322086, Krakow Court of Appeal Judgment of 22 I 2020, I ACa 338/19, LEX 3021570 or Lodz Court of Appeal Judgment of 13 VIII 2018, I ACa 53/18, LEX 2596855).

52 Cf. III.

system of regulations in force. The latter deals with references contained in the provisions of foreign law (of another country or non-binding international law) functioning in the same cultural and legal tradition or references created within this tradition solely on the basis of judicial decisions.

All cases of this form of use of extra-legal criteria in the process of applying the law are not only not model validation operations in the statutory legal order, but they essentially limit to some extent the operation of the principle of legality of the application of law, if it is understood as linking the clause applicability test with the formal validity of the provision containing it. However, it also means designating additional elements of the autonomy of the judiciary in relation to the policy of creating extra-legal references.

4.2.1. Use of reference that is "not yet in force"

The validation rule indicating the use of clauses from the applicable provisions does not prevent, albeit in exceptional cases, the use of a reference contained in a clause that is "not yet in force." Such a practice, which does not meet the formal requirement of legality of the application of the law, may take place in two different versions. The first of them occurs when such a clause is included in an issued and published legal provision, which, however, has not yet entered into force, while the second – when the provision containing clause is not yet officially published. Both of these situations, though rather exceptional, can be observed in judicial practice.

The first of these concerns invoking the criterion of the principles of social coexistence even before their formulation in normative texts.[53] This meant "judicial advance" (without emphasizing this fact in the justification of the decision) in relation to normative re-orientation of Polish law to a new axiology expressed by a criterion that was already present in the legislation of the USSR.

The second situation took place when the criterion of social harmfulness of an act was established in a situation when the clause of social danger of an act was still in force.[54] Here, in turn, the intention of the court was to apply the criterion of "harmfulness" instead of "danger" in the period of profound social change, which, firstly, had already appeared in Polish criminal statutes,[55] and, secondly,

53 Cf. SN Judgment 28 II 1950, Wa C 370/49, PiP 1951 No. 7, pp. 162–166.

54 Cf. SN Judgment 22 I 1991, WR 420/90, OSNKW 1991, item 44.

55 In Polish law, the situation with regard to the criterion of social harmfulness of an act was complicated since it appeared in art. 54 of the Code of Criminal Procedure of 1928 as amended in 1949, only to be replaced, in the KK of 1969 by the criterion of social danger, which finally disappeared in KK of 1997 (cf. R. Zawłocki, *Pojęcie*, pp. 46–35).

was already postulated in the doctrine as a criterion that was more measurable than "danger" and as a criterion limiting the possibility of politicizing its axiological content (which was the case earlier in relation to the social danger of an act).[56] Reaching for "non-binding" references in this manner may result from various circumstances, which certainly include the openness of works on draft new regulations, but also those that are related to the expectation for the axiological opening of a given regulation, usually supported by legal doctrine.

4.2.2. Use of reference that is "no longer in force" (formally repealed).

(1) Another of the above-mentioned situations is the use of a reference from provisions that are no longer formally binding due to their derogation. The basis here is the belief that the repeal of a legal provision containing an extra-legal reference does not preclude the use of the criterion contained therein as long as it is considered useful for some reason. It may result from habit, and even from a certain automatism in judicial reasoning, but it may also be associated with a conscious use of "old" criteria that are, in a sense, more useful in jurisprudence.

This practice adopts two distinct variants. The first is the use of a reference from a provision repealed in the result of changes in legislation as an element for the restructuring of the legal system in face of a profound social change, while the second – a provision repealed by an ordinary legislative derogation of legal provisions containing references.

The circumstance of a profound change in law has much deeper consequences not only in terms of the application of "old" references, but also its effects. It may not be consistent with the intention of the new legislator and may directly lead to axiological incompatibility. Of course, this does not mean that the use of the old (repealed) reference must always lead to such an effect, because as a rule, the references are so general that in most cases the content of the old references can simply be read in a way corresponding to the new values, and perhaps sufficient to emphasize the change of the content of the criteria. It does, however, create the possibility of such a disagreement, and in the case of political criteria, this disagreement is natural. However, the legislative anticipation of such a collision depends on the direction of the change.[57]

Therefore, this application may also be qualified as the application of the formally repealed but previously functioning criterion.

56 Cf. the discussion in I. Andrejew, *Zarys,* pp. 84 ff.. Cf. also on this topic: A. Wąsek, *Kodeks,* pp. 11–39, R. Zawłocki, *Pojęcie,* pp. 47 ff.

57 For example, in Poland it was manifested differently after 1945 and differently after 1989. After 1945, the autocratic legislator attempted to limit the use of old references

The situation of simple repealing of provisions containing references is less complex. Applying the "repealed" clauses usually does not cause an axiological collision with the new criteria, and if such a collision occurs, it does not have such intensity as in the case of referrals from the previous political system. The axiological content of the previous and current criteria remains the same as for their basic components. Therefore, there is mainly a shift of accents or proportions in determining the axiological bases. On the other hand, the very fact of applying the old clauses is a relatively normal consequence of, in a sense, delayed reaction of practice to the legislative change, which is particularly visible in the first period following the change of legal regulation.

(2) The conditions enabling the use of extra-legal criteria from the repealed legal provisions in both of the above variants include: (a) accepted methods of using the respective reference, as developed by in the current court practice and still accepted, (b) establishing a relatively permanent and precise, and at the same time universal and flexible content of such a criterion, (c) indicating its wide application if there is no collision of the content of the criterion established in this way with the current axiology, as well as (d) the conviction that this criterion is useful for constructing a normative basis for judicial decision in the context of the circumstances of the court proceedings in question.

Additional conditions enhancing this method for applying these criteria, especially important in a situation of profound social change, include their relationship with the tradition of legal culture that the respective judicial practice is

---

by establishing an axiological filter of their content (principles of the political system and objectives of the Polish People's Republic). After 1989, the democratic legislator not only did not establish such a filter, but also did not immediately abolish the old general clauses. It is therefore a situation similar to the social change that took place after World War II. The practice of applying the law reacted in a similar fashion. It does not change its habits right away. However, where the legislator changes the clauses, the practice seems to follow it (e.g. in the case of the clause of social harmfulness of an act, after the entry into force of the new KK of 1997, not a single case of using the old clause of social danger can be found). It seems that the decisive factor here is the nature of this change (towards the democratic system), which makes courts aware of the flaws in the solutions of the previous system, rendering it easier to overcome the habits of practice. What we are dealing here with is a continuation of the trend that emerged as a result of the resolution of the full composition of SN, which abolished the application of the guidelines on the interpretation and practice of the judiciary established before 1989 (cf. SN Resolution of 5 V 1992, Kw. Pr. 5/92, OSP 1993, item 218). As for the using the guidelines see also also SN Resolution of 19 II 1989, VI KZP 10/88, OSPiKA 1989, item 151).

identified with.[58] This practice seems to be relevant especially in the situation of an autocratic change, in which the judicature attempts, with usually some effects, at least for some time, to link the emerging new order with references characteristic of the legal culture, adequate for the changed legal order.[59]

Reaching for old references in a situation of profound change may also involve the use of a situation of "double negation" (negating previous negation). Within its framework, negating the previous political and legal system means at the same time a return (to an appropriate extent) to the system negated in the previous system, which is similar, in some respects, to the current system. If the current change is of a democratic nature, it means a different variant of referring to references that have been abolished or were not used in the previous (autocratic) formation, coming from an earlier (democratic) formation, which involves indirectly referring to references formed in the tradition of legal culture, that usually relates to a democratic system.[60]

4.2.3. Use of foreign law references

(1) The "separation" of the basis for the application of the reference clause from the validity of the provision contained therein also occurs when a reference is made to a legal provision of a "foreign" legal order. It can be both a normative regulation in force in another state and a normative regulation of international law that is not binding in the respective state. In both cases, the justification for the use of such references is the axiological relationship of the referential order and the order from which this type of reference is borrowed. At the same time, it is a form that does not imply the full reception of the reference, which could

58 This can explain the fact of using, for example, the classic reference to the principles of equity in the practice of applying the law in Poland after World War II, even though this criterion was replaced in the legislation by the reference to the principles of social coexistence (cf. e.g. SN Judgment of 14 XII 1973, II CR 692/73, OSPiKA 1975, item 94.

59 Cf. e.g. SN Judgment of 14 XII 1973, II CR 692/73, OSPiKA 1975, item 94 and SN Judgment of 28 V 1981, II CR 176/81, OSPiKA 1982, item 120.

60 This was the situation in Poland after 1989. The last thread of applying the "old" references after 1989 involves another issue. In may be not as much as solely applying references from before 1989, but also the use of references that existed even before 1939, i.e. a kind of return to the references that were repealed by the system immediately preceding. Among the signs of this practice one may mention the connection of the use of the criterion of principles of social coexistence in the light of the content of criterion of equity (cf. e.g. SN Provision of 21 V 1975, III CRN 86/75, OSNCP 1976, item 134).

occur at the level of legislation. As a result of such an operation we would simply be dealing in the processes of applying the law with an "own" referring clause (a clause from our "own" legal system). Leaving, by way of a kind of "legislative omission," the decision on the possible application of a foreign law clause to courts, as an element of the policy of creating (or actually "not creating") references, means a softer form of the flow of axiologically strongly involved legal structures between different legal orders, additionally shifted to the level of law application processes. This broadens the scope of judicial discretion with regard to the use of extra-legal references.

In a sense, the practice of using "foreign" references contained in the regulations of another country is related to the more general process of legal reception, but in this case such transplantation adopts the form of jurisprudence. As with the general reception process, therefore, it is possible primarily within the same legal culture[61] and, essentially, when the borrowed solutions appear to be more mature.[62] Nevertheless they can also be associated with a political influence, which, however, determines the legislative rather than the judicial borrowing of reference clauses.[63]

The situation is different when the decision maker uses, as part of its own process, the reference (i.e. borrows the reference) from a provision of international law that is not formally binding in the domestic legal order. Here, too, it is determined by the importance of the references and their applicability to the specific decision-making process. In a sense, the maturity of the order itself, to

---

61 Cf. K. Zweigert, H. Kötz, *Introduction*, pp. 89 ff., 133 ff. (concerning the Roman or German family of law). Cf. also the interchangeability of institutions referring to natural justice in Far Eastern systems (C. Choi, "Ancient," pp. 80–89, M.K. Young, "The Japanese," p. 28, L. Leszczyński, *Gyoseishido*, pp. 65–67). On the other hand, it can be treated as an element for standardization of legal solutions (cf. M. Sawczuk, "Uwagi," pp. 70 ff.).

62 As was the case with the reception of European law, mainly German law, in East Asia, and especially in Japan (cf. H.K. Lee, "Die Rezeption," pp. 158–170, Z. Kitagawa, "Theory," pp. 1–16) or the English law in India (M. Galanter, *Law*, passim). Generally, about the "intercultural" reception, cf. E. Levy, "The Reception," pp. 233–245. This reception may deep enough for the practice and doctrine to find themselves unable to liberate from adopting also the ways of understanding and applying specific institutions (e.g. using the construction of administrative recognition in Japanese practice, shaped on the basis of German practice (cf. K. Yamanaka, "Kritische," pp. 67 ff.). Generally, on the application of foreign law, cf. U. Drobnig, S.V. Erp, *The Use*, passim.

63 For example, in Poland after 1945, such borrowing from the legal order of the USSR takes place in legislative practice but not in judicial decisions.

which international references are borrowed, goes to the background, although in the case of mature, democratic and law-abiding orders (immature orders, usually containing some elements of autocracy, are not inclined to develop such a practice), the references used come from multilateral conventions, although not binding in a given country, but playing an important role in international legal order.[64]

On the other hand, it would make a slightly different sense to use references to international customs and generally recognized principles of international law, if these, as not having their normative form in international law (or being less normatively grounded), would contain criteria with the features of extra-legal values or norms (e.g. the principle of good faith or principles of equity[65]). The dissimilarity of this particular situation is related to the recognition of their validity, which, without relying on the theoretical justification, depends on the general relationship between the national and international legal order in the respective country.[66]

(2) The model way for applying an extra-legal criterion contained in a provision of foreign law is to treat it as a factor "only" supplementing the content of the normative basis of the decision, constructed with use of the *stricti iuris*

---

64 This is how it is possible to justify the practice of Canadian courts referring to the open criteria of the ECHR, which is not binding in Canada (Cf. Canadian Supreme Court's Judgmenet Brownridge v. La Reine (1972) R.C.S. 925) as well as M.I. Berlin, L. Metivier, *Le droit*, pp. 53 ff.

65 Cf. e.g. W. Czapliński, A. Wyrozumska, "Ogólne," esp. pp. 2–5, A. Lizer-Klatka, "Pojęcie," pp. 60 ff.

66 To some extent, it depends on belonging to democratic countries of rule of law, albeit it is also related to specific legal regulations. This can be seen on the example of the Polish legal order, in which the reference to both sources was different before 1989 (when no *ex proprio vigore* rule, even in relation to ratified and properly published international agreements, made direct implementation of international law impossible) and after 1989. In this last period, despite the fact that the regulation of the Constitution of the Republic of Poland of 1997, under Art. 9 of the Constitution of the Republic of Poland ("The Republic of Poland complies with the international law that binds it"), an open situation is left as to the generally recognized principles of international law and as to international customs, we can still find examples of the application of the principles by Polish courts after 1989.

However, it would be difficult to observe the use of on the occasion of such decisions, typical reference clauses resulting from these principles, despite the undoubtedly large load of axiology, and that sometimes of a universal nature (cf. e.g. SN Judgment of 17 X 1991, II KRN 274/91, OSNKW 1992, item 19). See also the justification of this practice: K. Skubiszewski, "Prawa," pp. 20 ff.

criteria and possibly references from the applicable (national or international) law. Therefore, there is no question of using such a criterion as the sole basis for constructing such content (especially as the criterion contained in the applicable national provision does not have this role either). This means, in fact, a smaller role of such criteria in decision-making processes than what would result from the sole distinction of such a basis for their application. This in turn mitigates all the real effects of using references from formally non-binding regulations.

Borrowing references from foreign law may be performed in a stronger version, when the domestic court refers directly to a normative act and incorporates the reference contained therein into its own decision-making process, and in a weaker version, when the use of such a reference takes place through the use of a judgment of a foreign court or an international court, applying the general clause that is useful in the current decision-making process. The latter version is a manifestation of a specific "judicial debate" between different courts, unrelated to formal judicial relations within the framework of a supranational structure. It is of particular importance in statutory law orders, where direct reference to foreign regulations is not only significantly more difficult to justify but is also much less frequent and less influencing for the judicial processes.[67]

It should be additionally pointed out that the reference regulation in both of the above-mentioned orders usually means a regulation in force (in a "third" country or in some "foreign" territory), but may also include (which creates a wider version and occurs even less frequently in practice), regulations already not binding, but referring to criteria that to some extent turn out to be useful in the respective decision-making process.

4.2.4. Borrowings and the judicial discretion

Each of the discussed situations differs from the borrowing of the reference *per analogiam clausulae*, albeit there is still an element of borrowing in each of them. In the case of the application of the *per analogiam* referring clause, we were dealing with its borrowing from another part of the applicable legal system, whereas in the case of the above-mentioned situations it cannot be said that the provisions from which the reference is derived remain formally in force.

The theoretical qualification of these applications (or non-applications), taking into account the features of the statutory legal order, despite the lack

---

67 Cf. SN Judgment of 26 I 2018, II CSK 191/17, LEX 2455728 (analysing the reference to criterion of "Treu und Glauben" of § 242 of BGB as discussed in several German Supreme Court Judgments).

of formal justification, should, however, be weighed against the effects of such application. And these transfer the basis for qualifying such an operation to what specific axiological content is linked with the application of the "not formally binding" clause. This relates to each of the three situations outlined above.

These situations, however, form a sequence that scales the departure from the basic properties of the statutory law order. It is relatively strongest in the first two situations – the application of a clause from a legal provision that is not yet binding (which has not yet entered into force) and the application of a clause from a provision that is no longer binding. The axiological and functional effects of such a departure may, however, prevail over formal arguments when, in the context of the juxtaposition of requirements of the actual decision-making process and the condition of regulation, it appears that applying this criterion is justified. We must not forget about the references contained in the most general provisions, which authorize the authorities applying the law to take into account the criterion of justice or equity in their decision-making. Therefore this type of broad reference does not preclude the use of "formally non-binding" references as long as the axiological content that can be determined on the basis of them falls within the scope of such broad authorization. In this context, the feature indicated above should be understood that it is the content of the reference that determines the consequences of departing from the formula of the theoretical justification for the application of the reference clause.

The situation of using a reference from a regulation of another state, in turn, should be classified differently. It is important here to define, as a condition for the correctness of such application, the homogeneous cultural and legal circle within which this type of borrowing can take place as well as the meeting of other requirements of the legal order (e.g. features of a branch of law) on the basis of the needs of the current decision-making process, as always important in such situations. Also in this case it is so that the most important feature is the axiological content of the criterion used. The cultural and legal community of both orders forms a general guarantee of their axiological unity. However, it does not eliminate the precautionary requirement, as the detailed aspects of social axiology may also differ within this general framework. On the other hand it is essential, from the point of view of the characteristics of the decision-making process, for the reference thus borrowed to be accompanied by a reference that falls within the national legal order. In this way, a foreign reference does not become the only axiological argument in validation, and its application assumes the characteristics of a reference to the established method of using an extra-legal criterion, usually in a more juridically mature legal order.

It seems that the same conditions and properties should be noted with regard to the use of references contained in formally non-binding regulations of international law corresponding to the characteristics of the same legal culture. For everywhere, the axiological coherence of the national and international order is the most important.

4.3. The issue of "jurisdictional creating" of an extra-legal reference

The above-mentioned methods for applying extra-legal references concerned clauses contained in various forms in legal provisions, regardless of whether they are in force or non-binding. The separate issue is the application of a reference created by jurisprudence, which is related to the consideration of the possibility of judicial "creation" of an extra-legal reference. There is still the question, how should one treat the application of an extra-legal criterion, which does not appear in any legal provisions. In other words, the question is whether is it possible, under the conditions of the statutory law, to treat such use of the criterion as its "additional creation" when making a court decision?

(1) The issues that arise in relation to this question can be presented in the form of three terminological variants – the additional creation of a general reference clause, of a reference itself and of an extra-legal criterion.

There is no question of additional creation of a reference clause by judiciary, as it is a structure of the text of a normative act.

Additional creating the reference is more real, not in the sense of including it in a normative text however but in a collection of carriers, which become the basis for the reconstruction of norms and the construction of the normative bases for decisions. In this sense, a second step is to reach for a reference clause contained in a provision "clearly distanced" from the provisions currently applied, regardless of whether it is a specific or general provision. However, it is in fact additional creation of references only for that part of the system to which it is adapted and only in the context of a specific decision-making process. In this sense, the above-mentioned situations of referring to clauses contained in formally non-binding provisions may also be treated as an additionally created reference (for the purposes of a specific decision-making process). There is no doubt, however, that "borrowing" sounds better than "additional creation."

On the other hand, a real "judicial creation of a reference" would be a situation of formulating (creating) an extra-legal criterion that is not known in the system of normative regulations. In the statutory law order, it would mean going beyond the scope of judicial discretion acceptable in therein with regard to determining the set of carriers from which the applied norms would be reconstructed.

It could mean some kind of "judicial objection" to the actions of the legislator, introducing an open collision as part of the framework of extra-legal axiology (which may occur, in particular, in a situation of a deep social change). If, on the other hand, it would fit into the axiology determined by the legal principles of the respective order (both constitutional and cultural-legal ones), it would mean at most a modification of specific axiological aspects not included in the legislative provisions in the form of creating a new (differently named) criterion or modification of the names of the existing criteria.

The assessment of the actual effects of such actions would, however, involve the analysis of the name of the criterion created in such a way and the resulting axiological content. The very condition that it should be a criterion unknown for the legal order (which of course is possible) is a situation so extreme that it is practically unrealistic. It would have to be associated with "inventing" a completely new name, which would also create the possibility of either associating an absurd content with it (e.g. the criterion of the "interest of the monarch" in the republican state) or giving such a new criterion a content inconsistent with the axiology (principles) of the respective legal order (e.g. the criterion of "market interest" in the system of centrally controlled economy) or the content axiologically inconsistent with the very essence of the law (e.g. the criterion of "interest of a criminal group" or, which would be even more pronounced, "good of the criminal group"). In this case this would not only denote a type of judicial axiological "objection" against the legislature, triggering significant effects whenever it could be confronted with the dominant social values, but would also fail to fit in the framework of the model term of law application process.

In this context, however, the situation in which the organ applying the law, knowingly or mistakenly, changes some component of the name of the criterion (e.g. instead of "social interest," uses the name "public interest"[68] in relation to the same reference, especially if this changed criterion also appears in the provisions of this normative act or regulatory system) cannot be treated as additional creation of a criterion. Although such a practice does not prove interpretative diligence, it is rather moderating the axiological dimension than changing it. These issues, however, are all the more related to determining the content that the entity applying the law would adopt for the respective extra-legal criterion, and not to considering the problem of additional creation.

(2) Additional creation of an extra-legal criterion, regardless of the intention behind it or lack thereof, may become an element of judicial imitation in the

---

68 Cf. SN Judgment of 18 XI 1993, III ARN 49/93, OSNIC 1994, item 181.

form of a specific precedent, both in the case of referring to a single decision as well as to the case-law line. It is evident that the use of absurd or inconsistent with the legal axiology criteria cause practical problem of axiological coherence of the legal order. It would be difficult to ascribe such effects to the cases in which the name of the criterion was changed within the scope discussed above. Although it would not correspond to the model of faithful use of references contained in legal provisions, it could be qualified, at best, as applying a criterion of modified by jurisprudence, perhaps even better reflecting the current (e.g. in the case of profound social change) dimension of the extra-legal axiology. In this context, too, it could therefore, albeit with some exaggeration to it, be treated as an application of the "judicial reference."[69]

---

69 This may be more a case in *common law* order, as functionally the courts use the extra-legal criteria in more independently way than in statutory legal order if the relations to statutory regulations are considered (cf. J.M. Marshall, *Examining*, pp. 55 ff.).

Chapter III Determining the content of the extra-legal criterion

The inclusion of the general referring clause in the set of validation arguments presented in the previous chapter initiates four subsequent types of reasoning and action, that ultimately lead to the issue of decision on the application of the law. The first is to establish the content of the extra-legal criterion (referral), the other – to include the established content of extra-legal criteria in the process of reconstruction of the rule (behaviour pattern) from the provision containing the reference, the third – to include the extra-legal criteria in the process of constructing a normative basis for the decision, and the fourth – participation of these criteria in determining the content of judicial decision (in terms of qualifying facts and determining the normative consequences of such qualification).

The present chapter will present various aspects of determining the content of extra-legal criteria. Regardless of the fact that these findings are made together with other activities and reasoning, as part of the process of judicial interpretation, only the "certainty" obtained as a result of these findings as to the determined content of these criteria allows this content to be included in activities consisting in reconstruction of the norm from the provision containing the reference and in the construction of the full normative basis for the decision. Therefore, the analysis of the processes of determining the content of the criteria, as logically prior, should precede the analysis of the role of these criteria in the overall process of operational interpretation (that will be presented in Chapter IV).

1. References to facts and references to values (assessments)

Determining the content of an extra-legal criterion that was appropriately named by the legislator means referring either to facts (e.g. established customs) or to a "system" of extra-legal values (e.g. equity) or norms (principles of social coexistence) as well as, if it is an estimation clause, to a comparative assessment (e.g. important reasons).

1.1. Determining the content of references to facts

(1) The relatively simplest situation concerns determining the contents of a reference to facts. As a model, it means a statement of their occurrence, for which an axiological declaration is not required. Evidently this is not a typical descriptive

statement due to the adjudicating judge's inability to independent, based on empirical research, determination of their actual existence. Examination by judges, both in the controlled and controlling instance, is based on already established knowledge (e.g. descriptions of respective customs), on expert knowledge (that reaches the procedure on *an ad hoc* basis) but also on own observations, experiences and intuition.

The issue of taking into account customs is also related to their "decision power." This, in turn, results from the possibility of giving normative character to certain facts. This would mean assuming that the occurrence of these facts is so common, permanent and strong that it makes it possible to build a structure on their basis for the application of standards, that would protect these customs (customary standards). This distinction cannot be made on the level of naming the respective criterion "customs." It is determined by "measuring" the intensity of the occurrence of specific customs in the particular social reality. Recognizing customs as customary norms strengthens their interpretative and decision-making role, which is visible in the subsequent stages of operative interpretation.

(2) Yet another semantic configuration evokes the criterion referred to as "legal (juridical) customs."[1] It is in a sense similar to the situation of the axiological edge between intra-legal axiology and extra-legal axiology (e.g. in the form of invoking "natural legal principles" or "principles of the legal order"[2]), except that this boundary situation does not contain an argument stemming from axiology. However, it is not a "legally established social custom" that would result from some legal (judicial) confirmation of a legal practice "but some kind of established legal practice" (e.g. a kind of "custom of judicial decisions" in one, and no other way). It is, therefore, a method of referring to facts or norms justified by some tradition that is separate from the above-mentioned one.

1.2. Determining the content of evaluation referrals

(1) The basic way of determining the content of an evaluative extra-legal reference (necessitating some kind of evaluation) is to refer to an axiology that has not been defined in terms of content in the basic type of sources of law for the respective legal order, and therefore it does not form part of the legal axiology, the most expressive construct of which are the principles of law. For the statutory legal order such a basic source will be legal provisions that contain such

1 Cf. e.g. Art. 1 of KH.
2 Cf. (respectively) § 7 of ABGB and Art. 6 of PPM.

references, although some components of this axiology may also result from the judicial decisions.[3]

Determining the content of extra-legal references in the processes of applying the law is associated with a much higher degree of valuation than in the case of the model interpretation of legal provisions, where the axiological arguments form one of the elements of the interpretation process, that is related to functional, teleological or systemic[4] arguments. Such activity however plays the role of basic argumentation interpreting the referring clauses themselves, "leaving" other arguments somewhat "in the background" of its own interpretative role.

(2) References to extra-legal axiology (not included in the legal system in the form of legal principles) adopt two basic forms. The first is to establish an estimate, while the second is to establish an assessment based on the value that forms part of the axiological system.

Formulation of estimates takes place in using estimated reference clauses in the decision-making process. They take a different linguistic normative form, while in the context of their place in the legal system, they should usually be located within the detailed provisions of a normative act. Examples of such constructions are references to important reasons, due diligence, appropriate age difference, permanent and complete breakdown of the marital relationship, special merits, etc.

Establishing the content of an estimated reference consists of two "operations." The first is to establish a fact (e.g. to establish that a given fact is the cause of an event or that there is an age difference, etc.), and the second is to estimate the scale of this fact (the reason must be important, the age difference has to be appropriate, etc.).[5] This estimation consists in evaluating (precisely "estimating") the degree (scale, scope, etc.) of occurrence of the estimated fact specified in the second term. Therefore, there is no reference to the systems of extra-legal values (e.g. moral or political), while the estimation itself is performed in close connection with a specific decision-making situation (hence such estimation can be called "situational evaluation").

One should indicate another two issues, complicating this relatively clear system of interrelations between the two components of the estimated reference.

---

3 Cf. II.4.3.

4 Cf. J. Wróblewski, *Sądowe*, pp. 128 ff., Z. Ziembiński, *Problemy*, pp. 274 ff., M. Zieliński, "Współczesne," p. 12 (assigning less importance to these distinctions), S. Wronkowska, Z. Ziembiński, *Zarys*, pp. 164 ff.

5 Cf. I.1.2.

Firstly we must note that within the framework of many estimation references, the fact itself may have some axiological component that requires its preliminary estimation. For example, the notions of "marital life" and "breakdown" themselves are not devoid of axiological elements (a similar situation occurs e.g. in a situation where "diligence" is found in a "due diligence" or "merit" in a "special merit" reference).

The second one relates to the practice whereby the content of estimated references is not determined independently but in conjunction with the criteria of general reference clauses.[6] In such situations, on the one hand, there is a generalization of the estimation criterion, and, on the other, a stronger connection between the general reference to extra-legal axiological systems and the "situational evaluations" that require estimation. The aforesaid combination can occur in two variants. The first one results from the linking of both references in the course of the decision-making process on the basis of the emerging need, while the second – from the wording which, already at the level of the name of the referring clause, combines extra-legal values with the need to estimate the scale of its inclusion in building the content of the decision to apply the law (e.g. "legitimate interest of citizens," or "important social interest").

(3) The latter of the above modifications affecting the basic method of determining the content of an estimated reference leads us to the very essence of general reference clauses. Anticipating the analyses carried out below, we can state at this point that, than different than with estimated references, determining the content of axiological general references (e.g. to the principles of equity or to the principles of social coexistence) takes place by referring to "systems" of values (or norms) that are extra-legal, falling within moral, political or economic axiology.

2. Determining the content of general reference clauses

Determining the content of the references contained in general clauses (references to "systems" of extra-legal values) initiates with the identification of the components of the clause's name and the selection of the type of values that

6 Cf. SN Provision of 22 IV 1968, III CRN 30/68, OSNCP 1969, item 3, SN Judgment of 24 XI 1971, I CR 512/71, OSNCP 1972, item 79, SN Resolution of 8 V 1975, III CZP 31/75, OSPiKA 1976, item 231 or SN Judgment of 6 XII 1976, III CRN 230/76, OSNCP 1977, item 190.

can be associated with the respective criterion from a national, collective, group (categorical) or individual perspective.[7]

Determining this content allows for the transition to further actions in the decision-making process, consisting, among others, (a) in determining the scale of mutual support of the individual extra-legal axiological contents and the scale of creating conflict situations between these individual contents, evaluations and criteria, (b) in establishing the relationship of generalizing the axiological content to concretizing the expressed evaluations (including situational assessments), (c) in determining the proportions between the characteristic content (verifiable in some sense) for the particular criterion and the interchangeable content of references (within particular references and between these references) resulting from combining axiological content, determining the relationship between the interpretation of general reference clauses and the interpretation of evaluation clauses, or (d) in defining the role of intra-legal axiology (legal principles and detailed legal criteria) in the interpretation of extra-legal references.

The specific manifestations of these properties are not completely reproducible in different decision-making processes. This is so as they will depend on many additional factors that significantly modify the overall picture in terms of the type of legal culture, the type of application of the law, the branch of law, the structure of the legal act, the type of political and economic system and the situation of stability or changeability of the social situation. The need for such relativizations does not, however, discredit the importance of perceiving general characteristics.

2.1. Identification of the components of the referring clause name

Determining the content of the criteria contained in a clause referring to extra-legal values includes reasoning initiated with the identification of the type of extra-legal value, then advances to determining its content and comparing this content with the fundamental legal axiology and terminates with linking the axiology determined in this manner with the characteristics of the particular decision-making process. All these reasoning processes are related to the

---

7 That is why the interpretation of extra-legal criterion must combine linguistic, axiological and teleological rules of legal interpretation (cf. e.g. SN Judgment of 10 I 2020, I CSK 279/18, LEX 2785119 and SN Judgment of 3 VII 2015, IV CSK 595/14, LEX 1917369, SN Judgment of 15 VI 2007, V CSK 63/07, LEX 457644, SN Judgment of 16 IX 2016, IV CSK 751/15, LEX 2109289 or SN Provision of 15 III 2019 r., V CSK 431/18, LEX 2636827.

legislative name of the evaluation criterion. Therefore, despite the fact that they strive to establish axiological content, they rely on the linguistic layer of the referring clause.

(1) As a rule, the entity applying the law refers to the legislative name of the referring clause and its extra-legal criterion as its constituent. Nevertheless this does not mean that in each case the court develops the argumentation regarding the adopted nomenclature of extra-legal references on which it based its decision-making process.[8]

However, the court applying the law usually attempts to determine the form of value (e.g. defined by the name "interest," "good" or "purpose") or norms (e.g. "principles," "considerations" or "requirements") by the axiological formula (e.g. "justice," "equity," "coexistence"), as framed in the appropriate scale (state/national, general, group or individual). The social dimension indicated in the name (social interest or objective, social good, equity, good morals, social justice, social coexistence) causes the content to be directed towards moral axiology, which may also be related to the content of religious criteria (e.g. Christian values). On the other hand, the indicated state dimension (objective of the state or state interests) may be related to axiology in a political sense. The latter may also be associated with the definition of the broadest scale of the social dimension of the content of the criterion (general interest, public interest or goal). The political dimension may also appear next to the name of the economic criterion (e.g. interests of the national economy, economic objectives of the state), which, however, may also have an independent meaning (e.g. the interest of a company) or a meaning related to moral criteria (good commercial practices, fair trade principles).

Clause names that are applied in jurisprudence usually combine the components of the legislative name of the criterion. However, it is also possible that the courts will attach less importance to the precise reproduction of the name formulated by the legislator. It seems to be the result of shifting the emphasis in the application of extra-legal references from "fidelity to the linguistic layer" to determining their axiological content and the conviction that since the essence of the reference is to reach beyond juridical arguments, then

---

8 In some cases the reference to the regulation that formulates the reference, is sufficient, as is the case concerning Art. 3 of POPC of 1950 (SN Judgment of 17 I 1962, 3 CR 877/61, RPEiS 1963 No. 1, p. 344) or of Art. 5 of KC (SN Resolution of 25 IX 1978, III CZP 59/78, OSNCP 1979, item 49).

attaching importance to normative formulations does not have to be absolute and unconditional.[9]

(2) Changing the name of the criterion may be one of the manifestations of this opinion, expressing the will to judicial modification of the content evoked by the name, although it may also be the result of chance.

In some situations (e.g. profound social change) such actions of the court may constitute their voice in the debate on the departure from the previous name of the criterion, related to the previous political system.[10] This applies to both political criteria (where the principles of the political system appear in the jurisprudence under the names of political goals but also the policy of the state[11]) and moral criteria (referring to the principles of equity when referring to the principles of social coexistence[12]). Evidently, the consequences of such "disrespect" for the nomenclature of a normative act do not have to be in any particular way "dangerous" from the point of view of the content of the criterion, to the extent that they change the axiology of the legal system and the application of its norms in a decisive manner negate basic social or political preferences. All that falls within a certain framework of axiological decisions, determined by the entire socio-political system, and it is within this framework that the references influence the content of judicial decisions. However, if such a practice of changing the nomenclature of extra-legal criteria would become common, it could, for example, hinder the axiological orientation of the addressees of norms or even instance control. Regardless of the fact that it would fail to meet the requirements of a correct linguistic interpretation, it could lead to the formulation, in court decisions, of "clumsy" names (e.g. "the general social role of bees"[13]), which would in effect approach the situation of court creating an extra-legal criteria.[14]

---

9 As it happens in replacing the criterion of "social interest" by the criterion of "public interest" in application of Art. 7 of KPA (cf. e.g. SN Judgment of 18 XI 1993, III ARN 49/93, OSNIC 1994, item 181).

10 Cf. SN Judgment of 20 V 1997 II CKN 51/97, OSNIC 1997 item 194, SN Judgment of 23 III 2017, V CSK 393/16, LEX 2306389, SN Provision of 13 VII 2020, IV CSK 746/19, LEX 3051786 or SN Judgment of 22 II 2019, IV CSK 121/18, LEX 2625010).

11 Cf. e.g. SN Resolution of 2 II 1967, III CZP 110/66, OSPiKA 1965, item 52 and NSA Judgment of 10 II 1981, SA 910/80, ONSA 1981, item 7.

12 Cf. e.g. SN Judgment of 13 I 1953, II C 1631/52, PiP 1953 No. 10, p. 557, SN Resolution of 13 II 1981, III CZP 72/80, OSNCP 1981, item 207 or NSA Judgment of 10 II 1981, SA 910/80, ONSA 1981, item 7.

13 Cf. e.g. SN Judgment of 28 XII 1979, III CRN 249/79, OSPiKA 1982, item 62 (p. 150).

14 Cf. VI.3.2.

2.2. Selection of the type of criterion and the type of axiology

The significant scope of the court's discretion is already evident in the case of the first component of the name of the criterion, i.e. the choice of its type. The division into values and norms is not a separate division in the context of defining the content of the criterion, because it is not possible to determine, in every case, regardless of the form of the verbal reference, whether a norm protecting value was already shaped.[15] What is important, however, is that the reference norm (with the exception of the customary norm) has an axiological justification. Hence, for example, the content of the criterion of the principles of social coexistence is identified in judicial decisions with both norms and social values.[16] The effects of the choice of the type of criterion by the court, provided it takes place within a given type of normative axiology, are not, however, as significant as in the case of the findings in relation to the other components of the name of the reference, and in particular the linking of the name of the criterion and the type of extra-legal axiology.

The main indications for determining the content of extra-legal values are the choices of the type of axiology. This choice is focused on the extra-legal (i.e. not forming part of the normative system) moral, political and economic axiology. It is related to the names indicated in the clause by the legislator, which, however, is by no means a definite indication, especially since the division into these types of axiology itself is not a disjoint one. Even when the court refers to the type of value indicated in the form of the name of the criterion, it does not deprive itself of the discretion in determining the details of its content. In addition, it is also possible to change (entirely or partially) the type of axiology and combine its individual types in the course of judicial application of the law.

2.2.1. Political values

The criteria that fall within the political axiology are the relatively easiest in their identification and determining their content. Their feature is general dimension

15 In Polish legal literature, there is a division into general clauses of the 1st and 2nd degree which, in a sense, reflects the evaluative and normative nature of the references. The first-degree clauses contain the basis for an individual assessment of the respective case, while the second-degree clauses are constructs that condition the compliance of this qualification with standards based on extra-legal assessments (cf. Z. Ziembiński, *Teoria*, pp. 144–145).

16 Cf. SN Judgment of 23 III 2017, V CSK 393/16, LEX 2306389.

(public or state) of their content, expressed in the form of criteria such as public interest, public objective or state goals.[17]

The manner in which their content is determined depends largely on the type of political regime, which also initially influences their normative shape. In a democratic and rule-of-law system, these criteria do not play a significant independent decision-making role (especially with regard to private law). Here reading its content entails its generalization to the level of state interest or public interest (public order), albeit confronted with the socially justified general interest.[18] In the application of law in authoritarian systems, their content, firstly, affects the processes of applying not only public law, but also private law,[19] secondly, it acquires an independent decision-making role, thirdly, it may mean direct "transmission" of current political programs based on political or ideological documents, and fourth, it may influence the content of criteria aimed at social values (e.g. relating to a social objective or interest). Their connection with the official ideology leads to a particularly clear emphasis on the values introduced by it. When the jurisprudence refers (also in the field of private law) to the directly political language (e.g. pointing to the intensification of the class struggle,[20] dazzling with the word "socialist,"[21] sharp opposition of capitalist and socialist system conditions,[22] pointing directly to the position of a party organization[23] or directly referring to statements of leading politicians[24]) are just some of the ways of arguing, leaving no doubts either as to the role of political criteria, or as to the method that they should be referred to in jurisdiction. These are usually accompanied by the care of the centre of political power for the uniformity

---

17 Cf. A. Reve, A. Ware, "Interests," passim.

18 Cf. ECtHR Judgments: of 10 IV 2007, Evans v. UK (6339/05), of 25 XI 1997, Zana v. Turkey (RJD 199V).

19 Cf. SN Resolution of 20 III 1976, III CZP 77/75, OSPiKA 1977, item 74 and SN Resolution of 30 IX 1976, III CZP 97/75, OSNCP 1977, item 83.

20 Cf. SN Resolution of 26 IV1952, C. Prez. 798/51, PiP 1952 No. 7, pp. 113–18.

21 These are relatively frequent cases (cf. e.g. SN Resolution of 28 V 1955, I CO 5/55, PiP 1955 No. 11, pp. 847–9, SN Judgment of 20 V 1976, III CRN 373/75, OSNCP 1977, item 31 or SN Resolution of 22 V 1978, II UZP 14/78, OSPiKA 1979, item 21.

22 Cf. SN Judgment of 11 XII 1951, C 1573/51, PiP 1952 No. 12, pp. 881–2.

23 GKA decision of 3 II 1977, IP-8150/76, OSPiKA 1977, item 212.

24 Cf. e.g. SN Judgment of 5–30 VI 1951, C 649/50, PiP 1951 No. 2, pp. 312–17, quoting the statement of J. Stalin referring to the relation of social interest to individual interest, or SN Judgment of 16 X 1952, C 1940/52, PiP 1953 No. 5–6, p. 821, quoting the statement of B. Bierut (First Secretary of the Polish United Workers Party) regarding overcoming the disproportions between the development of industry and agriculture.

of such practices. It can be manifested either in the form of direct political influence (by means of "manual" imposition of current political content, which means a complete breakthrough of the limits of rule of law principle) or through the content of general and binding guidelines for all courts, which are issued by a politically controlled supreme court.[25]

The verification of the content of political criteria is associated with the recognition of state interests, also associated as public, which may be based on the principles of the political system and official ideology, and in some situations also in political documents. As part of this verification, the type of political system is reflected, because the more authoritarian features such a system holds, the more the content of the political axiology will be read ideologically or on the basis of political documents by courts.

This leads to two conflicting possibilities for determining the specific content of reference clauses. On the one hand, it is the axiomatization and ideologization of the criterion, and on the other hand – linking the content of the reference with the current political line. Both of them, beneficial for the achievement of its short-term objective by the centre of authoritarian political power, in fact mean the instrumentalization[26] of determining the content of the extra-legal criterion. That makes the latter gain greater opportunities to influence the shape of decision-making processes due to the institutionalization of political interests,[27] the existence of forces capable of actively supporting this influence, and the lack of independence of the judiciary.

---

25 E.g. interpretative instructions ("wytyczne") of Polish SN, having been issued between 1962 and 1990, directed to and binding for all courts functioning between 1962 and 1990.

26 On the understanding and various aspects of the instrumentalization of law, cf. W. Lang, "Instrumentalne," pp. 3 ff. L. Morawski, "Instrumentalizacja," passim; W. Gromski, *Autonomia*, esp. pp. 107 ff. This is evidenced by the examples of determining the content of criterion of interest of the state from the old (no longer binding) art. 417 and 421 of KPC in the light of housing, agricultural and financial policies of the state (ʿcf. e.g. SN Provision of 17 IV 1969, III CRN 11/69, OSNCP 1970, item 12). Similar, albeit significantly stronger a practice may take place in case of applying political criteria to determine the content of discretionary administrative decision (cf. A. Szot, *Judicial*, pp. 26 ff., 119 ff.).

27 A. Reve, A. Ware, "Interests," passim.

2.2.2. Economic values

A similar degree of certainty accompanies the establishment and verification of the content of the economic criteria.[28] Also in this it is the type of economic system, which is related to the type of political system, that will have the greatest influence. This is determined not only by the way the law is applied in economic matters, but also by the method of verifying their content. The politicized centralist system favours, on the one hand, administrative forms of resolving economic disputes, and on the other hand – politicized methods of "verifying" the content of economic criteria, that are readily appropriately politicized in the names of references.

The model of centrally directed economy, based on the method of socio-economic planning, which protects state property (social property administered by the state) to the greatest extent and always leads to some authoritarianism in the field of political and social relations, will result in a natural preference for the general social (state) context of understanding the references to economic criteria. Although the assumed and implemented model does not have to always coincide, and then (e.g. in certain periods of "thaw"), in practice, the dominance of the general interest will not be so strong, but it will not significantly affect the basic features. In this type of economy, the names of extra-legal references may directly support the assumption that general interests, as identified with the interests of the autocratic state as the main economic entity, are pursued (e.g. when determining the content of the reference to the interests of the national economy, planned tasks, etc.). Also, the criteria emphasizing the economics of production and trading or the principles of economic accounting, even though they relate in terms to a total of measurable and rational ways of conducting the respective economic activity, will be interpreted and applied in the macrosocial perspective with such axiology, limiting the importance of direct interests of economic entities.[29] The intensity of these preferences is changing even in the most permanent systems based on these ideological principles, and therefore there is always some fluctuation in the role of these ideological assumptions.

In market and democratic systems, verification is on the one hand more difficult if these criteria point to a combination of economic and moral content,[30] but

28 Cf. J. Górski, "Aksjologiczne," passim.

29 Cf. SN Judgment of z 25 IV 1961, 1 CR 503/60, RPEiS 1962 No. 2, p. 355 and GKA decision of 29 III 1971, BO-2185/71, OSPiKA 1972, item 13.

30 What results, among others, in looking for the economic aspects in the criterion of principles of social coexistence (cf. SN Judgment of 23 III 2017, V CSK 393/16, LEX 2306389 or SN Judgment of 12 X 2017, IV CSK 660/16, LEX 2401827)

on the other hand it is easier if these criteria indicate to a basis that is measurable. For here, the basis for concretizing their content may be data that can be quantified, also statistically, especially where we are dealing – generally speaking – with the economic efficiency or rationality of managemen.t[31] Therefore, in such type of a system, it becomes common to associate, in jurisprudence, the content of these criteria with market principles, which may additionally acquire an individual economic dimension[32] or moral context.[33]

2.2.3. Moral values

The processes of determining the content of moral values, though connected with various aspects of the criterion of equity,[34] are the most diverse and complex ones.[35] There are several reasons for this.

Firstly, it is so, among others, due to the linguistic method of specifying these criteria in legal provisions. Their names are the most varied and show lower (as compared with political or economic criteria) precision and semantic sharpness, and are, at the same time, characterized by a specific interchangeability.[36] And it results less from the intention of the legislator than from the nature of these names itself. By way of example, the following criteria may be mentioned: good of child, the good of family, good customs, good faith, equity or principles of equity, principles of social coexistence, social interest or social goal. In addition, they can be further linked with religious values (e.g. Christian values). Even if the judicial practice respects the nomenclature of the criteria of general references, the scope of the diversity of judge's moral choices does not change.

Secondly, it stems from the more dispersed sources that shape moral values and the fields and dimensions of identifying their content, as well as the related possibilities of various ways of combining their content. In the case of this type

---

31 Cf. A. Bator, *Użycie,* pp. 260 ff.

32 E.g. interest of company.

33 E.g. in the case of determining the content of the principles of commercial honesty or good commercial manners (practices).

34 Cf. e.g. W. Dziedziak, *O prawie*, pp. 205–276.

35 Cf. R. Pound, "A Survey," passim, Z. Ziembiński, "Argumentacje," passim, M. Rümelin, *Die Biligkeit*, passim.

36 This applies to all the constituents of the name of the criterion. An example may be the interchangeability of the construct of "interest of child" and "good of child," distinguished at the level of normative regulation but reduced to identical content at the level of applying the law (cf. TK Judgment of 16 V 2018, SK 18/17, LEX 2486896, SN Provision of 20 X 2010 r., sig. III CZP 72/10, LEX 786940).

of axiology, the influence of legally defined names is lower than in the case of political and economic values. The names of the majority of moral criteria do not precisely define the perspective of reading the content of these values, making it possible to take into account the most general dimension and, at the same time, they are the least verifiable in terms of adequacy to the axiological source, but also a more specific dimension. Apart from the general social dimension (social interest), there is the possibility of linking their content with the universal dimension, somehow humane, going beyond the values of the respective society (e.g. universal values and general human values,[37] or Christian values[38]), there is the possibility of taking into account the axiology associated with a specific category of people (e.g. good of child), group axiology (e.g. corporate values on the basis of professional deontology[39]) and individual axiology (professed moral principles[40]).

Social axiology, affecting legal phenomena and legal turnover, may tip the balance in favour of preferring either general society or in some sense "balanced" (combining general and individualistic perspectives) understanding of the references cited.[41] For example, the most representative reference within this group – that to principles of equity, can be interpreted both in general and in individual terms. The reference to good faith or to good customs obviously expresses the importance of supra-individual rules on the basis of which specific assessments are made in the process of applying the law, but at the same time they do not create an automatic preference for the general public interest. We deal similarly case with references to the good of child or the good of family. However, the reference to the principles of social coexistence, social interest or the social danger of an act (in criminal law) at the starting point presupposes a

---

37 Cf. Preamble to RP Constitution.

38 E.g. Art. 21 sec. 1.6 of the Polish Broadcasting Act of 29 XII 1992, which, points out that the public media respect the Christian system of values based on the principles of universal ethics.

39 Cf. Art. 1 sec. 2 of the Polish law of 6 VII 1982 on the legal councillors (cf. also: G. Ławnikowicz, S. Pilipiec, "Nieskazitelność," pp. 247–256).

40 Cf. Art. 85 of RP Constitution as the reason for refusing military service.

41 Cf. various treating of the relation between criterion of "social interest" and "legitimate interests of citizens" of Art. 7 of KPA. They may "cooperate" in reaching joint content (cf. NSA Judgment of 18 XI 2020, II OSK 1901/19, CBOSA) but they may also be placed in a position of collision (cf. NSA Judgment of 20 IV 2021, III OSK 584/21, CBOSA) or weighing (cf. NSA Judgment of 23 VI 2020, I OSK 291/20, CBOSA or NSA Provision of 11 V 2021, III OSK 182/21, CBOSA).

point of view that is supra-individualistic in determining the content of the criterion. In a favourable "environment" of official axiology, confirming these content intuitions, the general social understanding of these criteria gains an advantage over their interpretations from the perspective of a social group (especially groups that are not large social groups). Thus, the "supra-individuality" affects the general social perspective and, in its extreme form, may lead to abandonment of efforts for empirical verification, or even to the impossibility of such verification, which in turn is associated with the axiomatization of understanding and taking care only that the assessments derived from these criteria are consistent with assumptions of official ideology.

The ideological assumption of preferring the social interest, as present in the practice of the authoritarian state, leads to the establishment of a valuation context in the use of reference clauses, in which general social values and, in a weaker variant, group values (mainly those of large social groups), will be treated as superior, i.e. having priority in the event of a conflict, in relation to values that are significant for individuals. Therefore, the ideology, in a sense, total, holistic, and consequently authoritarian, conditions these preferences in the opposite way to axiology, that is, generally speaking, liberal, democratic and pluralistic. The former is always "stronger" in terms of means of influence than the latter. The vision of the basic relation between society and the individual determines the foundations of the evaluation context also when using the structure of the extra-legal references. Evidently we must also be aware of the extremely general character of the aforesaid determination of dependencies. However, they indicate the most basic relationships and find their further confirmation in more detailed analyses.

Thirdly, in each case of determining moral content, there is a difficulty in reading social preferences during the decision-making process, on the basis of which the content of these criteria should be determined (even if it is correlated with the environmental or individual preferences of the decision-maker). Finding social preferences in the case of these criteria cannot be based on certain sources, let alone documents (e.g. even codes of professional deontology do indicate but do not specify axiological content). The possible source of verification is informal and is shaped spontaneously, without a clear "projection of the system" of evaluations or norms. The efficiency and accuracy of reading the social axiology also depends on its stability and on social activity that would express and reveal this axiology. Although the degree of social activity in manifesting individual moral convictions may help in identifying these preferences, it cannot be an indicator that excludes errors in their determination. Sociological surveys of public opinion (especially those of "random" nature) have similar characteristics, and they would be difficult to carry out anyway for the purposes of the specific application of the reference clause. Therefore, and for evident reasons, the basis here are the judge's own, unstructured observation, life experiences and moral intuitions. The wider the dimension of the referential moral axiology (with the dimension of general human axiology at the fore), the more difficult it proves to verify it in terms of detailed evaluations. What is also of significance in this context is the type of the political system in question. The democratic type determines the lower influence of political values as part of their connection with moral values and creates conditions for easier identification of social axiology (due to the greater activity and openness of democratic societies), which may be associated with a smaller scope of judicial "discretion."

Fourth and finally, determining the content of moral criteria may, to a greater extent than in the case of political and economic values, also take into account judge's preferences in the form of "group" values accepted by the members of judiciary or even the assessments of an individual judge making the decision. It is usually so that this type of preferences are included, as they are overlapping in various ways with the reading of social values. In the context of verification, taking into account one's own preferences is a factor that strengthens the credibility of such an activity, but it may also violate the already fragile possibility of compliance of assessments expressed in the process of applying the law and moral content in the social dimension.

Thus, in the case of determining the moral axiological contents, the scope of the autonomy of the judiciary is relatively the broadest. It always requires referring to autonomous judicial preferences, even if in certain situations it is not excluded to refer to documents (e.g. in the case of religion values[42] or corporate values, conditioning e.g. disciplinary liability). In the case of generalizing the content of moral values, i.e. presenting them in the general social dimension (e.g. social interest, principles of social justice), there is also the greatest probability of approaching the political content.

2.2.4. *Differentiating factors*

The practice of determining the content of references to general clauses depends on many factors, the most important of which is the type of political system, influencing, among others, the scope of the discretionary power that determines the results of these activities. In the authoritarian type, the legislator itself may limit the judiciary's axiological choices by means of the names of criteria (the

42 G. Maroń, *Integralność*, esp. pp. 309–472.

scope of the court's discretion in determining, for example, the objectives of the state building communism[43] is basically illusory). This concerns mainly the political values and politicized economic values (the principle of planned economy), although it is not completely irrelevant in the case of socially recognized moral values (social interest, socio-economic goal).

Regardless of the type of political system, the determination of all values is also influenced by the situation of social change, the effects of which may be revealed in jurisdiction. However, they will depend on the direction of such a change. For example, the democratic social and legal change (e.g. in Poland after 1989) triggered the judicial anticipation of a new, emerging axiology of a democratic society, also without a change in legal provisions and in naming of the extra-legal criteria. This applies in particular to determining the content of general social criteria (e.g. rules of social coexistence) that are most exposed to the politicization of their content. Authoritarian change has the opposite effect, although in this case the judiciary, built on the principle of independence, maintains (at least for some time) the potential to continue practices related to the democratic system and rule of law.[44]

The image of the operation of both of the above-mentioned factors in the social environment of law would be even more complete if they were also imposed on other ones. The most important of these include the properties of the branches of law in which the extra-legal criteria function as a component of the clause (the presence of clauses in public law may strengthen all effects resulting from the features of autocratic political system) or the type of law application (the same effect is achieved by the application of law by administrative bodies).

3. Effects of combining the content of extra-legal criteria

In addition to determining the content of values, expressed in the form of an appropriately named extra-legal criterion and falling within the framework of moral, political and economic axiology, there is a situation of combining the individual values in judicial practice. It occurs in various configurations, leading to various effects in terms of types of axiology and types of individual values. These may be related to one criterion as well as with more than one criterion

43 Cf. I.1.2., I.3.2., I.5.

44 What was one of the reasons of connecting the content of the criterion of principles of social coexistence with classin criterion of equity (cf. e.g. SN Judgment of 23 III 2017, V CSK 393/16, LEX 2306389, SN Provision of 13 VII 2020, IV CSK 746/19, LEX 3051786 or SN Judgment of 22 II 2019, IV CSK 121/18, LEX 2625010).

expressed both in several references, which together constitute the extra-legal axiology applied in the respective process.

3.1. "Mutual supporting" (enhancement) of extra-legal content

(1) The most common juridical situation is the use of reference or references to strengthen their role in a given decision-making process in relation to the role of the *stricti iuris* criteria and sometimes also in relation to the criteria of legal axiology (legal principles).

Different criteria in different configurations may be subject to this method of "mutual support." The decisions may combine criteria of the same kind (e.g. moral and moral, political and political), but also criteria of different types. In the latter practice, usually certain types play a stronger, fundamental role, while others play a reinforcing role, often forming an additional justification of the former. Certain criteria create strong ties, others – weaker ones.

(2) Combining the same types of criteria usually creates strong connections, supporting the strength of axiological argumentation. Connections in moral arguments are strong, especially when they represent a single-type interest (e.g. general social, group or individual). In an authoritarian state, it is usually the general interest not only in the scope of moral axiology,[45] but also in combining economic criteria.[46] Arguments resulting from political criteria are commonly supported by each other and this is also visible with particular force in this type of political system, e.g. due to the lack of conflict situations within this axiological order that is based on the preferences of a single centre of political power.[47]

Combining the same types of criteria may be associated with establishing different axiological contents. It is most profound, regardless of the type of political system, in the case of moral values (e.g. as regards the general social and group context with the criterion of social good or interest). In comparison, political and economic values are more condensed in content, but the degree of their condensation will depend on the political system. A similar situation takes place in

45 Cf. SN Judgment of 7 XII 1949, C 1675/49, PiP 1961 No. 1, pp. 145–148 and SN Judgment of 10 III 1977, II CR 24/77, OSNCP 1977, item 240.

46 Cf. SN Judgment of 30 XII 1976, III CRN 297/76, OSPiKA 1978, item 165 and GKA decision of 18 V 1976, DO-2206/76, OSPiKA 1977, item 14.

47 This applies in particular to the criteria of no longer binding art. 4 of KC, which formulated two different political criteria, usually appearing in the application of the law together, uniformly defining the content of the decision (cf. SN Resolution of 9 VI 1976, III CZP 46/75, OSNCP 1976, item 184). Cf also Z. Ziembiński, "Moralność," 103, Z. Ziembiński, *Etyczne*, 185–186.

the case of establishing single-type content expressed in the criteria contained in various referring clauses (e.g. the common axiology resulting from the criterion of social interest and the principles of social coexistence).

Creating a strong combination of various extra-legal criteria usually takes place in the decision-making practice when one of them is political evaluation.[48] Here, too, the strength of these relationships is determined by the type of political system. The use of political references in an authoritarian system strengthens both the role of the established content of economic criteria, of course those that prefer the general economic interest (on the scale of the entire national economy),[49] and the content of moral criteria understood in the general social context.[50] In turn, in a democratic system we do not witness the combination of different kinds of criteria in such a way that moral or economic criteria only justify the domination of political criteria. On the other hand, in a market system, the criteria of rationality at the level of the operation of an individual economic entity may be associated with the invocation of moral criteria (e.g. the principle of fair trading).

The mutual support of individual arguments can also be observed in the case of the joint interaction of moral and economic criteria.[51] A special role in this connection is played by the common occurrence of references, e.g. to the principles of social coexistence and the socio-economic purpose of law, especially if they are formulated in a single legal provision.[52] The latter criterion[53] easily passes into the general circulation and is usually an additional criterion, defining the meaning of the principles of coexistence, mainly in terms of economic criteria (where the element of "economic purpose" has a clear advantage in decisions over the element of "social purpose").[54] It is a more general feature, because most often when it comes to using economic and moral criteria, the former, as more

48 Cf. e.g. SN Judgment of 5 I 2011, III CSK 119/10, LEX 738400.

49 Cf. SN Provision of 16 IV 1968, III CRN 51/68, OSNCP 1969, item 52 and GKA Resolution 25 IV 1977, 1/77, OSPiKA 1977, item 173.

50 Cf. SN Judgment of 21 X 1950, C 345/50, PiP 1951 No. 4, pp. 740–41 (for the above-mentioned example of formulating the principles of social coexistence with political content or SN Provision of 11 IV 1968, III CRN 55/68, OSNCP 1968, item 159.

51 Cf. SN Resolution of 3 VI 1965, III CO 27/65, OSNCP 1966, item 34 and SN Judgment of 5 I 1978, II CR 478/77, OSNCP 1979, item 51.

52 As it is in Art. 5 of KC.

53 Cf. e.g. SN Judgment of 11 X 1968, I CR 378/68, OSPiKA 1970, item 152 (cf. also Z. Łyda, "Funkcjonowanie," pp. 68 ff.).

54 Cf. e.g. SN Judgment of 9 II 1977, IV PR 377/76, OSPiKA 1978, item 105.

defined, especially when they refer to the understanding of rational management, play a more fundamental role.

The combination of different types of values may therefore take place within two criteria of a reference contained in a single provision (as was the case in the situation in question) as well as within a single bi-component criterion, contained as the sole reference in the provision (socio-economic purpose). It is always associated with the perception of the need for "inter-typical" relativization, or with the mutual strengthening of both types of values.

The practice of combining single-type or multi-type contents of extra-legal axiology can be observed so often that it should be considered an important property of determining the content of criteria and of applying extra-legal references in general.[55] This is the result of the belief of entities applying the law that it is because of, *among other things*, openness of this structure and a lower degree of verifiability of the content of such criteria, the application of only a single extra-legal criterion from one reference is simply "not enough." Such an entity, enhancing and deepening its axiological argumentation, applies not only the criterion related to a given provision but also other criteria, "justifying" the application and determination of the content of the underlying reference. Such practice, in most cases, is not subject to critique by the glosses.[56]

Combining the content of various extra-legal criteria may also mean the impact of the content of some criteria on others, when the former become an element of an interpretative directive that covers provisions, whose part may also include references. Such situations are not frequent and are usually associated with the application of an interpretative norm created in order to correct the content of the criteria contained in the provisions adopted from the previous political formation. They usually lead to giving these criteria a new content (consistent with the axiology of the new system), but it cannot be excluded (in civil law in particular) to apply them in strengthening the axiological argumentation that would take into account the content of the "old" criteria.[57]

---

55 Cf. e.g. SN Resolution of 30 I 1970, III CZP 102/69, OSPiKA 1971, item 31 and SN Resolution of 20 III 1973, III CZP 52/71, OSNCP 1973, item 185.

56 It is sometimes possible to observe suggestions of the need to apply other references in decisions than those applied by the court (cf., for example, the glosses by A. Stelmachowski (1). and T. Zieliński).

57 Cf. SN Resolution of 28 V 1968, III CZP 49/68, OSPiKA 1970, item118, SN Judgment of 14 XII 1973 II CR 692/73, OSPiKA 1975 item 94 or SN Judgment of 28 V 1981, II CR 176/81, OSPiKA 1982, item 120.

(3) The effect of mutual supporting of arguments from open axiology in the variants discussed above may be such an accumulation of the criteria that a specific "axiological entanglement" of the content of the decision arises, apparent in the content of its justification. In a sense, this is a rationalization argument for the decision, consisting in the formation of a conviction of the recipients of the decision, concerning the significance of extra-legal axiological argumentation. At the same time it is not only the result of difficulties in determining the content of one criterion, separated from the set of references, but also the support of these values or the" justification" of some values by others, occurring regardless of the need for a specific solution.

This may lead to such an intensification of the practice of combining extra-legal criteria in a given decision[58] that the very basis of this decision becomes illegible, and the "total content" interpreted from all the criteria used is so extensive that it actually allows a decision to be made in every possible direction. This renders it difficult to understand the actual axiological choices, to recognize which criterion or criteria constitute the actual premise of the decision's content, and which are limited to further specifying the basic criteria. Characteristically, this practice is not as dependent on the type of political system as other elements of determining the content of the extra-legal criterion,[59] except for the possibility of directing axiological "entanglement" to the political ideologization of the content of criteria in an authoritarian system.

(4) The combination of axiological arguments can also be observed in the case of determining the content of the criteria of estimation clauses, when they

58 Cf. e.g. SN Judgment of 8 VIII 1980, III CRN 144/80, OSPiKA 1981, item 28 and GKA Resolution of 7 X 1974, No. 7/74, OSPiKA 1975, item 4.

59 A few examples of decisions relating to new references, introduced after 1989, can create this impression. This applies to the reference to "Christian values" juxtaposed with the principles of law, morality, social good, universal ethics, etc. (cf. TK Resolution of 2 III 1994, W.3/92, OTK 1994, item 17 and TK Judgment of 7 VI 1994, K.17/93, OTK 1994, item 11) and the rules of social justice, which became subject, in justifications of judgments, of not only referral to numerous other criteria (cf. TK Judgment of 29 V 1996, K.22/95, OTK 1996, item 6) but also reasoning of a doctrinal type, comparing different concepts and their applicability to operationalization (cf. TK Judgment of 22 VIII 1990, K.7/90, OTK 1990, item 5). This may also apply to the references brought forward from the previous system, e.g. rules of social coexistence, for which there are attempts to find their new content, including such that would refer to the meaning of classic references (cf. NSA Judgment of 26 VIII 1988, SA/Wr 773/87, OSP 1990, item 355 and SN Resolution of 17 XII 1991, III CZP 131/91, OSP 1992, item 129).

are explained not by themselves,[60] but through the criteria of reference clauses. The evaluation is then not only related to the facts, but also to the general criterion of the clause. This applies to various evaluative expressions, as long as the values indicated in general clauses become an element of determining their content. For example, to criterion of "important reasons," defined, for example, in the context of the criteria of the rules of coexistence, rules of morality, the good of child or the good of family.[61] That applies also to other estimation clauses, explained on the basis of various general criteria (e.g. due diligence,[62] exceptional cases,[63] special circumstances,[64] permanent and complete breakdown of the marriage,[65] substantial damage,[66] etc.). Of course, it should be remembered that the very determination of the meaning of an apparently descriptive term (breakdown of marriage, diligence) may also require, as is the case with any legal concept, reference to some more general criteria and thus relation to evaluation.

References to customs work somewhat differently. They will usually preserve their separateness,[67] or even competitiveness[68] in relation to the content of evaluative criteria. This is related to the relatively greater certainty of establishing the existing customs, and thus greater verifiability of such an extra-legal criterion, compared to determining the content of typically evaluative criteria. It is difficult to avoid any connection with evaluation, if the name of the criterion is axiologically tinted. This is the case with the criteria of "good customs" (good manners).

---

60 These are basically exceptional cases (cf. e.g. SN Judgment of 6 XI 1972, III CRN 250/72, OSPiKA 1973, item 159 and SN Judgment 26 V 1981, SA 974/81, OSPiKA 1982, item 58).

61 Cf. e.g. SN Judgment of 28 I 1960, 4 CR 208/59, RPEiS 1961 No. 1, p. 373, SN Resolution 27 III 1972, III CZP 69/70, OSNCP 1973, item 20 and SN Judgment of 30 VI 1979, IV CR 194/of 79, OSPiKA 1980, item 87

62 Cf. SN Judgment of 18 V 1974, III CRN 88/74, OSPiKA 1975, item 138.

63 Cf. SN Resolution of 8 V 1975, III CZP 31/75, OSPiKA 1976, item 231.

64 Cf. SN Resolution of 20 V 1976, II UZP 9/76, OSPiKA 1977, item 45 and SN Resolution of 17 XII 1991, III CZP 131/91, OSP 1992, item 129 as well as NSA Judgment of 26 VIII 1988, SA/Wr 773/87, OSP 1990, item 355.

65 Cf. SN provision of 22 VI 1972, III CRN 133/72, OSPiKA 1973, item 123 and SN Judgment of 3 III 1980, I CR 2/80, OSPiKA 1980, item 229.

66 Cf. SN Resolution of 16 I 1997, I KZP 32/96, OSP 1997, item 121.

67 Cf. SN Judgment of 8 X 1980, IV CR 383/80, OSNCP 1981, item 84 and SN Judgment of 13 IV 1972, I PR 153/72, OSNCP 1972, item 184.

68 Cf. SN Resolution of 15 XI 1968, III CZP 104/68, OSNCP 1969, item 154.

3.2. Creating and solving collision relations

The effect of combining values may be not only their mutual support in order to enhance arguments stemming from extra-legal axiology in decision-making, but also their "conflict" and the subsequent resolution of the resulting conflict. This applies to both collisions within single and different types of values, and it can manifest itself either in the soft or hard version. Each of these types of collisions may be visible in the justification of a court decision or, in various dimensions, hidden in the presentation of the reasons for the decision.

Creating axiological collisions may involve the use of the shape of a normative regulation containing various references to one type of criterion (e.g. in the case of a single legal provision referring to the social interest and the legitimate interest of citizens) or a "two-part" reference, indicating, for example, the need to take into account two different types of values (as is the case when referring to a socio-economic purpose). In both types of collisions created in this way, it is related not so much to the verbal shape of the reference itself, but to the juxtaposition of these values in the process of applying the law in relation to a specific factual condition. A collision may directly result from the court's "authorial" reading of the relationship between the types of values or between single-type values, which, in its opinion, should be confronted.[69]

The collision relations analysed below and the methods for solving them, differing depending on whether we are dealing with single-type or multi-type values, do not show significant differences depending on whether these criteria (both single and multi-type) are formulated in a single reference or several references. Maybe except for that, assuming that if entities applying the law "respect" the systematics of provisions in a normative act or branches of law, they treat references from different provisions, especially if they are related to different names, as references indicating different intentions of the legislator.[70]

69 E.g. the principles of social coexistence, which can be understood both in the collision relationship of moral and political axiology (cf. SN Resolution of 1–15 XII 1951, C 15/51, PiP 1952 No. 12, pp. 887–891 or SN Judgment of 4 VII 1969, III CRN 231/69, OSNCP 1970, item 72) as well as the collision relationship of the perspective of the entire social axiological system and the values adopted by the particular social group (cf. e.g. SN Provision of 11 IV 1968, III CRN 55/68, OSNCP 1968, item 159 or SN Resolution of 8 V 1975, III CZP 31/75, OSPiKA 1976, item 231).

70 Cf. e.g. SN Judgment of 3 VII 2015, IV CSK 595/14, LEX 1917369 and SN Judgment of 10 I 2020, I CSK 279/18, LEX 2785119.

The effects of collisions between the determined axiological contents depend on various factors, among which the most important is the type of political system, which affects the methods of judge's reasoning also in relation to the creation and "resolution" of this type of collision.

3.2.1. Collisions within the single-type criteria

The collision of axiological content of single-type criteria occurs on a different scale depending on the type of criteria.

(1) There are comparatively smallest conflicts observed within the political criteria. It is so because they are always (and therefore also in democratic systems) presenting state point of view. Nevertheless, it proves possible to confront general and permanent values (e.g. political ideology in an authoritarian system or permanent state values in a democratic system) with current political objectives (also different ones manifested in both types of political regimes).

The features of the political system are also associated with collisions occurring in the case of economic and moral criteria. For in both of its basic types, they are solved in radically different ways. Importantly, in the case of both of these types of values, soft collisions can easily turn into hard collisions if, as regards the authoritarian system, generalized versions of the content of both types of values are combined with the influence of political axiology, which will allow these values to be transformed into generalized – and in essence – political values.

(2) In the case of economic criteria, content conflicts run along the axiological edge between the market economy and the centrally planned economy, resulting to a greater extent from the names of criteria indicated in the regulations.

Basing the economic system on the principles of central planning and protection of social property leads to a natural link between the content of these references and political values, and thus a preference for their "evaluation" in the event of a collision with individual interests (e.g. entrepreneurs, taxpayers). It results from normative formulations,[71] which additionally leave no doubts as to the presentation by the authority settling economic disputes in such a system (which is not usually a court in the strict sense[72]) of a politicized hierarchy of

71 Cf. e.g. the criteria of the regulations which are no longer in force: Art. 386 of KC (economic plan duties, profitability of production and economic relations as well as securing the national economy against losses), Art. 826 i Art. 827 of KC (interest of national economy) and art. 1 of PAG (economic efficiency, social interest).

72 Cf. Art. 1 of PAG indicating that Central Arbitration Commission and Regional Arbitration Commissions are obliged, among others, to strengthen discipline of state economic units in executing the national economic plans and to improve cooperation

values related to the economy.[73] The constant relation of the superiority of the economic interest in the scale of the entire national economy over the criteria defending the economy within the specific economic unit (even if it is a state owned enterprise),[74] or the preference for the position of such an enterprise in a dispute with a natural person[75] may be slightly weakened only in exceptional cases.[76] The criteria of profitability and economic efficiency of operating on a micro-scale, i.e. the typical criteria of market economy references, may, on the other hand, constitute the basis for a decision to apply the law only in respect of legal relations within the framework of private economic sector.[77] Contrary to the above practices, the characteristics of a market economy system usually result in weighing the overall social and individual dimension of the content of economic criteria, linking its result to a specific decision-making situation.

(3) The most complex is the situation of content-related collisions within moral values, mainly due to the variety of their linguistic forms and greater vagueness of "evaluation" of their content and a different relationship with

---

between them according to the direction of socio-economic development of the country.

73 In this system such authority does not necessarily have to be a court, but rather a quasi-court, as it happened in Poland, where arbitration commissions were not independent entities. It were the rulings of this body that determined the content and importance of economic criteria in line with political axiology (cf. GKA decision of 16 IX 1969, BO-5521/69, OSPiKA 1970, item 175 and GKA decision of 5 I 1983, OT-8547/82, OSPiKA 1983, item 209).

74 Cf. GKA decision of 11 V 1970, BO-1279/70, OSPiKA 1971, item 19.

75 Cf. SN Judgment of 21 II 1974, II CR 840/73, OSNCP 1974, item 216 and SN Judgment of 29 I 1975, III PRN 69/74, OSNCP 1975, item 124 as well as NSA Judgment of 12 XI 1981, I SA 2279/81, OSPiKA 1982, item 171 and GKA decision of 27 XII 1981, IP-7002/81, OSPiKA 1983, item 71.

76 The social change that occurred in Poland in the mid-1950s, ("the post-Stalin thaw") liberalizing to some extent the system of real socialism (a change of a corrective nature in relation to the foundations of the system), resulted in a temporary recognition of the category of economic profitability involved in the activities of state-owned enterprises referred to as "units of the socialized economy" (cf. GKA decision of 25 IX 1958, RN-65/58, RPEiS 1959 No. 4, p. 274–5), but after two years the previously dominant tendencies came to the fore again (cf. GKA decision 29 III 1971, BO-2185/71, OSPiKA 1972, item 13). Certain changes also took place in the early 1980s (during "the Solidarity period"), as evidenced by the decisions made after the introduction of the foundations of the economic reform in 1981–82 (cf. e.g. GKA decision 27 XII 1981, IP-7002/81, OSPiKA 1983, item 71) though more decisive changes had been done at the end of this decade.

77 Cf. NSA Judgment of 30 VI 1981, II SA 198/81, ONSA 1981, item 66.

actually manifested social preferences, etc. However, this type of value is also sensitive to the type of political system.

The influence of official ideology and political axiology on determining the content and resolving conflicts within moral criteria, also in the authoritarian system (as long as it does not take on the features of a fully totalitarian system), is not completely linear and is sometimes confronted with the autonomous axiological choices of judicature. The legal tradition plays a certain role here, which, within the framework of continental European culture, is associated, especially in private law, with the reference to the classical judicial jurisdiction. In the authoritarian systems, this can manifest itself in two distinct ways. Firstly, by referring in decisions directly to the principles of equity, requirements of good faith or good customs,[78] originating from the previous, democratic formation, and secondly by referring to the content of such criteria when applying a new referring clause, already named otherwise (e.g. principles of social coexistence[79]). As the new system solidifies, the latter method grows in popularity, although sometimes the will to emphasize the "content distinctiveness" of the new reference will become apparent.[80]

"Ranking" of the moral axiology dimensions is of particular importance when comparing the social (general) interest and the group or individual interest. It can take place in two variants. The first of them means the confrontation of both interests in a situation where the criterion of social (general) interest is clearly indicated by one of the clauses, while the second – in a situation where the social (general) interest is taken into account and confronted with a group interest without separately targeting the extra-legal axiology to this criterion in the reference clause in question.

---

78 For example, it became evident that the decisions of the principles of equity and the principles of social coexistence were interchangeable, also under the rule of KC, which did not mention the former criterion; (cf. SN Judgment of 1 VI 1965, I PZ 34/65, OSPiKA 1966, item 61 and SN Resolution of 28 V 1968, III CZP 49/68, OSPiKA 1970, item 118).

79 It was first expressed in POPC of 1950. The postulation of treating these principles as a continuation of the reference to equity is also emphasized in the literature by A. Stelmachowski, *Wstęp*, pp. 137 ff., J. Wróblewski, *Wartości*, p. 226; I. Szabo, "Pojęcie," pp. 674, 676–678.

80 For example, in the form of an opinion that this clause negates the tradition of "bourgeois extralegal references" (cf. SN Judgment of 6 V 1960, 3 CR 561/59, RPEiS 1961 No. 1, p. 371). See also J. Nowacki, "Niektóre," p. 105.

Nevertheless the differentiation of the effects will depend not on the fact that the criterion of social interest appears in the reference clause itself, but on the type of political system. In authoritarian systems, irrespective of the fact that the reference to the social interest appears as an independent clause,[81] the content identified with this criterion always generates other axiological contents, approaching their "axiomatization" independent of the direction of evaluation indicated by the name of the criterion. Thus, it becomes an essential element of the understanding of all extra-legal references of this legal order, a category in a sense "identifying" of such an understanding of the function of law, the relationship between law and other social norms, and the place of the individual and its relationship to the whole, which is consistent with the official political ideology, assuming, among others subordination of individual or group interests to general interests associated with the political interest of the state.[82] Recognizing the primacy of the public interest is such an evident in the way of determining the content of the reference to moral criteria in this system that there are rarely any attempts to specify the role of this interest in a specific case nor to weigh the general and individual interest. It is enough to use an appropriate adjective (such as: universal, general, social, national, etc.), "strengthening" the rank of interest, which by its nature has to prevail over individual interest. At best, it is indicated, in a way to undermine the "impression," that this general interest was determined in a manner that also takes into account the interests of citizens,[83] or that the accepted overriding power in the public interest is justified in exceptional circumstances.[84] This picture is not changed by certain "adjustments" to this relationship in favour of group and individual interests in situations of crises (e.g. the so-called "thaw") of the authoritarian system, weakening the impact of the official political axiology.[85]

---

81 E.g. Art. 236 of KC.

82 Therefore it also concerned the most referred clause in the Polish law, which was (and still is) the clause of principles of social coexistence.

83 Cf. SN Resolution of 30 VIII 1968, III CZP 68/68, RPEiS 1969 No. 2, p. 235 and SN Judgment of 26 VI 1976, II URN 21/76, OSNCP 1977, item 36.

84 Cf. SN Resolution of 20 II 1969, III CZP 2/69, OSNCP 1969, item 195 (drawing a thesis that the individual interest "existing" since 1926 cannot be automatically abolished by the general public interest). In SN Resolution of 22 IX 1972, III PZP 12/72, OSNCP 1973, item 22 the Court expressed the belief that these interests cannot be automatically juxtaposed, and even the rule of protection of social property that is dominant in this system, does not operate automatically.

85 Taking place in the decade of the 50-ties (cf. SN Judgment of 11 XII 1951, C 1573/51, PiP 1952 No. 12, pp. 881 ff. and SN Judgment of 27 V 1958, 2 CR 547/57, PiP 1959 No. 3,

Conversely, it is the “weighing” of both interests (which does not imply, however, the unconditional primacy of the group or individual perspective) that is the essence of judicial practice in democratic systems, both those that are already mature and, in an appropriate proportion, those that are still on their path to such a state.

(4) A clear example of a change that takes place in the context of determining the content of the social criterion and the interests of citizens are the two rulings of Polish courts concerning the reporting of the content of the criteria contained in the Polish code of administrative procedure (KPA). They have been made before and after 1989, i.e. under the conditions of the autocratic system and in the situation democratic socio-political change.

The KPA, adopted in 1960 and still remaining in force (although amended numerous times), formulates, in Art. 7 thereof, which remained in force at the time of taking both decisions, a general guidance for administrative bodies regarding each decision-making process. It reads as follows: “In the course of proceedings, public administration bodies shall uphold the rule of law and shall take ex officio or at the request of the parties all actions necessary to clarify the facts of the case in detail and to settle the case, taking into account the social interest and the legitimate interest of citizens.” Therefore, it includes two open criteria with different orientation of their axiological content (social interest and the interest of citizens, which requires its additional qualification as a legitimate one), which should be further related to the obligation of public administration to act in accordance with the rule of law.

On the basis of this provision we observe emerging space for two collisions. The first one covers the collisions between the extra-legal (both open criteria) and the intra-legal (principle of rule of law) axiology, while the second, one that is more interesting here, between the general and individual dimensions of both types of interests. As part of the latter “clash,” two completely different jurisprudence positions can be noticed, formulated in different political environments of judicial control of the administration. The first of them dates back to 1981 (i.e. to conditions of an authoritarian state) and was formulated by the Supreme Administrative Court (NSA), which defined this relation as follows: “The content of Article 7 of the Code of Administrative Procedure means that the scope of protection of a legitimate individual interest reaches the limits of the collision with the social interest, which is the overriding value in a socialist state.”[86] The

pp. 586–7 and in the years 1980–1980 (cf. GKA decision of 6 V 1982, IP-2565/82, OSPiKA 1983, item 38).

86 Cf. NSA Judgment of 11 VI 1981, SA 820/81, OSPiKA 1982, item 22.

profound social and legal change that took place after 1989 radically changed this perspective. It was initiated by a judgment of the Supreme Court (SN) of 1993, which defined this relation, still subject to the same normative condition of Art. 7 of the Code, as follows: "…in the rule-of-law state there is no place for mechanically and rigidly understood principle of the primacy of general interest over individual interest (...), in each case the administrative authority is obliged to indicate what general (public) interest is at stake and prove that it is so important and significant that it absolutely requires the limitation of individual rights of citizens. Both the existence of such an interest and its importance, as well as the reasons for the need to prioritize the public interest over the individual in a specific case, must always be subject to close control of higher administrative organ and of judicial review."[87]

So far, it is the latter judgment, resulting from the adoption of the democratic-liberal axiological convention, that determines the decision-making practice of administrative bodies and judicial review of their activities.[88] It specifies the method of weighing both values despite the use of a term that is unknown to art. 7 of this code, i.e. "general (public) interest" instead of the term "social interest" used there. It also sets the jurisprudence of administrative courts by explicitly subjecting this weighing to judicial review, which is not an obvious task when the Polish model of this control is concerned that, in fact focuses on examining the activities of the administration from the point of view of its compliance with the legal provisions (as an element of the concept of "compliance with the law"[89]).

3.2.2. *Collisions between different types of values*

(1) The relationships between the general social, group and individual perspectives are also visible in the context of the collision between different types of criteria. It is actually so that the relationship in this respect can be reduced to a collision between the political and non-political content of both moral and economic criteria. The power the political axiology exerts in authoritarian systems means the "resolution" of these collisions either by omitting the moral or economic axiology as a component of the "joint content" of the respective criterion, or by politicizing such moral or economic content.[90] The clauses referring

---

87 CF. SN Judgment of 18 XI 1993, III ARN 49/93, OSNIC 1994, item 181.

88 Cf. citation of this judgment (e.g. NSA Judgment of 11 V 2021, II OSK 2179/18, CBOSA

89 CF. Article 1 of PUSA.

90 Cf. SN Judgment of 22 VI 1972, III CRN 126/72, OSPiKA 1973, item 55. A "softer" version of conflict occured between socio-economic considerations and the new

to the interest of the state, system principles and state goals, appearing not only in public law, but also in private (civil) law, especially if they are formulated as meta-references creating an official directive on the application and interpretation of law,[91] affect the way of understanding the references to moral and economic criteria in the process of applying the law. The relationship with the "strong" official ideology allows, even if it is not a common practice, to treat the reference to political criteria as a practice so natural that it becomes no longer necessary to justify the determined content of these criteria.[92] Sometimes a specific "last sentence of the statement of reasons effect" can be observed, in that the statement of reasons does not refer to the political context of the reference, except for one, usually the last, sentence thereof, which simply states that the interest of the state was infringed.[93] An additional reinforcement of this kind of argumentation may be found in the use of emphasizing expressions such as "always," "undoubtedly," "grossly," etc.[94]

Despite different ways of confronting, the effect of both types of domination of political values is the same or almost the same. The effect of such "conflict" may be the politicization of the content of references to moral and economic

---

agricultural policy of the state (cf. SN Judgment of 6 VII 1967, III CR 117/67, OSNCP 1968, item 67). Another, more general effect, may, for example, link the content of moral judgments with social justice based on the main formulas of justice in a socialist system, or directly on "socialist morality which was an argument for the recognition that the state through its policy (implementation of its objectives) determined the content of social norms" (SN Resolution of 1–15 XII 1951, C 15/51, PiP 1952 No. 12, pp. 887–91). Similarly, SC formulated a specific principle of social coexistence, stating that "everyone should support the objective set by the state" (SN Judgment of 21 X 1950, C 345/50, PiP 1951 No. 4, p. 741). On the basis of the influence of communist ideology, the tendency to politicization of the extra-legal axiology occurs also in the case of references to economic criteria, which is understandable in view of the close connection of both spheres and the justification of the existence and functioning of the socialist economic system, mainly by means of political and ideological arguments (cf. GKA Decision of 3 II 1977, IP-8150/76, OSPiKA 1977, item 212).

91 It happens so that all these references appeared together in the justification of the ruling of a decision, mutually strengthening the power of their influence (cf. SN Judgment of 19 I 1972, III CRN 471/71, OSPiKA 1973, item 29).

92 Cf. SN Judgment of 28 IX 1976, I PRN 59/76, OSPiKA 1978, item 18 (where the Court considers precisely the elements of the criterion "interest of Polish People's Republic" in particular case). Cf. also SN Judgment of 19 I 1972, III CRN 471/71, OSPiKA 1973, item 29.

93 Cf. e.g. SN Provision of 12 IX 1973, III CRN 188/73, OSNCP 1974, item 183.

94 Cf. e.g. SN Provision of 24 I 1974, III PRN 1/74, OSNCP 1974, item 180.

criteria. Political assessments, sometimes formalized and with institutional support behind them, influence the content of decisions more strongly than informal and non-institutionalized moral assessments and economic criteria. It may result, for instance, in linking the content of moral judgments with social justice based on "the main formulas of justice in a socialist system,"[95] or directly on "socialist morality."[96] A characteristic (though not common) example of politicization of the moral criterion was the formulation by the Polish Supreme Court in 1950 of a specific principle of social coexistence, stating that "everyone should support the objectives set by the State,"[97] which was a hidden argument for the thesis that this state, through its policy (achieving its objectives), actually determines the content of social norms that it deems worth accepting. On the basis of the influence of communist ideology, the tendency to politicize occurs also in the case of references to economic criteria,[98] which is understandable in view of the close connection of both spheres and the justification of the existence and functioning of the socialist economic system, mainly by means of political and ideological arguments.

Similarly to the determination of political content itself, the standardization of such practices can be performed either directly by the "manual" imposition of current political content (which corresponds to "totalitarization" of the system) or by actions performed within the framework of legal discourse, consisting in issuing, by a politically controlled court of the highest instance, guidelines that apply to all courts.[99]

(2) Lack of such a strong influence of political ideology in democratic systems, which is also associated with the multiplicity of political decision-making centres, manifesting itself in "weighing" the content of different kinds of values, which not only does not automatically giving the advantage to political axiology but also seeks "axiological compromise."

An example of balancing the state, social and individual dimensions is the practice of referring to the open criteria contained in the ECHR. This Convention, regulating content that is strongly "saturated" with axiology, does

95 Cf. e.g. SN Judgment of 5–30 VI 1951, C 649/50, PiP 1951 No. 2, pp. 312–17 and SN Judgment of 14 V 1966, I PRN 28/66, OSPiKA 1967, item 65.

96 Cf. e.g. SN Resolution of 1–15 XII 1951, C 15/51, PiP 1952 No. 12, pp. 887–891.

97 Cf. SN Judgment of 21 X 1950, C 345/50, PiP 1951 No. 4, p. 741.

98 Cf. GKA decision of 24 VI 1970, BO-3113/70, OSPiKA 1972, item 159.

99 E.g. interpretative instructions ("wytyczne") of Polish SN ceased to function in 1990 and recognized by SN in 1992 as non-valid for the judicial practice after deep social change (cf. SN Resolution of 5 V 1992, Kw. Pr. 5/92, OSP 1993 item 218).

not resign from authorizing both the courts of the member states of the Council of Europe and the ECtHR to refer, in the judgments, to the criteria which additionally open up the axiological normative regulation of the Convention.

The most important role in this context is played by the criterion of "necessity in a democratic society," which refers to the social axiology (democratic society) understood pragmatically (necessity) and purposefully (related to other criteria defining the purpose of a Member State's action, consisting in limiting the scope of the law set out in paragraph 1 of articles 8, 9, 10, 11 and art. 2 of Protocol No. 4).[100] This clause therefore refers to the value, the scope of protection of which depends on the assessment of the purpose and manner of state interference in the content of the respective right. The ECtHR has repeatedly defined the content of the entire standard. When referring to the criterion of "democratic society," it emphasized the presence of the values of pluralism and tolerance.[101] In turn, the term "necessity" was distinguished by the Court, from the term "required" or "desired,"[102] additionally nullifying the scope of the necessity test depending on the type of right or even the type of good protected by the respective law.[103] What proves important for the application of the standard is its imposition on a specific (most often in the form of axiological terminology) purpose of state interference (e.g. interest of national security, public safety, economic well-being, protection of morals, public order), which may justify it when the interference, being provided for by law,[104] was a matter of urgency and the adopted measures themselves were proportionate. This is what it means not to exceed the limits

---

100 Cf. D.J. Harris, M. O'Boyle, C. Warbrick, *Law*, pp. 283–301.

101 Cf. § 49 of ECtHR Judgment of 7 XII 1976 Handyside v. UK (A.24) or § 42 of ECtHR Judgment of 19 II 1998 Bowman v. UK (RJD 1998-J).

102 "The Court notes at this juncture that, whilst the adjective "necessary," within the meaning of Article 10 par. 2, is not synonymus with "indispensable" (…) neither has it the flexibility of such expressions as "admissible" (…), "ordinary" (…), "useful" (…), "reasonable" (…) or "desirable" (cf. ECtHR Judgment of 7 XII 1976 Handyside v. UK, A.24).

103 Cf. e.g. ECtHR Judgment of 25 III 1985, Barthold v. Germany, A.90, where the Court determined that the assessment of the member-state's necessity to interfere with a commercial statement is less restrictive than in the case of political or artistic statements.

104 This condition also has a more universal meaning than just a formal definition of interference by national law, referring to axiologically indifferent standards of the rule of law, which are common to the member states of the Council of Europe (cf. e.g. ECtHR Judgment of 25 VI 1997 Hallford v. UK (RJD 1997-III).

of necessity, "measured," on every occasion, in the context of the specific legal situation.[105]

The set of extra-legal criteria developed in this way creates a wide discretion in judging courts, both domestic and the ECtHR. The axiological contents are distinguishable at the level of individual societies and states,[106] but they also have their universal dimension, which is markedly visible in the jurisprudence of the ECtHR,[107] later adapted by the courts of the Member States. The functional relations between the criteria, as elaborated by this Court, are established in the order of taking them into account and determining the axiological content specific to the case and type of protected right. They are mainly of a social (moral) nature, but they do not shy away from pragmatically (but no longer ideologically) treated political aspects, especially where the interests of state security or of public order are at stake, understood in a climate appropriate for the democratic and rule-of-law systems of the Council of Europe member states.

4. Comparing the content of extra-legal criterion with intra-legal axiology ("juridization")

(1) The verification of the content of the preferences indicated by the references must, however, be associated with taking into account one further group of criteria. We are talking about fundamental legal criteria (as expressed in legal provisions or explicitly recognized as intra-legal values on other grounds), beyond which the construction of reference clauses would reach their essence, but which, in the process of applying the law, "return" as part of the process of applying references. This "return" takes place mainly through the creation of a general framework of axiological choices that the decision maker cannot ignore. In other words, it has always to compare the extra-legal criteria "deriving from" the reference clauses against these fundamental legal criteria in making a decision based on an extra-legal reference.[108]

105 Cf. e.g. ECtHR Judgments: of 26 IX 1995 Vogt v. Germany (A. 323), of 26 XI 1991, The Sunday Times No. 2 v. UK, A.217 and of 22 X 1981 Dudgeon v. UK (A.45) defining this relation in the light of protection of morality or ECtHR Judgment of 25 XI 1997 Zana v. Turkey (RJD 1997-V) defining this relations in the light of the protection of the public order.

106 Cf. ECtHR Judgments: of 20 IX 1994, Otto Preminger v. Austria (295-A), of 7 XII 1976 Handyside v. UK (A.24) of 10 IV 2007 Evans v. UK (6339/05) and of 25 XI 1997 Zana v. Turkey (RJD 1997-V).

107 Cf. e.g. § 49 of ECtHR Judgment of 25 VI 1997 Halford v. UK (RJD 1997-III).

108 Cf. below: 4.

The intra-legal axiology may be included in the process of determining the content of extra-legal criteria in two basic ways. The first is the juxtaposition of the content of these criteria with the principles of law, while the second is the juxtaposition of this content with the axiology shaped by jurisprudence and precedent practice. As can be seen, the legal (intra-legal) axiology understood in this way may or may not be related to the preferences of the legislator. Thus, it is more an axiology of the legal order than an axiology of the legal system (system of normative regulations),[109] although, evidently, it must take into account the latter as to the most fundamental values for a given law.

(2) The context of the role of legal axiology constituting the framework for determining extra-legal axiology evokes the above-mentioned relationship between the constructions of reference clauses and legal principles. The differences in their structure are to some extent transferred to the axiology expressed by both of these categories. Such a transfer of features results from the type of reference which, as a reference that is open "only" in indicated areas, does not cover the entire axiology of the decision-making process, but only some of its dimensions, leaving the areas "unfilled" with extra-legal axiology open to the influence of the axiology of legal principles. Nevertheless, it is also connected, and this is even more important from the point of view of the general axiology of the decision-making process, with the role of the principle of the rule of law in this process, requiring courts to base their decision-making process on law in the understanding of competence, procedural and substantive legal grounds.

The juxtaposition of both types of values is a form of a specific "juridization" of the content of non-legal criteria, and in this context the dominant role of the principles of law, as carriers of legal axiology, in this relationship is emphasized.[110] The content of extra-legal criteria is juxtaposed on the content of the principles of law under the assumption that the determined extra-legal axiology cannot break the content of the fundamental principles of law. This applies in particular to the principles of the entire legal order, that cause the strongest impact on the axiology of the judicial interpretation. In its entirety, this relation refers to

---

109 Cf. B. Liżewski, "Klauzule," pp. 191–208.

110 That results sometimes in close connections between the content of extra-legal criterion and legal principle (cf. TK Judgment of 11 X 2011, K 16/10, LEX 992832 or SN Judgment of 31 I 2018 r., IV CSK 442/17, LEX 2483681) or to the treating of this criterion as a principle of given branch of law (SN Judgment of 11 II 2016, V CSK 302/15, LEX 2023169).

constitutional principles,[111] to a significant extent concerns also the principles of the fundamental branches of law (civil, criminal, administrative), gradually reducing its impact in the case of the principles of hybrid branches (e.g. labour law, agricultural law), or the rules of certain sub-branches (e.g. tax law as a sub-branch of administrative law).

The position and influencing power of the axiology generated by legal principles depend, however, on their type. For if there is a difference between the principles expressed in normative acts and the principles having only an indirect connection with the law-making processes, then the scaling of the power of their impact will be aimed at emphasizing the role of the former principles. They have the authority of the legislature, which, being legitimate to create law, also has the right to shape legal axiology. Evidently, it is completely different in a democratic system than in an authoritarian system (where principles can become an instrument of politicizing extra-legal axiology also in the context of judicial application of law[112]). Against this background, the principles shaped "solely" doctrinally or as a result of referring to the "cultural and legal tradition" (which are influenced by legislative processes, but indirect and at the scale of the entire legislative practice) not only play the role weaker in terms of influencing the extra-legal axiology used in the process of law application but also limited to the legal order functioning in a democratic political system.

The confrontation of the extra-legal axiology of the respective criterion and the legal axiology of a given legal principle is different if the content of the legal principle cannot be determined without referring to the extra-legal axiology. This

---

111 Unless this juxtaposition of rule of law and extra-legal criterion takes place in the convention adopted by the Polish constitution-maker, who formulated, in art. 2 of the RP Constitution provision potentially confronting both types of axiology and leading to various relations between them ("The Republic of Poland is a democratic state of law that implements the principles of social justice"). As a result of its application, the necessity to adjudicate collisions between legal and extra-legal axiology is not an exception (cf. S. Tkacz, *Rozumienie*, pp. 147 ff. and the TK judgments indicated there). There is however a connecting point between the criterion of "principles of social justice" and "democratic rule of law state" in the concept of "procedural justice (cf. on that issue: TK Judgment of 16 XI 1999, SK 11/99, OTKU ZU 7/1999 item 158, TK Judgment of 28 VII 2004, P 2/04, OTK ZU 7/A/2004, item 72 or TK Judgment of 17 XI 2008, SK 33/07, OTK ZU 9/A/2008, item 154).

112 Cf. SN Judgment of 11 XII 1951, C 1573/51, PiP 1952 No. 12, pp. 881–882, SN Resolution of 26 IV 1952, C.Prez. 798/51, PiP 1952 No. 7, pp. 113–118, SN Judgment of 3 IV 1959, 4 CR 1045/58, RPEiS 1961 No. 1, p. 373. or SN Judgment of 23 III 1967, III PRN 2/67, OSNCP 1967, item 22.

is particularly evident when the linguistic form of the principle itself contains a reference or cannot be specified (e.g. in terms of the scope of protection) without referring to extra-legal criteria. It is here that the content of the principle is compared with the extra-legal content, e.g. in the case of establishing the content of the principle of not granting legal protection to actions constituting an abuse of law, in a situation where the essence of this abuse is defined in the light of principles of social coexistence[113] or the content of the principle of protection of the exercise of property rights in the context of the limits of its compliance with the principles of social coexistence.[114]

Both types of juxtaposition of both types of values prove the lack of a general collision between referring to extra-legal axiology in the processes of applying the law and the principle of the rule of law, regardless of the possibility of creating various detailed relations that appear, depending primarily on the type of political system. On the other hand, in each of the above-mentioned cases, the practice of juxtaposing and weighing both types of axiology means the formation of a specific "axiological edge," allowing judgments to move on the border of both axiologies and to take them into account in various proportions, depending on various factors, including – the needs and circumstances of the decision-making process.

(3) A separate way of incorporating legal axiology is the second form of "juridization" of the content of extra-legal criteria. It involves courts that, in the course of specific decision-making processes, refer to the content already established by past jurisprudence. This form, therefore, does not result from direct legislative actions. It also does not depend on the type of political system to the extent as it is the case with other elements in determining the content of extra-legal criteria. On the other hand, it is more related to the type of legal culture in which case law plays a smaller or more significant a role in judicial decision-making processes.

The connection of both types of axiology consists in the use of previous court decisions (individual judgments or jurisdictional lines), in making of which the content of the extra-legal criterion was established and in the justification of which was revealed.[115] Although it operates softer than, for example, clearly

113 Cf. SN Resolution of 20 VI 2013, III CZP 2/13, LEX 1425316.

114 Cf. SN Judgment of 12 VII 2012, I CSK 676/11, LEX 1228770, SN Judgment of 26 IX 2019, I CSK 384/18, LEX 2766082 and Warsaw Court of Appeal Judgment of 15 IX 2020, V ACa 496/19, LEX 3112276.

115 Cf. L. Leszczyński, "Implementing," pp. 231–244.

formulated normative legal principles, nevertheless, taking into account the fact of widespread use of the jurisprudence, also in legal systems where there is no strong precedent practice,[116] it links the determined extra-legal content with the pre-existing juridical discourse. As a result, we are approaching the socially significant value of the uniformity of judicial application of law, which proves particularly difficult to achieve in terms of determining the content of the extra-legal criteria.

The shaping of such "jurisprudence axiology of the legal order" is stronger if it is sufficiently durable, and thus demonstrated in an appropriately stabilized jurisdiction, presented in particular by the highest court instances. Although determining its content requires additional interpretative efforts (taking into account a number of judgments in order to identify such a line), it results in clearer and stronger axiological content. Nevertheless it also happens that individual judgments may, usually to a slightly more limited extent, play the role of determining the specific content of an extra-legal reference.[117]

Pointing to the role of legal axiology shaped by jurisdiction requires emphasizing that it is possible to formulate jurisprudence theses that are treated as principles of law with a clear axiological content.[118] This is, in a sense, a supplement to the set of the above-mentioned "non-legislative" principles. An example of such a situation are certain rulings of the CJEU, without which the formulation of one of the most important principles of the primacy of EU law would prove impossible.[119] And the fact that such jurisprudence principles in the EU legal order are treated, at least from a functional point of view, as part of primary law, proves their actual "normative" role. And it is not uncommon for a rule formulated in such a judgment to contain a legally undefined criterion, combining both types of axiology from the point of view of intra-legal axiology.[120]

---

116 Cf. L. Leszczyński, "Extra-Legal," pp. 1073–1086.

117 Especially if such practice is accompanied by cataloguing the principles of social coexistence by the Polish SN in the 1960s and 1970s (cf. A. Łopatka, Z. Ziembiński, "Próba," passim).

118 Therefore, it is not about "legal principles entered into the book of legal principles," formulated, for example, by the Polish Supreme Court in the form of resolutions, because the essence of these principles is to indicate the method for resolution of an important and complex legal issue, not necessarily of an axiological nature.

119 Cf. e.g. CJEU Jugments: of 15 VII 1964, 6/64 Flaminio Costa v. E.N.E.L. C:1964:66 and of 13 II 1969, 14/68 Walt Wihlem, C:1969:4.

120 Cf. e.g. CJEU Judgment of 20 II 1979, 120/78 Cassis de Dijon, ECR 0351.

5. "Normativization" and "concretization" of the content of the extra-legal criterion

(1) Determining the content of an extra-legal criterion is subject to a specific normativization at the next stage of "axiological processing." It consists in transforming the value defined on the basis of the above-mentioned reasoning and actions into a behavioural pattern (norm) based on it. The same operation takes place in the case of determining the existence of a custom (as a result of determining the content of a reference, e.g. to established customs), but the norm so determined will have no axiological justification.

In the case of references to extra-legal values, normativization understood in this way takes place both when the content of the reference is determined "non-normatively" (e.g. good of child, good of family, social interest) and when the content of the reference enables more direct linking of the value with the norm having an axiological justification (e.g. good customs, principles of equity, principles of social coexistence). The linguistic layer plays a secondary role here, since, for example, a reference to equity (without including the normative reference name of "principles" or "considerations") does not preclude giving such a criterion a normative aspect precisely at the stage of operative interpretation.

The sole difference is in the way in that axiological and normative contents are related. In the case of normative reference, it takes place in a "natural" manner, by combining the "ready" normative aspect with its axiological grounding. This is the case, for example, in the case of establishing the content of a specific norm based on a socially shaped moral value (e.g. "one should help the weaker") as the principle of social coexistence. On the other hand, in the case of a "non-normative" reference, the normativization of the content of the criterion includes an additional activity consisting in formulating a behavioural pattern based on the determined value. The scope of normalization and the scope of application of the behavioural pattern are determined, which are then related to the norm protecting the value indicated in the reference so defined. For example, determining the axiological content of the criterion "good of child""means determining the protected value in a general form, assigning it a normative content in the form of a norm ordering the protection of the general content so determined, and subjecting it to situational specification, on the basis of which the scope of normativity (set of prescribed behaviours) and the scope of its application (set of situations, to which the order applies) are finally defined.

(3) An attempt to catalogue given extra-legal criteria may be treated both as a way of normativization and concretization of the content the extra-legal references. This operation is typical of the arguments by lawyers, who are used to

systemic thinking. In fact, it constitutes not a typical concretization of the content of references, but rather their ranking and determination of the "standardization scope" with these criteria. Cataloguing takes place in relation to these criteria, which can be presented in the form of standards.

We may use the practice of cataloguing the principles of social coexistence by the Polish Supreme Court in the 1950s and 1960s as an example. It met with criticism of the doctrine, which, it seems, led to the abandonment of creating a moral normative system that was, in a sense, competitive to the legal system.[121]

Cataloguing also concerned the clause of systemic principles referred to in Art. 4 of the Polish civil code, that remained in force until 1989. However, unlike cataloguing the rules of coexistence, it was a rather short-lived practice. It was not accompanied by such a negative position of the doctrine, mainly due to the position of these principles, overlapping, at least in part, with the legal norms expressed in regulations.[122] It would be difficult to consider these enumerations as an exhaustive catalogue; it was at best an indicative set. What also remained unclear was the legal status of these principles, as some of them were listed in the PRL Constitution, others remained outside it, and for some it would be difficult to find a direct normative basis. It seems that the intention of the SN was to outline, and not to construct a catalogue, so that it would constitute an axiological (ideological and political) orientation in making decisions based on these principles.

---

121 The principles of social coexistence established in the jurisprudence of the Polish SN (usually equated with specific civic obligations) include: the duty to support the objectives set by the state covering, obligation of social work, the inadmissibility of profit without work, the obligation to observe loyalty of mutual relations, the duty of gratitude for the good received, the duty to avoid irritation in social coexistence, the duty of employees to care for the welfare of the workplace, etc. (cf. A. Łopatka, Z. Ziembiński, "Próba," pp. 810 ff.

122 In this context, the Polish Supreme Court stated, for example, in 1972 that the basic principles of the political system include: a socialist economic system (nationalization of industry, agricultural reform, protection of social property, development of industry and crafts), protection of workers and people incapable of work, the development of scientific and inventive creativity, various forms of cooperative activity (work, housing, production), and finally the rule of law in the activities of the judicial authorities, including nullity of the proceedings, or judgment incriminating without legal basis, or depriving an obviously due benefit (cf. SN Judgment of 19 I 1972, III CRN 471/71, OSPiKA 1973, item 29, p. 67). In another decision, the principle of "to everyone according to their work" and the principle of planning were also considered as such (cf. SN Judgment of 21 V 1952, C 278/52, PiP 1953 No. 3, pp. 451–2)

(3) The described determinations of content in relation to extra-legal references are "subsequently" subject to specific concretization, regardless of the type of value, the scope of generalization of the content and the ways for combining them in the form of supporting or conflicting values. It consists in connecting these findings with the characteristics of a specific decision-making situation (various forms of the facts, the content of a legal document, the content of a controlled judgment or administrative decision, etc.). Ultimately, therefore, there is also a specific "situation" (which can also be called "contextualization") of the extra-legal axiology, which forms the core of the decision-making process. It is important for the entire decision-making process and its participants, insofar as "only" within its framework the relationship between the established extra-legal axiology and the subject of the process can be defined.

The basic way of making the content of the reference more specific is to express an assessment directly superimposed on the decision-making situation. Such an evaluation, while not taking a generalized form, indicates the basis of the evaluation and links the content of the evaluation appearing in the decision-making process with social preferences that are in some way visible (verifiable). Certain difficulties may arise whenever the clause refers to universal values, which can not only be verified but also identified without causing certain difficulties, also in conditions of a democratic system.[123] Generally speaking, it is an intuitive, and where possible – "empirical" statement of the existence of certain preferences (e.g. by using the results of systematic empirical research on social awareness).

The observation of the methods for determining the content of the references allows us to state that there are several ways in that the courts may concretize their content.[124] They certainly include, among others, analysis of partial assessments,[125] determination of social phenomena covered by the respective criterion and the related decision-making rules,[126] determination of elements of

123 Cf. TK Resolution of 2 III 1994, W.3/92, OTK 1994, item 17 and TK Judgment of 7 VI 1994, K.17/93, OTK 1994, item 11) based on Art. 18 and 21 of the Polish Broadcating indicating Christian values (cf. also K. Daniel, "Kontrowersje," pp. 157 ff., W. Sadurski, "Wartości," pp. 3 ff.).

124 The most characteristic criterion in this context is the "nature of the legal relationship" expressed in Art. 353[1] k.c. (c.f. J. Guść, "O pojęciu," passim).

125 Cf. SN Resolution of 4 IV 1968, III CZP 27/68, OSNCP 1969, item 6, SN Provision of 18 IV 1975, III CRN 247/74, OSNCP 1976, item 130 and SN Judgment of 11 VII 1978, I PRN 32/78, OSNCP 1979, item 18

126 Cf. SN Judgment of 19 IX 1968, II CR 291/68, OSNCP 1969, item 200 and SN Resolution of 20 V 1978, III CZP 39/77, OSPiKA 1980, item 38.

a specific facts related to the content of that reference and the scope in which this relationship occurs,[127] providing examples of situations that would not correspond to the content of the criterion,[128] presenting extremely different situations and comparing their possible qualifications in relation to the criterion,[129] presenting a situation opposite to that being subject to classification on the basis of the criterion,[130] establishing a hierarchy between the given criteria not in an abstract form, but in relation to the situation that the decision concerns,[131] or also establishing the scope relations between criteria of similar content.[132]

The significance of this type of concretization of the content of the criterion results from the fact that the prior determination of this content in general is associated with constructing the content of the court decision in the context of the specific facts of the case and other properties of the so-called court case materials. Therefore, it forms not only a presentation of axiology for cognitive (determination of the applied values) or declarative (the axiology desired according to the position of the adjudicating court) purposes, but also has a directly practical (decision-making) significance. It can also be treated as a specific neutralization of the effects of generalization, which appear commonly in determining the content of the extra-legal criterion.

The foremost issue related to the concretization of the content of the references is the determination of the limits of judicial discretion with regard to applicability of one's own preferences and/or preferences of the judges' community in the process of determining the content of extra-legal criteria (and particularly moral values). Evidently we cannot exclude the participation of both these types of axiology in determining the content of such criteria. It is further impossible to establish a general model of the proportions of such participation, neither between these two types, nor between these types and the social axiology identified in the decision-making process. The crux therefore lies in that

---

127 Cf. SN Judgment of 10 V 1966, II CR 97/66, OSPiKA 1968, item 5, SN Judgment of 20 I 1975, II CR 784/74, OSPiKA 1975, item 241 and SN Resolution of 28 XII 1979, V PZP 5/79, OSPiKA 1981, item 41 or NSA Judgment of 5 V 2021, III FSK 746/21.

128 Cf. SN Resolution of 3 X 1966, III CZP 17/66, OSPiKA 1969, item 1 and SN Resolution of 19 V 1981, III CZP 18/81, OSNCP 1981, item 228.

129 Cf. SN Judgment of 11 III 1974, III CRN 9/74, OSNCP 1974, item 202.

130 Cf. SN Resolution of 25 V 1971, III CZP 29/71, OSPiKA 1972, item 131.

131 Cf. SN Judgment of 17 XII 1965, I CR 309/65, OSNCP 1966, item 132 and SN Resolution of 9 VI 1976, III CZP 46/75, OSNCP 1976, item 184.

132 Cf. SN Resolution of 18 III 1968, III CZP 70/66, OSPiKA 1968, item 151 and SN Resolution of 19 XII 1972, III CZP 57/71, OSNCP 1973, item 37.

the sourcing from axiology that is accepted by the judicial community, or even some “personalization” of this axiology, would not depart from the manifested social preferences. The imposition of these preferences on a specific decision-making situation is important since it is the judge (bench) who knows the facts that has to be qualified best and who is willing to assume its own “axiological competence” concerning the treatment of one’s own preferences as a criterion for qualifying facts.

(4) Estimation references are a completely natural construction that allows to concretize their content through linking the evaluation with the current decision-making situation. Since they contain the authorization of the entity applying the law not only to determine facts (age difference, marriage breakdown, diligence) but also to estimate the scale, scope or intensity (valid, permanent and complete, appropriate) of their occurrence, such an estimate cannot be judicially realized without reference to facts and own axiological “vision” of the criteria for such an assessment.[133] In this case, referring to social axiology is only a landmark. It may be useful, for example, in the case of superimposing a general reference on the need to estimate its importance (e.g. for the criterion of important social interest), but it is not a reliable point of reference, e.g. in the case of the necessity to estimate the significance of the reasons for failure to meet the condition or the deadline for performing a specific action. In such cases, it is the “jurisprudence axiology” understood as the “practice of estimation” (weight assessment) that harmonizes with the properties of a specific actual state is what plays the decisive role.

Linking such an “evaluation” with the actual condition causes that the estimation takes place in connection with the linguistic argumentation (determining the meaning of the phrase describing the actual condition) and cognitive argumentation (determining the occurrence of the condition). Situalization and, consequently, the concretization of such an assessment usually do not raise any doubts.

Whenever the estimate references are not explained by themselves,[134] but in conjunction with the criteria of the general reference clauses, the estimation is

133 Cf. e.g. SN Judgment of 2 X 2015, II CSK 757/14, LEX 1936713., SN Judgment of 29 XI 2017, II CSK 86/17, LEX 2417587, SN Provision of 26 III 2014, V CSK 344/13, LEX 1460985, SN Resolution of 20 VI 2013, III CZP 2/13, LEX 1425316, SN Judgment of 3 II 2011, I CSK 261/10, LEX 784986 or SN Judgment of 14 IX 2016, III CSK 339/15, LEX 2135368.

134 These are basically exceptional cases (cf. e.g. SN Judgment of 21 VIII 1974, I CR 332/74, OSPiKA 1975, item 140 or SN Resolution of 8 V 1975, III CZP 31/75, OSPiKA 1976, item 231).

not only related to the facts, but also to the general criterion of such a clause. The concretization of the content of the general reference then takes place somewhat indirectly, through the situational assessment of the estimated reference. This applies to various estimates, e.g. important reasons (concretizing, for example, the criteria of coexistence, rules of morality, the child's welfare or the good of the family[135]), due diligence,[136] exceptional cases,[137] special circumstances,[138] permanent and complete breakdown of a marriage,[139] serious harm,[140] etc.

However, it should be noted that the mere determination of the content of an estimated reference may combine descriptive and evaluative elements when determining the meaning of an apparently descriptive term that forms an element of an estimated reference. Moreover, the principles of law may also play a significant role in determining the content of the criterion contained in the estimate,[141] this being related to a specific juridization of the content of the situational assessment.

In the cases of joint clarification of the meaning of an estimate and the general reference clause, however, there is a clear shift in determining the content of the clause itself. Linking the general criterion to the actual condition creates a situational assessment also for determining the content of the clause criterion. This makes the issue of excessive generalization and axiomatization usually "disappear" then, because there is a direct need to reduce these criteria and general assessments to the actual circumstances. Determining the content of the extra-legal criterion in such cases acquires more of the features of a situational assessment.

---

135 Cf. e.g. SN Resolution of 27 III 1972, III CZP 69/70, OSNCP 1973, item 20, SN Judgment of 5 IX 1975, I. CR 526/75, OSNCP 1976, item 171 or SN Judgment of 20 V 1976, III CRN 373/75, OSNCP 1977, item 31.

136 Cf. e.g. SN Judgment of 18 V 1974, III CRN 88/74, OSPiKA 1975, item 138.

137 Cf. SN Resolution of 8 V 1975, III CZP 31/75, OSPiKA 1976, item 231.

138 Cf. e.g. SN Judgment of 18 XI 1965, III CR 202/65, OSPiKA 1966, item 216.

139 Cf. e.g. SN Judgment of 28 X 1980, III CRN 222/80, OSNCP 1981, item 90 or SN Judgment of 8 III 1977, I PRN 17/77, OSPiKA 1978, item 72.

140 Cf. e.g. SN Resolution of 16 I 1997, I KZP 32/96, OSP 1997, item 121.

141 Cf. e.g. SN Judgment of 14 X 1980, IV CR 381/80, OSNCP 1981, item 86.

Chapter IV The extra-legal references in the process of judicial interpretation of law

1. Operative judicial interpretation in the process of application of law

1.1. Law application process – the decisional model

(1) The decision model adopted in the present elaboration in order to define the essence, main components (actions and reasoning) and the course of the judicial decision-making process of applying the law as well as the participation of extra-legal references in it is based on the distinction between its two basic phases (terminating with the decision to apply the law), that together constitute the process of applying *sensu stricto* and two additional phases, which can be treated, in some approaches, as separate decision-making processes.

The first of the basic phases is the preparatory ("pre-decision") phase, including the simultaneous findings of the facts of the case and the determination of the legal basis, which in fact translate to an operative interpretation. The second phase is the phase of making the decision to apply the law. The additional phases, on the other hand, are the possible (depending on the submission of an appropriate application) control phase in relation to the issued decision, taking place in various procedural forms, and the executive phase, also taking place in various procedural forms. The last two phases can be treated as additional phases to the main phases of the law application process as a whole, but they can also be treated as separate decision-making processes, as they can also be divided into the preparatory phase and the decision-making phase, covering the same components, which are present in the process of applying the law *sensu stricto*.

The operative interpretation fully complies with the legal basis of the case as part of the preparatory (pre-decision) phase, but it also occurs in the decision-making phase, the subject of which is the reduction of general interpretative arrangements in the form of the established normative basis for the decision to the content of the decision on the application of law itself. The effect of these activities is an individual and concrete decision, which includes the qualifying and the consequential part. The first one covers the qualification of the established facts pursuant to the normative basis, a component of which may also include the extra-legal criteria (stating that the facts "fit" in the scope of normative regulation and application of the interpreted norm). On the other hand, in the consequential part of the decision, which in fact determines the ultimate result of the law application process, the normative consequences of qualification of the facts are established. It is also in this part that extra-legal criteria may participate in shaping the content of sanctions or other types of consequences (e.g. updating an obligation or establishing a new legal status).

(2) The activities of determining the facts are cognitive activities, albeit subject to legal regulation, they contain elements of the so-called formal truth that does not fit entirely the realistic understanding of "material" truth. The role of interpretation concerns these regulations (e.g. legal presumptions) and normative expressions defining facts (e.g. homicide). The facts are "described" to some extent in the text of a normative act or a precedent judgment. Without giving this name an appropriate meaning (linguistic interpretation), it is impossible to define the nature of the respective act or legal situation.

Determining the facts is therefore not a purely cognitive process, subjectable to simple logical falsification.[1] Thus, it is possible to define the scale of permissibility of formulating evaluations (axiological argumentation) in this process. The presence of cognitively-based assessments in the fact-finding process, also including assessments that are brought in by extra-legal references, is manifested in four aspects, different in terms of the type and effects of the assessment.

Firstly, the presence of assessments is related to the structure of the free assessment of evidence, granting the decision-making entity an authorization to qualify each piece of presented evidence as to its credibility (certainty of the occurrence of the fact described in it) and the relationships between the presented facts. Such an assessment also takes place when the evidence is related to specialist knowledge that cannot be shared by the judge on account of education or life experience (e.g. as part of the assessment of the credibility of an expert opinion or the determination of the credibility of various expert opinions).

Secondly, the relationship between cognitive and axiological findings in the form of the interference of assessments in the process of determining the factual state may consist in evoking a general belief that it is necessary to state the occurrence of given facts in a more definite manner and, consequently, to thoroughly explain and justify the occurrence of the respective actual state in conditions of inclusion of assessments in the cognitive process. It manifests itself in two aspects. Firstly, it may be associated with care that one's own decision will not

1 Cf. M. Zieliński, *Poznanie*, esp. pp. 187–199.

be overruled in the course of an instance control due to failure to explain or an inadequate explanation of all relevant circumstances.[2] Secondly, it may be linked with the need of activeness of an organ applying the law in finding facts irrespective of the activeness of the parties.[3] We may assume that the reasoning here is that if and so, through extra-legal references, assessments clearly "enter" the entire process of applying a legal norm, the whole fact should be determined, proven and justified in the most accurate and thorough manner.

Thirdly, in the normative regulation itself, facts (in abstract terms) can be defined (named) in an evaluative way in two variants. In the weaker version, the descriptive form of determining the facts is associated with preferences that are "hidden" in determining the meaning of legal concepts, assuming determining the content of the concept of an attitude with an axiological grounding (e.g. when establishing the concept of "human being" while in a stronger one, expresses by estimation clauses[4] (e.g. "important reasons," "special merits" or "exceptional circumstances"[5]), the expressed assessment is not a fundamental assessment (qualifying something as good or right or bad or unfair) but it is an assessment of the degree, scale, importance, etc. of the occurrence of the respective facts described by the second part of the name of the estimate. Apart from stating "basic" facts (reasons, merits, etc.), there is also their classification (importance, specificity, etc.) from the point of view of axiological assessment. As a result, in such a situation, the facts of the case are not, for example, reasons in general, but reasons assessed (evaluated) as important, or not any circumstances, but circumstances assessed as exceptional.

Fourthly, axiology may also affect the object of proving in the process of establishing the facts of the case also in such a way that it determines the redundancy of establishing certain facts from the point of view of the final decision made in the proceeding. This unique manifestation of the interference of assessments in establishing facts is at the same time the most powerful interference, as it negates the purpose of getting to know the truth. It determines, on the

---

2 Non-compliance with these criteria was the basis for initiating an extraordinary appeal directed to the SN. In this context, the state interest criterion became an extra-legal political criterion, which harmonized with intra-legal criteria, strengthening the necessity to properly establish the facts (cf. SN Judgment of 1 IV 1965, III PR 1/65, OSNCP 1966, item 20 and SN Provision of 9 I 1981, III CRN 310/80, OSPiKA 1981, item 137).

3 Cf. e.g. SN Judgment of 10 IX 1982, III CRN 201/82, OSNCP 1983, item 81 or SN Judgment of 17 VII 1975, I PZP 9/75, OSPiKA 1976, item 136.

4 Cf. I.1.2.

5 Which means a use of estimation reference clauses (cf. II.1, III.1.2.).

basis of an extra-legal criterion, which facts will be subject to proving (and thus, which facts will not be subject to proving). The presence of a reference does not change the qualification of the facts, but, under certain conditions, it will render it impossible to treat them as the facts of the decided case. It consists in recognizing that a full explanation of the facts and taking into account the results of cognition could hinder or even annihilate the protection of the value expressed in the extra-legal reference. It states, in other words, that the extra-legal criteria are more important than the determination of the objective truth in the respective case. This is not a typical function of a reference, as it occurs only in certain processes of applying particular norms (in fact, it is limited solely to family law), and that only then, when the institution of presumption exists therein. In particular, in the role of "eliminating the truth" from the decision-making process, the criteria of good of child,[6] interest of the child, or the social interest in cases of denial of paternity or motherhood (establishing the actual state of parenthood could be contrary to the good of the child in a situation where the child recognizes another person as parent).[7] Such a structure is usually conditional, and its usefulness is associated only with a specific decision, without leading to the formulation of a thesis about the supremacy of the extra-legal criteria in every case. Nevertheless it forms such a characteristic role of references in establishing the facts that it cannot be overlooked and we cannot fail to separate it from the other ones. The uniqueness of such a role of references from the point of view of the entire practice of applying the law may be confirmed, and its effects – balanced, by the statements of courts about the general preference for the principle of objective truth in a situation of its conflict with extra-legal criteria.[8]

---

6 In the context of Polish judicial practice, the role of such a "cognitive filter" is the extra-legal criterion of "good of child." It may, under certain circumstances of the application of family law, block the determination of the actual parent, if such determinations could disturb the mental balance of a minor child, which is an essential component of the criterion of "good of child" (cf. e.g. SN Resolution of 17 I 1969, III CZP 124/68, OSNCP 1969, item 169, SN Judgment of 14 II 1969, I CR 570/68, OSNCP 1969, item 186 or, recently, SN Judgment of 19 X 2011, II CSK 87/11, Lex 1027165 and SN Provision of 22 VI 2012, V CSK 283/11, Lex 1232479).

7 Cf. SN Resolution of 17 I 1969, III CZP 124/68, OSNCP 1969, item 169 or SN Judgment of 15 II 1973, II CR 711/72, OSNCP 1974, item 86 where a reference is made to a similar argument resulting from the 1825 Civil Code of Kingdom of Poland (structure created after Vienna Congress of 1815).

8 Cf. e.g. SN Judgment of 14 XII 1973, II CR 692/73, OSPiKA 1975, item 94.

The first two of the above-mentioned types of participation of assessments in determining the facts are indirectly, and the last two – directly related to the role of extra-legal references in the decision-making process and the reasoning of operative interpretation.

1.2. Operative interpretation of law and its phase sequence

(1) The operative interpretation of the law, which in fact covers the determination of the legal base of the process of applying the law, includes a particular sequence of reasoning leading to the decision to apply the law. It can therefore be presented in a phase structure.[9]

This is due to the features of the operative interpretation that emphasize its "decision-making" and not solely cognitive or explanatory nature. The most important of them include: (1) making it in order to issue a decision, (2) leading to its "positive" (i.e. enabling a decision to be made) result, (3) its "situational nature," consisting in a close relationship with the established parallelly facts, which narrows the scope of interpretation, (4) the width of the base, which involves the requirement to take into account all possible sources of reconstruction of the applied norms, which makes it necessary to include validation findings in the interpretation, (5) joint and parallel orientation of interpretation to competence, procedural and material (substantial) norms in the context of the respective decision-making process, (6) locating the process and the result of the interpretation in the frames of judicial practice in the context of following it or, less frequently, contradicting it to some extent, and (7) its phase structure, separating individual reasoning and interpretative actions leading to a decision to apply the law.[10]

The process of operative interpretation includes several phases. The first of these is the orientation (initial) phase, covering the original, and in no way definitive for the course of the decision-making process, impressions from the interpreter's first contact with the materials of the case, relating mainly to the legal nature of the case. The second phase includes validation arrangements, under which the decision maker (operative interpreter) selects the legal carriers (from a set of legal provisions, other decisions on the application of law (precedents), and extra-legal criteria on the basis of which (as part of the subsequent phase) the relevant legal rules (behaviour patterns) will be reconstructed. The third

9 The operative interpretation is also made in the process of constructing normative bases for legislative decision (also on the basis of constitutional norms).

10 Cf. L. Leszczyński, "Wykładnia," pp. 12–22.

phase includes the reconstruction of the norms contained in each individual above-mentioned carrier (source of law in the decision-making perspective). This forms the basis for the transition to the fourth phase, the subject of which is the construction of the normative basis for decisions of the application of law, consisting in combining the norms reconstructed in the previous phase, taking place in the regular (non-conflict), conflict or inferential course. The fifth phase of this process includes the reduction of the normative content of the decision base to the content of the concrete decision in terms of both the qualification of the facts and the determination of their normative consequences.

The phased nature of the operative (judicial) interpretation process does not mean the "irreversible sequence" of the phases of this system. Referring to the above-mentioned parallelism of establishing the facts and legal base in the judicial process, it should be assumed that each finding of a fact that is both new and significant for the decision-making process, which triggered the need to include a new legal carrier, may also effect a "return" to the already "closed" phase of model interpretation in order to supplement the interpretative materials with the elements required for issuing a decision.

(2) Each of the above-mentioned phases generates the participation of various rules of legal interpretation, that occur there in their basic, contextual or complementary-corrective roles.

The basic role of the respective rules consists in that they initiate the process of interpretative decisions in a given phase and that they have the greatest impact on the results of these findings. The contextual role means the direct reference point (effect check) for the application of the rules that play the basic role. On the other hand, the complementary and corrective roles of the rules of interpretation are related to the need to additionally check the results of applying the rules in both of the aforesaid roles with the other rules of interpretation, which is important especially when, as a result of applying the rules of interpretation in the basic and contextual roles, there are any doubts or interpretation conflicts. The assumption of an additional check is based on such a meaning of the formula *interpretatio cessat in claris*, which is emphasized by the so-called interpretative holism, requiring that in any given process of operative interpretation the clarity of the result of this interpretation results from the application, of course in various roles, of all kinds of rules of interpretation. Therefore the potential impact of each type of interpretation rule, considered sufficiently applicable for making a judicial decision, should always be considered in such a decision.

The above-mentioned roles of individual rules (directives, arguments) of interpretation can be related to their classical set. It includes two types of linguistic rules (semantic and syntactic ones), two types of systemic rules (system-structural and system-axiological ones), teleological and functional rules, rules of open (extra-legal) axiology, as well as rules of conflict and inference. The imposition of these rules on individual phases of the operative interpretation allows for the identification of differences that can already be signalled, at least with regard to the basic roles. And so, as part of the orientation phase, both types of system rules play a fundamental role, with the possibility of including in this set the rules of open axiology (holding a contextual role in the model). In the validation phase, the system of rules that play the basic role depends on the type of source – when applying legal provisions, this role is played by system-structural rules, when applying legal principles – the system-axiological rules, when applying other decisions on the application of law – the functional rules, while when applying extra-legal criteria – the rules of open axiology. In turn, in the reconstruction phase, both types of linguistic rules play a fundamental role in relation to the meaning of normative expressions of legal texts (semantic rules) and the structure of a normative statement (syntactic rules), which, in the case of determining the content of an extra-legal criterion, further interact with the rules of open axiology. The construction phase evokes the basic roles of individual rules analogically to the validation phase (depending on the source of the reconstruction of interpretative norms that play a dominant role in the construction of the normative basis of decisions), while taking into account the specificity of collision and inferential reasoning. And finally, in the decision-making phase, the basic roles in building the content of the decision to apply the law are played by system-structural and linguistic rules.

The rules related to the use of axiology within this set have a twofold character – that of system-axiological rules and of rules for the application of open axiology. The latter, directly related to the presence of extra-legal references in the interpretation process, play a fundamental role in the validation phase (when applying the extra-legal reference as a carrier of normative content[11]), in the reconstruction phase (when determining the content of the extra-legal criterion[12]) and in the construction phase (when this criterion plays a significant role in the construction of the normative basis of the decision[13]). In other phases, the rules of application of open axiology play a contextual (orientation phase) or a complementary-corrective (other phases) role.

---

11 Cf. II.

12 Cf. III.

13 Cf. IV.4.5.

In each of these roles, these rules interact in a different way with the system-axiological rules. This is particularly evident when establishing the content of extra-legal criteria, which cannot break the intra-legal axiology established on the basis of system-axiological rules,[14] but is also present in other interpretative reasoning, which includes the rules of open axiology.

(3) The arrangements presented in the two previous parts of the book specifying the conditions and method for applying the extra-legal references (using extra-legal criteria) in the respective decision-making process and determining the content of the applied open criteria occur in realty of decision making and interpretational process together with the actions and reasoning analysed in the present Chapter. Their "exclusion" from the presently described presentation of the operative interpretation process (despite being a part of it) was related not to the order of their occurrence, but to the need for arrangements, in a sense, conditioning the participation of extra-legal references in the decision-making process. It is only after both these reasoning and actions were made that the content of the extra-legal criteria can be combined with rules (patterns of behaviour) reconstructed from other carriers (sources) of law. Only then can the scope and strength of their impact on the entire process of this interpretation be determined, including reasoning and activities related to legal provisions, other decisions of the application of law or legal principles (regardless of their provenance). This linking results from the fact that the content of the open criteria, finally formulated in a normative form (behaviour pattern), cannot constitute an independent building block of the normative basis of the judicial decision and then the content of this decision itself (which may be the case in jurisprudence based on *ius equity* or decision-making processes of various forms of ADR[15]).

Therefore these extra-legal references that render it possible to distinguish the validation phase (the basis for their application) and the reconstruction phase (determination of the axiological content of extra-legal criteria, transformed into a extra-legal normative pattern), first participate in the preliminary arrangements of the interpretation process (orientation phase), and "subsequently" in one that also includes other carriers (sources) of law – i.e. the validation, reconstruction, construction and reduction arrangements. Such a composition does not mean that in any decision-making process, both clearly separated activities are performed first in relation to all references used in the decision-making process, and only then are their results superimposed on the

14 Cf. III.4.
15 Cf. I.1.

interpretation process involving other legal carriers (predominantly provisions of law). In reality, the phases of the decision-making process converge, although distinguishing significant elements of the influence of extra-legal references on the activities discussed below presupposes making earlier arrangements as to the application of open criteria and determination of their extra-legal axiological content. This also applies to the orientation phase, although the content of extra-legal values is "established" only initially, and even intuitively within its framework. However, one cannot exclude the real parallelism of all these activities or their "spiral sequencing" (making subsequent, partial determinations within subsequent phases). Thus, as in the case of the entire phase system of an operative interpretation, it should be stressed that it is a model system that determines the logical subsequent dependence of some types of interpretation findings in relation to the remaining ones.

(4) The above-presented description of the participation of extra-legal criteria, with a predetermined axiological content, in the process of constructing the final decision on the application of law, combining various patterns of behaviour, includes the impact of references on several types of reasoning and interpretative activities carried out at different stages of this operative interpretation. The first of its aspects is the impact of extra-legal references on the recognition that the legal issue brought for consideration is worth legal protection (orientation phase), the second – their impact on validation arrangements with regard to the application of other legal carriers, especially legal provisions (validation phase), the third – the impact of the reference on the content of the basic (single) behaviour pattern reconstructed on the basis of a legal provision, a component of which may be a reference to an extra-legal criterion (reconstruction phase), the fourth the impact of the reference on use of all reconstructed behaviour patterns to construct the total (final) normative base for the decision (the construction phase), while the fifth – the impact of the reference on the reduction of the content of this basis to the content of the decision to apply the law (reduction phase). We will analyse these phases, one by one.

2. Influence of extra-legal axiology on preliminary interpretative findings (orientation phase)

(1) The phase of validation findings *sensu stricto*, i.e. the selection of specific legal carriers on the basis of which the normative basis of decisions will be constructed, is preceded by a phase that may be called indicative or orientation phase, phase of preliminary interpretative findings or, in a sense, interpretative intuitions.

This phase serves to define the operative interpreter's (decision-maker's) own position in the face of the legal issue that appears as the subject of the decision-making process and not separate, and certainly not an extensive reasoning. It forms a kind of "first impression," often not even fully recognized as a separate reasoning by the interpreter, resulting from the "review," the first "contact" with the case materials (presented in the indictment act, lawsuit, complaint or some other application) determining (from the applicant's point of view) the facts of the case ot its legal base.

The most important decision-making effect of this phase is to create the belief that the problem considered is a legal problem (i.e. it fits within the legal order) and that it "deserves" to be dealt with in the context of the decision-making process, and therefore "deserves" legal protection. This triggering of belief should be understood not so much as the effect of full supporting reasoning, but as the lack of doubts that could lead to the negation of the belief as to the indicated criteria for the initial "qualification" of a case brought to the court. This belief is triggered by the intuitive application of two kinds of systemic rules of interpretation – the system-structural and system-axiological ones. However, it cannot be ruled out that in certain situations a complementary role in relation to both types of system rules, and sometimes even a fundamental role in relation to the belief that there is a need for legal protection of the issue submitted for adjudication, may be played by the rules for using open (extra-systemic) axiology.

Usually both kinds of axiological rules work together to the extent mentioned above at this preliminary stage of the operative interpretation. Therefore, they create a certain "interpretative key," in a sense making the further course of the interpretation dependent on these axiological findings. The more experienced the operative interpreter is, the greater role it will play. Appropriate practice, usually associated with both deeper legal knowledge and a "decision-making sense," may affect the direction in which the process will go (it may, for example, focus on refusal to deal with the case), on the later roles of particular rules of interpretation at the subsequent stages thereof, on the proportions of their influence on the result of the interpretation or on the way they are applied in interpretative reasoning.

This does not mean, of course, that the position of axiology in the reasoning at this stage of interpretation is closer to the essence of reasoning appearing in the equity case-law (adjudication on the basis of equity), but it undoubtedly emphasizes the role of axiological rules in interpretation, including the open axiology. Its presence at this phase is not always associated with reference to specific extra-legal references indicated in the regulations of the respective branch of law within which the subject of the decision-making process is located. Rather, it concerns the "general" share of extra-legal (social or political) axiology, resulting, for example, from the "most general" clause for such a section, included in the initial provisions of a given act, and for this reason creating an extra-legal axiology for the entire branch of law[16] or even the entire legal order.[17]

(2) At the indicative stage of the interpretation, especially if this initial view results in the continuation of the decision-making process, it may also be prerequisite to carry out two more reasoning, requiring deeper consideration, and thus going beyond the interpretative orientation. However, these are then less related to the axiological rules of interpretation. The first of them appear when the matter is defined in the materials by a name (expression) that requires immediate explanation (n the base of semantic rules). On the other hand, the second does appear – if, in the course of this preliminary examination of the case materials, doubts arise as to the interpreter's decision-making competences (when, consequently, this competence issue should be resolved either independently or by entrusting it to another entity).

The lack of doubts as to all of the above issues allows for the transition in the interpretation process to further understanding and activities – considering the applicability and selection of extra-legal references relevant to the case and determining the content of the extra-legal criteria formulated therein.[18] In consequence of these findings, the extra-legal references with an already established axiological content may affect the application of other legal carriers as part of an operative interpretation, as presented in the next section of the present Chapter.

3. Impact of extra-legal references on the application of other legal carriers (validation phase)

(1) The participation of extra-legal references in the validation phase (apart from validative decision on the using the reference clause itself[19]) concerns mainly the application of regular legal provisions, but may also refer to the application of legal principles and other court decisions in the decision-making process.

Usually, this participation consists in a specific "validative correction" in the form of a refusal to apply these sources within the specific decision-making

---

16 As it occured in the case of references of § 7 of ABGB, Art. 1, Art. 2 and Art. 4 of ZGB or Art. 5 of KC

17 As it occured in the case of references of Art. 2 of RP Constitution (including the criterion of principles of social justice).

18 Cf. II and III.

19 Cf. II.2.2.

process. It takes place in the form of the use of the law applicability test, which corrects the application of formal provisions. The refusal to apply such a provision may be based on various criteria, such as: its retroaction, *desuetudo*, declaration of its unconstitutionality by the constitutional court with the delay of its derogation,[20] or a declaration by the court adjudicating that the provision is unconstitutional (as part of the so-called diffused constitutional review) or a sub-statutory provision conflicting with a statutory regulation. Each of these criteria of the test of the applicability of legal provisions may contain elements of extra-legal axiology, not always involving the application of specific reference clauses.

(2) The impact of extra-legal references on the application of legal provisions applies both to provisions that do not contain and those that do contain extra-legal references.

In both cases, the judicial validative correction due to the participation of an extra-legal reference means the weakening of the structure of the theoretical validity of a norm reconstructed from a provision of law. This may consist in declaring a provision invalid if it was already declared unconstitutional by a constitutional court[21] or in a refusal to apply the provision, adjudicated by a court with regard to the particular decision-making process. The effect of the latter practice is the separation of the basis of validity and the basis for application of a legal provision, which means the elimination of a norm reconstructed on the base of such a provision from a particular decision-making process (without affecting its formal validity) on the grounds of arguments not falling within it *stricti iuris*.[22]

The above-mentioned dependencies and effects also remain valid in the event of a refusal to apply a provision containing an extra-legal reference (which should not be confused with a refusal to apply the referring clause itself as part of such a provision[23]). Due to the axiological content of such a provision,[24] this

---

20 Cf. Polish normative construct, authorizing the TK to "postpone" the moment of derogation of an unconstitutional provision for a period of up to 18 months.

21 In the case of the Polish legal system, the role of such a clause may be fulfilled by regulation of art. 2 of the RP Constitution (reference to the principles of social justice). Cf. S. Tkacz, *Rozumienie*, pp. 69 ff. See also TK Judgment of 9 I 1996., K 18/95, OTK 1996, No. 1, item 1, TK Judgment of 12 IV 1994, U 6/93, OTK 1994, No. 1, item 8 and TK Judgment of 9 III 1998, U 7/87, OTK 1998, item 1.

22 What touches in some aspect the G. Radbruch's category of "*gezetzliche Unrecht*" (G. Radbruch, "Statutory," passim, J Zajadlo, *Formuła*, esp. 105 ff.) or H.L.A. Hart's concept of "minimal content of natural law" (cf. *The Concept*, pp. 190–194).

23 Cf. IV.

24 Cf. below: 2.

test and its possible outcome may, to some extent, be associated with an axiological correction of the content of the behaviour pattern reconstructed from such a provision, which usually reduces the effects and shifts the validation correction into a correction of the content of the behaviour pattern.

There is, however, one more factor that differentiates the above relationships and the scope and depth of their effects. It is the presence of an open criterion in the official (i.e. contained in the provision) interpretative directive. It deals particularly with a situation of profound ("revolutionary") social change, that encompasses changes in social and political axiology, resulting in systemic and legal changes.[25] This is because references containing corrective changes that may be present during the course of the same social system do not cause changes in the basic axiology of the system. In this case references may change the content of the interpreted norm, which comes from a different period in the functioning of a given formation, but will not result in the refusal to apply such a norm to a specific case.[26] Even more so, the reference does not fulfil such a quasi-validative function in a stable legal order with sufficiently durable axiological foundations.

Normative structures introducing such a role of references are located in a legal act that is sufficiently important for the entire legal order, in addition to its initial provisions, making it potentially applicable in all decision-making processes made on the basis of detailed provisions of this act or, more broadly, in the entire branch of law, or even the entire system of law.[27] They function differently in relation to the old regulations that did not contain any extra-legal references, and differently in relation to the old regulations, which contained references, obviously related to the axiology dominating in the previous model of state and society.

---

25 For more details about it cf. III.2.

26 SN Resolution 26 II 1969, III CZP 79/69, OSPiKA 1971, item 30 (p. 59). More on the relation between legal regulation and legal principle cf. J. Starościak, *Studia,* 103, J. Wróblewski, *Zagadnienia*, 263, 281.

27 This was the case of the rule constructed in Art. 5 of the Soviet decree on the court (allowing the application of pre-revolutionary law as long as it was consistent with the revolutionary conscience and revolutionary consciousness of the masses) or the rule of Art. 1 POPC of 1950, repeated in art. 4 of KC (referring to the principles of the political system and objectives of the Polish People's Republic). The latter provision formulated a norm on the manner of application and interpretation of civil law provisions in general, but could be applied in recognizing the applicability or inadmissibility of applying provisions adopted from the interwar period to a specific decision-making process.

Distinguishing these situations will allow for the definition of different roles of the references. For the application of the "old" (adopted) rules that did not contain references, it usually acted as a simple rule of refusal to apply.[28] On the other hand, for the application of the adopted provision, which itself contained an extra-legal reference, that rule creates a different starting point. Even if the reference was formulated in the old system by a name no longer applied in the new law (e.g. the principles of fair dealing, the principles of equity in the socialist legal order), the mere fact of the presence of the reference shifted the focus from deciding that the provision was inapplicable to interpretative arrangements. At that time, most often the content of the legal norm changed to the extent that the content of the extra-legal reference contained in the provision was altered. It was therefore "sufficient" to read the content of the old reference in a way that would correspond to the new values.[29]

However, the political context of such determinations in both of the above-mentioned roles of references is clear. It is not a coincidence that the legislators use the function of references discussed here, thus creating protective measures for the transformation of law towards an authoritarian system. Protecting oneself against the negative consequences of the application of the provision established in the previous (non-authoritarian) system for the new axiology seems to be an important task for the "new authority," which was rather apparent in the case of the validation role of the above criteria.

(3) The extra-legal criteria may also impact the application of other legal carriers, located differently in relation to legal provisions.

---

28 A characteristic feature is the 1955 resolution by the Supreme Court, including the following view: "As far as the regulation issued in bourgeois Poland is concerned, it cannot be applied also when its disposition is obviously incompatible with the principles of the political system and the objectives of the People's State. (...) and if such a situation developed, the inadmissibility of application of this regulation is an order of the popular justice, even in the light of lack of its formal abolishment" (SN Resolution of 12 II 1955, PiP 1955 No. 7–8, p. 288). Cf. also a similar statement in SN Judgment of 28 VI 1945, C I 5/45, PiP 1946 No. 5, pp. 185–7 (where the rules of social coexistence are additionally mentioned) as well as SN Resolution of 1–15 XII 1951, C 15/51, PiP 1952 No. 12, pp. 887–91. This does not mean that the thesis of this decision was universally dominant for the application of adopted regulations. It depended much on the branch of law, the period of Polish People's Republic that the decision was made in, etc. In most cases there was no such an explicit declaration by court authority, and the conformity with new axiology was reached by means of appropriate interpretation.

29 Here: to the principles of the system and the objective of the state (cf. SN Judgment of 19 XII 1961, 3 CR 377/61, RPEiS 1962 No. 4, p. 300).

With regard to the principles of law, it depends on whether they are contained in legislation or have a different source. In the first case, such an impact is particularly relevant if the principle of law is a component of the regulation adopted from the viewpoint of the previous constitutional system. The "new" references perform functions analogous to the refusal to apply an ordinary provision discussed above, but the effectiveness of the open criteria in this role depends on the scale of the axiological inconsistency of the old principle with the new axiology (in extreme cases, it is not impossible to even find a provision containing "old" reference unconstitutional). In the case of an impact on the application of "non-regulatory" principles (based on the legal tradition), such an operation of the new criteria is somewhat "easier" due to the lesser formalization of traditional principles. This applies to both substantive law and, to a lesser extent, procedural rules.

However, the basic measure of the effectiveness of extra-legal criteria in the above-mentioned role is the type of political system. For in the case of a change that is to shape an authoritarian system, such a refusal to apply the "old" principles of law takes place on the basis of the direct influence of the new political axiology, while democratic changes involve the refusal to apply the principles of the outgoing order with reference to permanent moral values and the axiology related to the legal tradition, which the new order aspires to.

Both of these relations can also operate within the same systemic formation, although here the position of principles as determinants of the axiology of the current legal system is usually stronger, and this is so in both distinguished types of political system. The relationship between references and principles focuses here on the content relationship,[30] and not the validative one.

When the refusal to apply earlier judicial decisions for axiological reasons is considered, the matter is much simpler. The open criterion works more strongly and more directly here. In the statutory law order, this may apply not only to an "ordinary" decision that the court would like to use, but also to decisions treated as precedent (shaping the line of jurisdiction) or to entire, mature lines of case law. Although the scale of the effectiveness of such an action decreases as it approaches the entire line of jurisprudence, the detailed relations will, again, depend on the type of political system and the type of extra-legal reference axiology (political values justify such a refusal most fully in the authoritarian system, in particular wherever such a line was formed during the previous systemic formation).

---

30 Cf. III.4.

(3) The possibility of the above-mentioned validative correction with use of extra-legal criteria does not apply in principle to the legal provisions from which the competence norm is reconstructed and the sources for reconstruction of detailed procedural norms. This correction is therefore the most clear in relation to the correction of the grounds for applying provisions formulating substantive legal norms, although here precise relativizations would have to be tied with the features of individual branches of law. This applies to the sources (in the form of both legal regulations and past court decisions) of implementation of both substantive legal norms – the qualifying and the consequential one.

The participation of extra-legal criteria in validative determinations in the form of a refusal to apply other legal carriers brings a change in the roles of individual rules of operational interpretation. The position of systemic and structural rules becomes somewhat weakened with regard to the basis for the application of legal provisions, which usually play a fundamental role in this phase of interpretation. The jurisprudential correction causes that they must be confronted with the rules of taking into account open axiology, and where relations with legal principles are at stake – with systemic and axiological rules. However, with regard to adjudication on the application of earlier judicial decisions, the rules of open axiology cooperate as basic rules with strongly operating functional rules.

4. Participation of extra-legal references in the reconstruction of behaviour patterns (reconstruction phase)

(1) The share of open criteria in the reconstruction phase of the individual pattern of behaviour, which will be combined with other such patterns in the subsequent stage in the process of building a normative basis for judicial decision, takes place after the linguistic content of individual criteria and the normative pattern of behaviour expressed by this criterion (e.g. the principle of social coexistence) or related to the protection of the verbally expressed value of the name of the criterion (e.g. good of child) were already established.

As a result of these actions, the established content is confronted with the *stricti iuris* criteria. The latter are included in the "juridical part" of a legal provision that includes an extra-legal reference or an earlier decision on the application of the law in which an extra-legal reference was applied. Therefore there is the potential, in both of the above cases, for the reconstructed pattern of behaviour to include both types of criteria, and their participation becomes real if the entity applying the law invokes them in a specific decision-making process.

Such a combination of legal and extra-legal criteria should not be confused with two other types of interpretative reasoning. The first is the checking whether the established content of the extra-legal criterion falls within the legal axiology in the form of legal principles or clearly shaped case law (precedents). The other reasoning is the participation of extra-legal criteria in the process of constructing a normative basis for a decision (the subsequent phase[31]), where various basic behaviour patterns are combined, and their set may also include basic patterns resulting from the reconstruction that already takes into account the extra-legal reference.

Two basic reasoning occurring in this phase – the clarification of the meanings of normative expressions and the reconstruction of the norm (behaviour pattern) generate a different share of extra-legal references. It is so as focuses mainly on the impact on the reconstruction of norms contained in regulations. Although the impact of the extra-legal criterion contained in a legal provision on the meaning of the expression in this provision is not excluded, this influence is not independent as it manifests itself through the scope of the norm reconstructed from the provision that this expression is part of.[32]

(2) The basis for the participation of open criteria in the reconstruction of the basic pattern of behaviour from a legal provision is the finding of some inadequacy of referring only to the legal criteria to determine the content of such a pattern. Most often it takes place in relation to the content of a legal provision containing a reference to an extra-legal criterion, because here the distinction between the essence of both types of criteria is the clearest and produces the strongest results. The consequence of participation of the extra-legal criterion in this reasoning, is that it most often complements the content of the pattern of behaviour reconstructed on the basis of the *stricti iuris* criteria contained in the same provision (the mildest influence). It may also consist in its correction (narrowing or extending the scope of the rule and its application), which may sometimes come close to not taking the *stricti iuris* criteria into account in a given decision-making process (the deepest interference, which in fact means situations of direct conflict and the result of refusing to apply the intrinsic legal criteria because of the content of the extra-legal reference). Obviously, the perspective of the above-mentioned share of open criteria applies only to the particular decision-making process, unless such a solution is adopted by precedent practice.

---

31 Cf. below: 5.

32 For example, the principles of social coexistence do not affect the content of the expression of "abuse of the law" itself but determine the content of the norm, reconstructed from the art. 5 of KC, defining the form and scale of abuse of the law.

Such an impact may result from the presence of a criterion in the applicable legal provision, but it may also be related to a separate interpretative directive contained in a "special" interpretative provision.[33] Then it will have a broader impact, including determining the content of an entire class of provisions, also in the absence of any references contained therein.[34]

The interaction of both criteria from the reconstruction of the base norm leads to two consequences, resulting from the conflict of both criteria. The first of them, which is definitely less frequent in decision-making practice, occurs when, in the result of the confrontation of both types of criteria, the extra-legal criteria prevail over the content of the base formula to such an extent that they will be of use for qualifying the facts (or determining the consequences of this qualification) and they virtually eliminate the participation of legal criteria in determining the content of this basic norm reconstructed in this provision. The second effect of the interaction of both types of criteria, meaning the balancing of the proportion of the participation of both types of criteria in the content of the reconstructed rule. In fact, both actions mean a harder or softer solution to a certain situation of collision between the intra-legal and the extra-legal criteria, bringing this reasoning closer to the application of strict conflict-of-laws rules.[35]

(3) These relations also apply to provisions containing legal principles. Although this relation is "more difficult" for extra-legal criteria, it does not exclude the complementary or even corrective role of the latter in relation to the intra-legal axiology.[36] On the other hand, supplementing or correcting the content of "non-statutory" legal principles by open criteria is so much easier and stronger that the "validity" of such a principle is justified not by the establishment, but by the very content of the extra-legal social values sourced from the legal tradition.

The share of open criteria is similar in the case of the reconstruction of a pattern from another decision of the application of law or entire line of jurisprudence. It is also in this case, that these criteria supplement or correct the content

---

33 Cf. Art. 1 POPC of 1950.

34 The role of such open criteria can be played by political criteria (former art. 4 of KC.) by moral criteria (Art. 8, 9, 10 and 11 of ECHR) or axiologically "neutral" criteria (Art. 31 of VCLT), which means that it applies to various political systems.

35 Cf. below: 5.4.

36 This can most clearly be seen in the example of art. 2 of the Constitution. An extra-legal criterion may also affect the content of legal principles as a "meta-clause" (cf. S. Tkacz, *Rozumienie*, pp. 13–41).

of the legal criteria of the judgments used, in a situation similar to an axiological collision. In the order of statutory law, the interference of extra-legal axiology in the content of a decision on the application of law may be even stronger than in the case of legal provisions. Especially if the reconstruction is aimed at identifying an appropriate fragment that allows to reproduce a pattern or compilation of several fragments of the justification of a specific decision of the application of the law (although it should be noted that there are differences between an "ordinary" judgment and a resolution of an extended panel of the court of the highest instance). However, when referring to a jurisprudence line, the juridical argumentation formed within it retains a stronger position.

(4) The relations that are signalled above concern mostly the reconstruction of the base of material law norms and, to a lesser extent, the reconstruction of procedural and especially competence rules. This is because the reconstruction of the competence norms does not assume the participation of open criteria in the purpose of correcting its scope resulting from the legal provision. And that affects its possible supplementation to a small extent.

The participation of open criteria in the reconstruction of basic behaviour patterns effects changes in the model roles of rules of interpretation. Of course, the role of linguistic rules, both the semantic and the syntactic ones, remains the fundamental one in each of the above cases of the participation of extra-legal criteria at this stage of operative interpretation. However, if this share concerns the reconstruction of norms from legal provisions containing a reference, the basic role of linguistic rules is supplemented by the same role of open axiology rules on the side of determining the participation of the extra-legal criteria in this interpretative reasoning. The rules of taking into account open axiology enter into analogous relations with the linguistic and systemic-axiological rules in the case of the reconstruction of the content of the legal principles and with the linguistic and functional rules in the case of the reconstruction of behaviour patterns contained in past court decisions applied in a given decision-making process.

5. Participation of the extra-legal references in building the normative basis for decision (construction phase)

5.1. Features of the construction phase

(1) The constructive phase of operative interpretation focuses in the most important features of the participation of extra-legal references in an operative interpretation from the point of view of the content of the normative base of final

judicial decision in this process. Its core consists in the construction of a base, which combines, in a dimension adequate to the "needs" of the decision-making process, all the basic behaviour patterns that were reconstructed in the preceding phase from various legal carriers.

The complexity of this phase consists in the fact that the normative basis of a decision is built not only for the final decision (court judgment, administrative decision), based on a substantive law norm but also for the "initial" competence decision (defining own competence to conduct the process) and partial procedural decisions (specifying the manner for performing individual activities in the decision-making process), leading to the final decision.

Determining the content of the above-mentioned types of norms is based on a model sequence of actions.[37] First of all, the basis of competence should be established (which sometimes requires a separate, somewhat incidental procedure, e.g. in the case of a need to resolve a competence dispute), and only after that should the procedural basis be established, which in turn precedes the substantive law determinations. In this context, it is important to distinguish between the procedural grounds covering the entire procedure (which takes place in the form of, for example, examination of the formal grounds for initiating proceedings or establishing the legal principles "governing" the respective type of procedure and the specific decision-making process) and the grounds relating to each specific action that is undertaken in a specific process (e.g. delivery, appearance in court, giving the floor to a witness, etc.). Nonetheless, while the determination of fundamental procedural norms, as well as both substantive rules (qualifying and consequential), takes place in each process and then usually becomes a component of the argumentation presented in the justification of the decision, a separate and precise determination of the competence grounds and detailed procedural grounds is performed, whenever it proves necessary (e.g. doubts as to the authority's own competence or this being questioned by a party or similar doubts or questioning the manner of carrying out a given activity in the decision-making process).

(2) Assuming that the behaviour pattern reconstructed from the extra-legal reference itself cannot constitute an independent basis for the content of the

37 Causing the use of various interpretative rules (cf. SN Judgment of 9 III 2018, I CSK 336/17, LEX 2485381, SN Judgment of 22 II 2019, IV CSK 121/18, LEX 2625010, SN Provision of 12 I 2018, II CSK 160/17, LEX 2483679, SN Judgment of 22 VI 2018 r, II CSK 539/17, LEX 2521685, SN Judgment of 10 I 2020, I CSK 279/18, LEX 2785119 or SN Judgment of 3 VII 2015, IV CSK 595/14, LEX 1917369).

application of law decision (or as a matter of fact any of the partial decisions), it should also be assumed that such a basis is not grounded solely on the content of norms reconstructed from legal provisions. If the participation of references in the decision-making process and operative interpretation (analogously to the participation of other decisions on the application of the law[38]) is to be real, it should not only be noticed but, what is more, its aspects and scope should also be defined. At the same time, this does not concern the participation of the content of the reference in the construction of the individual pattern of behaviour, that would combine the legal and extra-legal criteria contained in the specific legal provision (which was the subject of the previously discussed reconstruction phase[39]), but the share of this content in the construction of the final basis for the decision to apply the law, combining these previously reconstructed unit patterns.

The participation of extra-legal references in the phase of constructing the normative basis of a decision may take place in three courses: basic, inferential and collision. In each of them, open criteria appear in various connections with patterns reconstructed from other legal carriers, and their participation, triggering changes in the roles of individual rules of interpretation, leads to various interpretative effects in the context of the content of the normative base of decision.

5.2. Basic course

(1) The participation of extra-legal criteria as part of the basic course of the construction phase implies the inclusion of these criteria in the determination of some aspect of the normative content of the decision base.[40] The content of the reference acts here in two forms – either as an independent extra-legal content applied in the decision-making process "only" at this phase, or as a component of the base formula determined in the previous phase, combining both contents contained in the provision subjected to interpretation.

The independent operation of an extra-legal criterion takes place when the authority applying the law decides, at this stage of interpretation, to add, to the already reconstructed patterns of behaviour, some new, extra-legal criterion, that was not present in the provisions previously considered. Such a decision

38 More on that cf. L. Morawski, M. Zirk-Sadowski, "Precedent," passim, L. Leszczyński, "Implementing," passim.

39 Cf. above: 4.4.

40 Cf. M. Zieliński, *Wykładnia*, pp. 234 ff., 339 ff.

is therefore motivated by a decision-making need, indicating a certain scope of insufficiency of the already established patterns of behaviour, including, above all, the already established *stricti iuris* criteria to construct a full decision basis.

The extra-legal criterion applied in this way is sourced either from a general provision in relation to the applicable specific provisions or from another specific provision related to the applicable provision. The first situation occurs more often, because it is an element of complementing the reconstructed behaviour patterns by norms of a general nature, which in this case take the form of norms based on the extra-legal criteria. It is also possible that such a general provision expresses the principle of law, which additionally includes the relationship between intra-legal and extra-legal axiology.

The second situation means the "joint" operation of the extra-legal and the *stricti iuris criteria* within a single behaviour pattern, reconstructed from the specific provision of law (which is the result of the participation of open criteria in the interpretation of the provision containing the reference[41]). It is more frequent in adjudication practice than the situation of independent participation of an extra-legal criterion in the construction phase of interpretation. Even it has a stronger impact in "its part" as a component of the base norm, including both juridical and extra-legal elements, it has a slightly weaker impact on the final content of the normative basis of the decision, although the specific dimension depends on the result of their joint action with the *stricti iuris* criteria, as indicated above.

In the case of reconstructing a behaviour pattern containing legal and extra-legal criteria, the share of the extra-legal criteria in the content of the normative basis of the decision depends on the detailed proportions of their participation in the content of this pattern, on the position of the legal provision containing juridical criteria, on the axiological significance of the extra-legal criteria, on their relationship with legal axiology, and so on. However, it is always a share that is "weighted" with the legal criteria.

The above-mentioned relations of cooperation refer to legal provisions, however, also within the order of statutory law, they also may, to some extent, refer to juridical criteria derived from other judicial decisions, especially if they are treated as a precedent or they are formed in lasting jurisprudence lines. We can even state that the scale of the impact of the extra-legal criteria is greater here, which results from the model (in the statutory law order) of weaker position

41 Cf. above: 4.3.

of juridical arguments contained in other court decisions compared to such arguments contained in legal provisions.

(2) Combining different patterns of behaviour is the essence of building the content of the normative basis for the decision of the application of the law. In the model it is constructed on the basis of more than one pattern of behaviour reconstructed from legal carriers. The exception in this respect may be the process of constructing the competence base, which depends essentially solely on the *stricti iuris* criteria that might be expressed in a single legal provision. The share of open criteria in the construction of the detailed procedural basis should be defined as "half-way." Sometimes it happens so that the participation of the criteria could not be determined (e.g. as to giving the floor to a witness as a relatively uncomplicated procedural act specified in a specific provision). Extra-legal criteria, on the other hand, may constitute the fundamental part of the basis of a general procedural norm (e.g. a norm defining the conditions for a public prosecutor's participation in civil proceedings[42]). In its entirety, however, the condition of "multi-source" nature of this basis is actual in relation to the substantive legal basis, even regardless of the complexity of the facts of the case. In this context, the share of extra-legal criteria can be determined in the construction of both the base of decision that qualifies the facts, and of decision establishing the normative consequences of the said qualification.[43]

It is not uncommon in practice to face a situation in which the substantive legal basis for a given decision of the application of law is built on the basis of combining single norms reconstructed from various provisions of law (general and specific, national and international, statutory and sub-statutory, etc.), past court decisions (individual decisions and jurisdictional line), principles of law (expressed or not expressed in legal provisions) and various types of extra-legal criteria. Norms based on open criteria can combine with one, several or all types of norms reconstructed from various sources. In the latter case, the detailed relations will multiply on the basis of the relations established above in the dual connections.

The share of extra-legal criteria in this set of sources for reconstruction of behavioural patterns combined into the final basis of the decision cannot be based on a single determinant. This is determined by the very model features of the statutory order, assuming, first of all, that there are the basic norms reconstructed from legal provisions that play the leading role as an element of the

42 On the ground of Art. 7 of KPC.
43 Cf. below: 6.

normative basis of decisions, and, secondly, that the extra-legal criteria cannot constitute such an independent building block of such a basis. Relativization of the participation of extra-legal criteria is based on such factors as: the above-mentioned scope of participation of the extra-legal criteria in confrontation with the *stricti iuris* criteria in the reconstruction of the behaviour pattern from a provision containing a reference, a type of extra-legal axiology (associated with the type of political system, e.g. favouring in authoritarian regime political axiology), the content relationship of extra-legal axiology with the principles of law (also depending, among others, on the type of political system), the location of the extra-legal references in the structure of the regulatory system, and finally the type of branch of law (more or less axiologically involved).

The scope and impact the participation of the extra-legal factors has on the construction of the normative basis of the decision, regardless of the structural factors discussed above, are influenced by the properties of the facts of the case that is already determined at this stage of the operational interpretation. They can significantly strengthen the participation of extra-legal criteria in construction of this basis if, for example, the manner of abuse of the law is examined in the context of the relationship between such an action and the violation of moral norms or exceeding the limits of freedom of speech in the context of the need to protect morality or the public interest.

However it does not change the fact that the content of the normative basis of decisions in the statutory order is shaped predominantly on the basis of the basic behaviour patterns reconstructed from the provisions, whereas the open criteria, similarly to other court decisions, supplement or correct to some extent those elements of the content that result from such provisions. This does not mean, however, that in any particular decision-making process, the basis for a decision applying the law cannot be constructed mainly on the basis of open criteria or other court decisions. The fact that in this legal order it is not possible to issue a decision on the application of law, and therefore it is not possible to construct a normative basis for a decision without resorting to norms reconstructed from the provisions, does not mean that the criterion used in the provision does not fulfil the role of merely justifying the solution based on an open criterion when issuing a decision. This applies in particular to substantive bases, both qualifying and, to a lesser extent, consequential. For, similarly to the reasoning in the previously discussed phases, in the basis of detailed procedural decisions or, in particular, the basis of a competence decision (defining authority's own competence), the impact of open criteria can be defined either as complementary to the impact of the base norms of the reconstructed legal provisions or (in the case of the basis of procedural decisions resulting from provisions, in which the references are made), as a corrective influence.

(3) In the result of the participation of open criteria, the sequence of roles of rules of interpretation changes in the phase of constructing the normative basis for the judicial decision. The model of the statutory legal order, in which the basic role is played by systemic and structural rules, insofar as the basis for the decision is built on the basis of norms based on the reconstructed legal provisions, is subjected to modification. This makes the rules of taking into account open axiology aspire to the basic role, achieving it proportionally to the scope of their influence on the content of the normative basis of decisions. In the case of the participation of criteria with a pragmatic aspect, the latter rules can play such a role together with functional or teleological rules (e.g. as with an economic purpose or a socio-economic objective). As it is the case with each application of open criteria, the contents of an open axiology are confronted with the basic principles of the law of the part or of the entire legal system, which amplifies the role of system-axiological rules.

The above-mentioned, complementary or corrective role of norms reconstructed from open criteria in relation to norms reconstructed from provisions may have a different scope and scale of influence in the process of constructing a normative basis of decisions. In some of their dimensions, the supplementation formula for the full and final shape of basis may lead to the determination of the share of these criteria as components of inferential rules, while in the correction formula – as components of collision rules.

5.3. Inferential course

(1) The supplementing the normative content of the normative base for decision boult on the grounds of various norms reconstructed from various carriers, may be connected with the application of open criteria. Its scope may be so broad that it can be included to form part of interpretative inferential reasoning. Due to the complexity of inference as a kind of reasoning "from the norm about the norm," meaning a kind of "additional creation" of some important component of the normative basis of a decision, that is impossible to reproduce (reconstruct) on the basis of ordinary interpretative reasoning, the inference itself and the participation of the extra-legal criteria therein fit several different phases of the model of operative interpretation presented here.

Firstly, it occurs in the validation phase in the absence of an extra-legal reference in the respective legal provision, if the "decisional situation" indicates the need to base the operative interpretation on a reference borrowed from another specific provision (*per analogiam clausulae*) or from a general provision with a varying degree of "systemic distance" from the applicable provision. Secondly, it occurs in the reconstruction phase, when the *stricti iuris* criteria from a given provision are insufficient to reconstruct the basic unit norm and there emerges a need to supplement the content of this norm with an extra-legal criterion not included in this provision. And finally, thirdly, in the construction phase, when the set of the reconstructed base norms combined here is insufficient to build a normative basis of the decision and there is a need to additionally supplement this set with some extra-legal criteria that were not taken into account till that stage.

(2) The inferentiality of reasoning in the construction phase means inferring an additional normative component from the already established set of norms in order to "close" the content of the normative basis of the decision and to make it ready to be reduced to the decision to apply the law. In this sense, we can talk about additional construction of this missing part of the normative basis of the decision.

Such an addition may apply to virtually any type of the inferential reasoning. It participates however relatively most expressly in axiological inferences. In both forms of *a fortiori* (*a minori ad maius* and *a maiori ad minus*) reasoning and in *a contrario* reasoning, it consists in the fact that the assessment which form the basis of a prohibition or an order results not from a legal but from an extra-legal axiology. The same occurs with axiological inference *per analogiam iuris*, except that here the open criteria expressing extra-legal axiology complement the legal axiology created by the legal principles.

The inferential function of extra-legal criteria usually remains, also in the construction phase, related to "supplementing" norms reconstructed from legal provisions. Nevertheless this role of open criteria should be applied also to that part of the basis of a decision that was reconstructed from earlier court decisions, especially since some of them either create legal principles or grant such status to certain norms expressed in legal regulations.

As was the case in the basic course, also in the inferential course of the construction phase, the open criteria may act in the form of independent axiological contents or as a consequence of combining these contents with the *stricti iuris* criteria in the reconstructive phase. The previously presented distinction of the scale of the impact of open criteria on supplementing the competence, procedural and material-legal bases also remains valid.

5.4. Collision course

The participation of open criteria in the collision course of the construction phase is optional insofar as a collision is found within the framework of combining various base norms, which prevents the continuation of the process of building a normative basis for decisions without its resolution. The share of these criteria in the resolution of collisions has four variants. In the first of them, various open criteria come into conflict with one another in determining the content of an extra-legal reference.[44] In the second, the open criteria conflict with the criteria from the legal provisions within the framework for reconstruction of the basic behaviour pattern from the provision containing the extra-legal reference. In the third variant, which is similar to the second, the open criteria collide with norms reconstructed from other legal carriers – mainly from provisions, but also from other decisions of the application of law, or even from principles of law.[45]

Finally, in the fourth variant, the open criteria play a separate role from the above-mentioned ones, as the criterion for determining a normative collision between patterns from single-type carriers (from provisions, decisions or principles of law) and from different types of carriers (between norms from provisions and court decisions, between norms from legal provisions and principles, between norms from principles of law and other court decisions). In each of them, the participation of open criteria results in different scope of their influence on the result of collision resolution. As in the reasoning discussed earlier, open criteria can enter into these collision relations both in the form of an independent axiological content (moral, political or economic) and a content linking these values with juridical criteria.

(2) The participation of open criteria in the role of a criterion for solving any of the above-mentioned collisions takes place after failed application of system-structural rules of collision solving (*lex posterior derogat legi priori*, *lex superior derogat legi inferiori*, *lex specialis derogat legi generali*, assuming that "*derogat*" means priority and not derogation *sensu stricto*), systemic-axiological rules (the priority of a rule of law or norm having a stronger connection with the rule of law) and functional rules (priority of a norm holding more important social functions). On the other hand, the participation of open criteria can occur either in the form of reference to "objectified" values (in some sense verified socially or

---

44 Cf. e.g. SN Judgment of 6 VII 1967, III CR 117/67, OSNCP 1968, item 67 or SN Judgment of 22 VI 1972, III CRN 126/72, OSPiKA 1973, item 55.

45 For both variants cf. above: 4.

politically) or, which is completely unique, in the form of reference to the "personal preferences" of the operative interpreter.

The interpretative role of open criteria in the course of the collision, regardless of the above relativizations, serves to achieve two successive "post-collision" results. First, it serves to achieve an interpretative compromise (with extra-legal axiology determining the proportions in taking into account both conflicting norms as part of the "compromised" norm) and then, shall this prove impossible, it leads to the refusal to include the "axiologically weaker" (on grounds of the extra-legal axiology) rule into the content of the normative basis decision. The share of open criteria in the achievement of both objectives of removing collisions is stronger if their content is based on a verified axiology (which means different things for different types of values). This applies in particular to the construction of the substantive legal basis for a judicial decision, where this role is relatively the broadest.

6. Impact of extra-legal references on the content of judicial decision (decisional reduction phase)

6.1. Features of the reduction phase

The reduction phase is usually associated with the final decision on the application of the law, which has a substantive nature (court judgment, administrative decision). The real complexity of this phase, however, rests in the fact that the reduction also applies to the established basis of a competence decision (determining the operative interpreter's own competence to conduct the process) and of a procedural decisions (determining the manner the respective activities of the decision-making process are conducted in).

What is more, the final decision on the application of the law may be presented either in the form of two content-related decisions (which has a praxeological justification) or in the form of one two-part decision (which has a procedural justification). The first part (or a separate "first" decision) is the normative qualification of established facts of the case (e.g. behaviour in penal law, contracts in civil law, administrative decisions in judicial review of administrative activities, etc.), consisting in reducing the content of the substantive base of decision, containing a behaviour pattern for the addressees whose behaviour is qualified. The second element (or the "second" decision) is the determination of the legal consequences of the aforesaid qualification of facts, consisting in reducing the relevant components of the content of the substantive base defining these consequences to the result of the previously performed qualification of facts.

Distinguishing both parts of the final decision makes it possible to relate both types of reduction to the concept of a sanctioned and sanctioning norm, as distinguished by the theory of law.[46] Due to the fact that determining the consequences does not only result in the application of classic legal sanctions, but may also lead to the determination of other consequences of qualifying facts (e.g. establishing the legal status or updating a right or obligation) that are different from sanctions, it seems better to call this part of the decision consequential and not sanctioning (and analogically, the first part of the decision – the qualifying and not the sanctioned part).

The issuance of a decision in the qualifying and consequential dimension is based on conducting subsumptive reasoning. For it is subsumption, if it is understood as any "bringing" of a given fact under the norm, that also includes establishing the consequences that result from subsuming it under the norm determining the consequences, but not so much of the established facts as their qualification. In this context, subsumption means the superimposition of the criteria of the qualifying and consequential norm on the actual findings, ultimately leading to the reduction of the general substantive legal norm to be applied (normative basis of the decision) to the content of an individual decision on the application of law in both of its dimensions.

The share of extra-legal references in this phase of the decision-making process covers both the above-mentioned basic elements of the decision on the application of the law.

6.2. Share of open criteria in the qualification of the facts of the case

(1) The reference clause does not form a separate element of the qualification decision. It enters into these activities to the extent it appears in the content of the normative basis of the decision. This is related to the qualification of the facts in the form of a relative assessment, comparing both real facts (e.g. action in the exercise of property rights, appropriation of someone else's property) and legal facts (e.g. conclusion of a legal transaction, content of a contract, content of a controlled administrative or court decision) with legal criteria and optionally with extra-legal criteria (principles of social coexistence, local relations, public interest, etc.).

---

46 Cf. J. Lande, "Nauka," pp. 921–929.

(2) The participation of the criteria resulting from extra-legal references in the operation of comparing the already established facts (which may also be related to the application of extra-legal criteria as a part of estimation clause[47]) with the normative criteria occurs in three basic variants.

Firstly, the criteria of extra-legal referrals may shape the process of qualifying the respective factual state either jointly (with) or independently (without) of the legal criteria. This applies, for example, to assessing the relative[48] qualification of the content of the concluded contract[49] or the manner of exercising a subjective right[50] from the point of view of the principles of social coexistence, since an activity that is inconsistent with these principles is invalid, or since making the right of use contrary to the socio-economic purpose of the law or the principles of coexistence does not benefit from legal protection. The open criteria of criminal law also operate in this manner, when determination of the social danger of an act (the degree of which cannot be insignificant) is a condition of recognizing the act as a crime.[51]

This variant usually results in the interaction of open criteria with legal criteria, although the dominant role of the former in shaping the result of qualification cannot be excluded.[52] It may lead to two relations indicating the strong entering of open criteria in the place of legal criteria as the basis for qualifying the facts. As part of the first, it enables the qualification of the facts (e.g. a concluded contract as a type of legal transaction) only on the basis of such a criterion (e.g. the principles of coexistence), which is already its independent operation. On the other hand, under the second, it may lead to disregarding of those intra-legal criteria which would result in a qualification inconsistent with the applied extra-legal criteria.[53]

---

47 Cf. II.1. (where the child's welfare test may even exclude the fact-finding itself).

48 Cf. J.Wróblewski, *Sądowe*, pp. 177 ff., 188–189.

49 Art. 58 of KC.

50 Art. 5 of KC.

51 Cf. Art. 26 of KK of 1969 irrespective of the fact that in the case of an act whose degree of danger is insignificant, the proceedings could be conditionally discontinued.

52 This is expressed in indications of such a framing of the facts as to make them directly suitable for comparison with the clause criterion, that is, whether they are explained "in terms of," (or "in light of," "according to") the criteria in question (cf. SN Provision of 3 XII 1966, III CR 301/66, OSNCP 1967, item 220, SN Provision of 11 X 1974, III CRN 235/74, OSPiKA 1977, item 103 or NSA Judgment of 21 V 1981, SA 797/81, ONSA 1981, item 44).

53 Cf. SN Judgment of 30 I 1976, I PRN 52/75, OSPiKA 1977, item 47.

Secondly, the participation of extra-legal references in the qualification of the facts also takes place when the reference plays the role of an element that enhances the role of the already determined similarity between the facts that are regulated and non-regulated by the respective qualification norm. What is used in such cases is the structure of an analogous application of law that may be based on a reference in the sense that the social importance of the extra-legal criteria determines the requirement to qualify both of these types of facts (i.e. regulated and not regulated by the norm) from the point of view of the same normative criteria.[54] Here the open criteria have a twofold action: firstly as a reinforcement of analogous juxtaposition, and secondly as an additional criterion with which the facts are compared (if the extra-legal reference is an element of a borrowed basis).[55]

And thirdly, as strong as in the first variant, the impact of extra-legal criteria on subsumption arguments occurs when, on the basis the extra-legal criteria, the juxtaposition of the facts with the legal criteria is waived.[56] This is a situation similar to the failure to apply a legal norm, e.g. adopted from the previous system, due to its non-compliance with given extra-legal criteria, and its effects are similar to the resignation from establishing the facts of the case for axiological reasons stemming from the reference.[57] That is combined with the previous negative validation argumentation in the process.

6.3. Open criteria in establishing the normative consequences of qualification of facts

(1) The selection of legal consequences when making a decision on the application of the law may be effected without and with the participation of an extra-legal reference. Also in the argumentation of the choice of consequences, one can distinguish several ways in which the criteria resulting from the referrals may participate.

---

54 On rules for establishing similarity in argumentation cf. J. Nowacki, *Analogia*, pp. 9–44 (esp. p. 13), K. Opałek, J. Wróblewski, *Zagadnienia*, p. 319, A. Korybski, "Analogy," pp. 27 ff. C. Perelman speaks of recognizing one such factor as apparent (cf. *Logika*, p. 163). Cf. also R. Dworkin, "Hard," passim, H. W. Jones, "An Invitation," pp. 1028–1030 (indicating category of "trouble cases").

55 Cf. SN Judgment of 23 III 1967, III PRN 2/67, OSNCP 1967, item 223, SN Resolution of 11 XII 1975, III CZP 63/75, OSNCP 1976, item 259 and SN Resolution of 13–27 X 1952, C 2104/52, PiP 1953 No. 3, pp. 456–9.

56 Cf. SN Provision of 21 VI 1979, III CRN 68/79, OSPiKA 1980, item 30.

57 Cf. above: 1.2.

Firstly, the criteria of extra-legal references may form an element of the directive on the choice of strictly legal consequences. Referral may constitute a formal element of the consequences choice directive when the legislator orders to take into account appropriately named extra-legal criteria, e.g. when assessing the punishment.[58] However, it may also shape an informal element, when such an order is not expressly formulated in the provision establishing the sanctions selection directives, but law enforcement entities apply extra-legal criteria that are expressed in legal texts. In both cases, it is valid when the entity applying the law has a choice between the types of sanctions or has the possibility to moderate the sanctions (when the sanction is gradual), because then the reference may play the role of a criterion for the selection or dimension of selected legal consequences. In addition to criminal law, this also applies to civil and administrative law (affecting e.g. the amount of compensation or determining the scale of the obligation to perform the service).

Secondly, in consequence of application of a reference, the entity applying the law may deviate from the application of the legal criteria in determining the consequences, which means that the reference, as a more significant criterion, has a negative impact on the choice of the consequences prescribed by the legal provision. This is a situation similar to establishing the inapplicability of a legal norm in a specific case,[59] except that here it only concerns the consequential norm and the choice of consequences that are based on it. It is characteristic that such a role of the open criterion may also apply to criminal law[60] and that it can occur (outside of criminal law) both when applying a norm created in the same type of regulation[61] and a norm adopted from the previous system.[62] Such decisions are usually justified by the accumulation of various axiological arguments, which are to counterbalance the application of legal sanction.[63]

Thirdly, the participation of extra-legal references may take place when the legislator "suggests" the possibility of relying in the argumentation of the choice of consequences solely on extra-legal criteria, which means that the references have an independent role in determining the consequences.[64]

---

58 Cf. Art. 50 § 1 of KK of 1969 in regard to the criterion of social danger of an act or Art. 53 § 1 of KK of 1997 regarding the criterion of social harmfulness of the act).

59 Cf. above: 1.3.

60 E.g. exclusion of liability due to the lack of social harmfulness of an act under Art. 1 of the Penal Code of 1997).

61 Cf. SN Resolution of 27 XI 1978, III CZP 79/78, OSNCP 1979, item 94.

62 Cf. SN Resolution of 13–27 X 1952, C 2104/52, PiP 1953 No. 3, pp. 456–9.

63 Cf. SN Resolution of 27 XI 1978, III CZP 79/78, OSNCP 1979, item 94.

64 Art. 417^2 KC as the basis of state responsibility.

(2) The independent participation of open criteria in determining the consequences, as discussed above, is included in three additional options.

The first option would entail the absence of any legal measures for the selection of consequences, which would usually also be accompanied by the absence of stipulation of any extra-legal criteria that could be taken into account. It would be a situation of a particularly strong and wide gap in relation to the selection of consequences. An institution meeting these features would be the construction of a completely free recognition as to the content of the decision (and within the latter – as to the choice of consequences), which currently is not present in the judicial type of application of the law.[65]

The second option, involving the provision of measures of determining consequences in the most general way possible, would create a more limited scope of discretion in the sense that, firstly, it would be placed within the framework of legal order, and secondly, it could be defined (at least generally) in terms of the legal institutions in which it could be applied, and thirdly, that it would be subject to general axiological conditions in the processes of applying the law. Creating a gap as to the selection of consequences in this variant, which, however, does not entail the lack of indication of consequences at all (which is a feature of *equity* jurisprudence), occurs in the order of statutory law or in the form of a maximally general, formulation of the basis for a decision expressed in the preliminary provisions of an act, or in the form of the reference indicated in its specific provisions.

We deal with the use of the general form of indicating the consequences in case of the natural legal principles under § 7 ABGB or the principles of equity under Art. 4 ZGB. A decision made entirely on their basis, even if it is subject to a finding that the *stricte* legal basis is insufficient to make a decision, may independently include various arguments for applying the law, and thus also arguments regarding the selection of consequences.[66]

---

65 However, it may take the form of an administrative decision, as is the case, for example, in Poland, e.g. in the form of a President's decision to pardon or refuse to appoint a judge or award the title of professor.

66 Polish regulations do not include such authorization, although the norm of Art. 4 of KC, which was in force till 1989 and defined the manner of applying the law, could also, at least in a sense, act as the basis for a decision establishing legal consequences, based on the principles of the political system and the objectives of the state. However, it would not be an unambiguous basis, nor one that would prove easy to operationalize, hence there are no examples of such argumentation.

Creating a discretion as to the choice of consequences through references appearing in detailed provisions, setting a sanction that can be moderate without specifying the criteria for its measurement, on the other hand, creates a more limited scope thereof. The effect may be virtually the same as before, except that the discretion in the specific provisions is more connected with the properties of the legal institutions in which it can be practiced (for example, the role of the rules of equity as a basis for determination of the obligation to compensate for damage caused by the activity of the public authority[67]). A decision made under such conditions, similarly to the first variant, is usually accompanied by reinforced axiological argumentation present in its justification.[68]

And finally, the third option, slightly different from the two previous ones, creates a relatively limited discretion, but at the same time it is definitely the most common in the practice of applying the law. It consists in the fact that the provisions indicate both legal and extra-legal bases for the choice of consequences, but the entity applying the law, in recognizing the greater importance of the extra-legal criteria for a given decision, applies the extra-legal criteria as the actual basis for the assessment of consequences, which are only "additionally justified" by the legal criteria.[69]

The overlapping of the two bases for the selection of consequences may have different proportions. It may also cause a certain "distortion" of the argumentation of the justification of the decision, which by rationalizing the decision with the use of reinforced axiological argumentation (i.e. by emphasizing the extra-legal bases) may deviate from the actual proportions in the use of both bases in the decision-making process.

(3) The listed types of participation of extra-legal references in creating the basis for the choice of consequences are not uniform. In some cases, the extra-legal criteria take on a decisive role, and may even independently affect the application of a legal sanction in general, and the scope of such a sanction, which is included in the catalogue of sanctions indicated in the legal provision. The application of extra-legal grounds for the selection of consequences does not, however, lead to the imposition of extra-legal sanctions, typical, for example, to political norms or moral norms, which, of course, may appear in some situations as accompanying sanctions (e.g. loss of social prestige, loss of political position), but which are not imposed by the organs applying the law.

67 Art. 417^2 of KC.

68 Cf. SN Resolution of 28 V 1968, III CZP 49/68, OSPiKA 1970, item 118.

69 Cf. SN Judgment of 30 IX 1949, C 1066/49, PiP 1950 No. 3, pp. 118–120.

Chapter V Some comparisons

The functioning of extra-legal references, both in the context of creation and that of application of law, is influenced by various factors, that have impact on both of the above aspects in a different way and on a different scale. It seems that in order to capture the comparative dimension of the analyses and findings disclosed in the previous chapters, it will be reasonable for us to indicate four groups of such factors of different provenance that are influencing the functioning of the references in different ways. The said include: the type of legal culture (allowing for the juxtaposition of the culture of statutory law with other legal orders), the type of social environment of law (leading to the juxtaposition of the democratic system and the autocratic system, also taking into account the specific situation of social and legal change), the structure of the legal system (allowing to reveal the influence of systematics and the type of a normative act as well as the branch of law concerned) and the type of decision-making process (leading to the recognition of the features of the administrative type of law application and the impact of the type of court and court decision).

1. Type of legal culture

The present work focuses on the processes of creating and applying extra-legal references in the statutory law culture, combining its features with the analysis of reasoning and activities undertaken in these processes taking the Polish legal order as the main consideration point. Nevertheless, it seems so, that for the purpose of "comparative signalling," some space should also be devoted to juxtaposing the role of references in other orders of this culture (on the example of the German legal order) with their role in different legal cultures,[1] an example of which may be the *common law* culture and the Far Eastern legal culture presented on the example of the Japanese legal order.

1 As for the differentiation of legal cultures, cf. K. Zweigert, H. Kötz, *Introduction*, pp. 57–67, R. David, *Le grands*, passim. On ground of Polish literature cf. *Główne*, pp. 11 ff., R. Tokarczyk, *Komparatystyka*, pp. 109–152.

1.1 European culture of statutory law (case of Germany)

(1) Owing to the fact that the extra-legal references in the form of general clauses appeared in European civil law codifications in the nineteenth century, it is within this culture that a model and a point of reference for both the creation and application of law should be sought. The most important general characteristics for this order are:

- civilist genealogy of references, however, shifting – from the beginning of the twentieth century – to the regulation and application of public law (especially – constitutional and administrative law, but also criminal law),
- the existence of references not only in democratic but also authoritarian systems, as evidenced by the referrals in the legal orders of the USSR, fascist Germany or the countries of Central and Eastern Europe after World War II,
- different positions of references in systematics of legal act, with the predominance of placing them in general parts of codes or in general parts of the respective chapter, but also present in specific provisions,
- the differentiation of the names of extra-legal criteria and the normative structures in which they appear, with the common occurrence of some names (e.g. good customs, good faith, principles of equity) but also the appearance of "rarer" names (e.g. natural legal principles, principles of proper economy),
- the main focus of referring to social-grounded moral values, leading to balancing the general and the individual content,
- no practice of politicizing references in democratic systems and a different scales of politicizing moral and economic content in authoritarian systems,
- adaptation of references in the international law rooted in this culture, with the example of the references of the European Convention for the Protection of Human Rights and Fundamental Freedoms functioning in the jurisprudence of the European Court of Human Rights.

(2) When we transfer our considerations to the level of the European state, characteristic features can be observed in the German legal order, shaped under the influence of concepts of the *Begriffsjurisprudenz* and the *Rechtstaat*. Breaking through the authoritarian past after World War II, it became an example of a legalistic and rational approach to creating and applying extra-legal references. Although there is no space here for a detailed analysis we still need to signal some of the basic properties.

As for the forms in which the references appear, the German legislator refers to the classic names of the criteria of good faith (*Treu und Glauben*) and good customs (*gute Sitten*), as well as equity (*Billigkeit*), locating them mainly in references of private law.[2] On the other hand it also links the criterion of public interest (*offentliche Interesse*) to the public law, as applicable in administrative law as an element of administrative discretion (*Verwaltungsermessen*).[3] The criterion of equity becomes a determinant of the content of decisions also based on provisions that do not refer to this criterion on their own.[4] In turn, the criterion of justice is related to the content of Art. 20 of the German Constitution, in particular with the principles of *Rechtstaatsprinzip*[5] and *Sozialstaatsprinzip*,[6] but this is not automatic, because it is usually accompanied by an in-depth analysis of the scope of content connections and the role of these criteria in determining the content of the decision, which is typical of legalistic legal culture.[7]

The references that are most characteristic for this legal system are found in civil law. This applies in particular to the criteria of good faith (in the so-called objective sense) and good customs (manners). When we consider the role of good faith (*Treuund Glauben*), the most important function is played by Art. 242 BGB, in which, apart from customary relations (*Verkehrsitte*), it plays the role of

2 Criterion of *Treu und Glauben* appears, among others, in § 242 (scope of obligations of debtor) of BGB, whereas criterion of *gute Sitten* – in § 138 (validity of legal act), and among others in § 817 and 819 of BGB. In turn, the criterion of *Billigkeit* becomes a part of independent reference, among others, in § 15, 660, 920, 1246, 1331 and 2048 of BGB.

3 In relation to that it is emphasized that it is not completely free. H. Maurer (*Allgemeines*, p. 95) writes directly: "*Das Ermessen vermittelt keine Freiheit oder gar Beliebigkeit der Verwaltung. Es gibt kein freises Ermessen.*" The standards of judicial review of a discretionary decision are set out in art. 114 of the German Code of Administrative Procedure, making it possible to control not only its legality, but also, to a certain extent, the purposefulness and legitimacy of issuing the decision itself and exceeding the legal limits of recognition and means of achieving the objective. More on mistakes in making such decisions, cf. R. Alexy, "Ermessensfehler," passim).

4 Cf. F. Henf, *Billigkeit*, esp. pp. 119–181.

5 Cf. e.g. Judgment of German Bundesverfassungsgericht: E 21, 378 ("*Im Rechtsstaatsgedanken ist die Idee der Gerechtigkeit enthalten*").

6 Cf. e.g. Judgment of German Bundesverfassungsgericht: E 59, 231 ("*Das Sozialsstaatsprinzip begründet die Pflicht des Staates, für eine gerechte Sozialordnung zu sorgen...*").

7 This also applies to the role of clauses of § 138 and § 242 of BGB in deciding in issues of public law and their relation with art. 2 of the German Constitution concerning the right to protect personality (cf. e.g. the judgment of German Constitutional Tribunal of 19.10.1993 r. (1BvR 567 u. 1044/89, Juristen Zeitung 8/1994, p. 408 ff., with H. Wiedemann, "Gloss," pp. 411 ff.).

a criterion for qualifying the behaviour of debtors.[8] On the other hand, for the role of good manners (*Gute Sitten*), it is the Art. 138 BGB that is basic, according to which they constitute a criterion for the validity of a legal transaction.[9]

The analysis of content and function of Art. 242 BGB makes us admit that German doctrine and jurisprudence are attempting to specify the meaning of this clause, and even the very meaning of both words considered. The content of this concept is understood as a specific legal and moral principle, leading to the treatment of the case-law based on it as a case-law of equity (the entire rule is similar to the content of Art. 2 ZGB). The scope of this discretion does not, however, clearly depart from the need to take into account also legal arguments when applying this clause ("it does not lead to pure equity" or "equitable recognition"[10]). The effort is aimed at finding an objective measure to determine the values on which the decision is to be based, and the search for the sources of this measure also includes Chapter I of the German Constitution, i.e. internal legal criteria. Fulfilling the content of the norm formulated in Art. 242 BGB involves the "considering" of general and individual interests in relation to the parties to the legal relation. Therefore, the detailed functions of the *Treu und Glauben* clause include: supplementing the debtor's obligations (also "side" obligations, that are not resulting from the contract), controlling the exercise of the right by the creditor and correcting the terms of the contract.[11] Therefore, on the basis of the doctrine and jurisprudence, there are no grounds for perceiving this clause as a specific key that would go beyond legal criteria and principles.

What leads us to similar conclusions is the analysis of the content and functions of Art. 138 BGB, which includes the clause of good morals (*gute Sitten*). Understanding these criteria as a sense of decency, based on justice and equity, does not prevent the need to be cautious in linking its content solely with moral convictions. Rather, it is about the "minimum of morality" (morals), which finds its confirmation in the basic values of the applicable legal order. Also in the case of this clause, the reference to the Constitution (and in particular Art. 2 thereof, setting the standard of personal freedom) is clearly visible. Moreover, there is concern for defining the limits of generalizing the axiological argumentation

---

8 "*Der Schulder ist verpflichtet, die Leistung so zu bewirken, wie Trau und Glauben mit Rücksicht auf die Verkehrsitte es erfordern*".

9 "*Ein Rechtsgeschaft, das gegen die guten Sitten verstosst, ist nichtig*"

10 Cf. *Bürgerliches*, p. 161, K. Larenz, *Methodenlehre*, pp. 404 ff., K. Larenz, *Lehrbuch*, pp. 107 ff., F. Henf, *Billigkeit*, pp. 71 ff.

11 Cf. *Bürgerliches*, pp. 162–163 (with the jurisdiction indicated there).

that can be derived from this clause (since in a pluralistic society the role of the term "prevailing morality" is limited).[12]

Examples of these two clauses, even discussed very briefly, allow us for the conclusion that the "theoretical climate" built on the basis of positivist doctrine and then the works by M. Rümelin[13] and J. W. Hedemann[14] had a limiting impact on the consequences of applying general clauses in private law, being conductive to the legalistic treatment of this structure, the essence of which tends to weaken this legal value. This attitude is further enhanced by an even "stricter" treatment of clauses in the areas of administrative law and, in particular, criminal law.[15]

What is one of the basic issues in administrative law is to determine the scope of administrative discretion (*Verwaltungsermessen*), the role of not fully defined terms within its framework, and the judicial review of the said discretion. Administrative discretion (which is clearly emphasized that this is not a completely unlimited discretion[16]) is treated as an authorization for the administration to act, consisting in selecting from several possible forms of activity the one that best suits the performance of the administration's tasks. The presence of unspecified terms in such authorization means introducing an element of evaluation into a decision-making process.[17] What we should deem as limits for this discretion are those related primarily to the content of Art. 114 of the German Code of Administrative Procedure, which at the same time sets the standards for judicial review of discretionary decisions. The latter, not referring to the control of the purposefulness of issuing the decision itself, consists not only in detecting the exceeding of the legal limits of discretion, but also in controlling whether the purpose of the authorization is properly implemented.[18] This serves

12 Cf. *Bürgerliches*, 81–82 (with the jurisdiction indicated there).
13 M. Rümelin, *Die Billigkeit*, passim.
14 J.W. Hedemann, *Die Flucht*, passim.
15 Cf. F. Haft, "Generalklauseln," passim.
16 Cf. H.J. Wolff, *Verwaltungsrecht*, pp. 136 ff., H. Maurer, *Allgemeines*, pp. 95 ff.
17 Cf. H. Maurer, *Allgemeines*, pp. 99–104.
18 In pursuant to art. 114, the court control has to prove "*ob der Verwaltungsakt oder die Ablehnung oder Unterlassung des Verwaltungsakten rechtswirdig ist, weil die gesetzlichen Grenzen des Ermessens überschritten sind oder von dem Ermessen in einer dem Zweck der Ermachtigung nicht entsprechenden Weise Gebrauch gemacht ist*"; on the topic of different concepts of control of discretionary decisions in the German, Austrian and Swiss doctrine – cf. M. Mincer, *Uznanie*, 117–121, F.O. Kopp, *Verwaltungsgerichtsordnung*, passim.

to distinguish the types of discretionary errors (*Ermessensfehler*).[19] Caring for the precise determination of legal boundaries, types of errors and the scope of judicial control falls in line with the definition of the content of the public interest criterion (*offentliche Interesse*) by the doctrine and judicial decisions.[20]

On the other hand, in the field of public economic law, attention is drawn to a number of forms of administrative activities which are close to informal administrative recommendations. The doctrine resorts to terms such as *Verwaltungsleitung*, *Verwaltungempfehlung*, *Schlicht-verwaltende Einwirkung* or *Nicht-hoheitliche Wirtschaftslenkung* to describe the activities of the administration in this area.[21] The type of economic system, most often referred to, generally speaking, as social market economy,[22] assumes various forms of state (administrative) interventionism also in economic phenomena and processes.[23] These interventions are sometimes justified also with use of referring clauses. For example, in the field of antitrust legislation, the public interest clause may constitute the basis for a decision of the Ministry of Economy, allowing companies to merge despite a different court decision.[24] The decency clause works in the opposite direction, as compliance with this criterion is an element of non-violation of the principles of fair competition.[25] The bidirectional operation of economic law clauses is characteristic of a legal system in which certain economic tasks are performed by the state.

1.2. The references in *common law* and in the Japanese legal order

The nature of the present work prevents a detailed analysis of characteristics of both of these legal orders. They are based on various systems of sources of law, emphasizing either case law or statutory law as the main source. Even with only

19 Cf. H. Maurer, *Allgemeines*, pp. 96 ff., R. Alexy, "Ermessensfehler," passim, E. Eyermann, L. Frohler, J. Kormann, *Verwaltrungsrechtsordnung*, pp. 750–751.

20 Cf. H.J. Wolff, *Verwaltungsrecht*, pp. 123–129.

21 Cf. H. Bauer, *Informelles*, pp. 241 ff., R. Schmidt, *Offentliches*, pp. 494 ff., W. Brohm, "Rechtstaatliche," pp. 133 ff., R. Stober, *Wirtschaftsverwaltungsrecht*, pp. 155 ff., T. Fujita, "Die Rechtsprobleme," pp. 1 ff.

22 Cf. *Wirtschaft*, pp. 3–7; *Besondere Verwaltungsakt*, pp. 729 ff.; R. Stober, *Wirtschaftsverwaltungrecht*, pp. 34 ff.

23 *Besonderes Verwaltungsrecht*, pp. 213 ff.; H. Mossbauer, *Staatsaufsicht*, pp. 194 ff.; G. Puttner, *Wirtschaftsverwaltungsrecht*, pp. 49 ff., 259 ff.

24 Cf. R. Schmidt, "Wirtschaftspolitik," pp. 40 ff.

25 Cf. art. 1 of the Act on Combating Unfair Competition (*Gesetz gegen den unlauteren Wettbewerb*); also G. Leidig, *Dominante*, pp. 107 ff.

scarce common features, they still present a similar position regarding the independent use of social values and norms in decision-making processes.

(1) What is most important for the culture of *common law*[26] is the style the judicial decision is made in,[27] which includes the most important aspects of referring to extra-legal criteria, associated with the assumption that the basic source of law (at least in the field of private law) is a judicial decision (precedent) taken with a significant degree of autonomy in relation to the legislative act.[28] What is more, in the Anglo-Saxon culture, instead of referral in the form of general clauses, a "competitive" order of adjudication arises and functions on the basis of extra-legal rules and criteria in the form of the *equity* system. Since it is not relying, in principle, on legal texts,[29] it shifts the burden of applying these values and norms entirely to the adjudicating entities, which, moreover, corresponds to the general features of *common law*.[30] Therefore, it is not the relation to legislative references that comes to the fore, but the context of axiological judicial freedom, which, in the *equity* order of adjudication, is not tied to normative texts and constructions.

Returning to the clauses, we should state, in the most general terms, that in *common law* culture there was no common practice of referring to extra-legal criteria in this form, patterned after the codifications of continental Europe. While the lack of structure of the clauses is natural in the, as a rule, non-codified civil law, references may appear however in those matters in which there is a legislative form of regulation (i.e. mainly in public law). In the processes of applying such a law, however, specific features of adjudication will come into play, as characterized by the use of a broader discretionary freedom, for example due to a more competitive position of the judiciary in relation to the legislature, and in

26 Cf. e.g. R. Pound, "Common," passim.

27 Cf. e.g. R.J. Aldisert, *The Judicial*, esp. pp. 98 ff., R. Sartorius, "The Justification," passim.

28 Which does not mean that the altering relations between the two legal cultures, which in total lead to the mutual acquisition of a number of properties, do not allow for the extension of at least some observations noted here also to the use of references in Scandinavian, German or French law, which by no means do not belong to *common law* culture, but in which previous court decisions play the role of precedents in determining the basis for making decisions on the application of law (cf. K. Zweigert, H. Kötz, *Introduction*, esp. pp. 284–292, C. Perelman, *Logika*, pp. 104–139, D.N. McCormick, R.S. Summers, *Introduction*, passim).

29 Cf. I.C. Kamiński, *Słuszność*, pp. 80 ff.

30 Cf. e.g. R. Pound, "Common," passim, J. Levin, *How Judges*, esp. pp. 13–104.

particular where a strong line of jurisprudence is formed.[31] Whenever the shape of the law is determined by precedent practice (private law), the use of extra-legal criteria will be associated with references arising in the course of making a precedent decision and disclosed in its *ratio decidendi*.[32] Therefore, what is of greater importance is not the fact of the appearance of a reference in the Act, but rather whether the content of the *ratio decidendi* of the precedent decision considered contains any moral, political or economic criteria, which also appear in a form that is "indeterminate" enough to be treated as extra-legal. Thus, the extra-legality consists in any form of participation of moral, political, economic or custom criteria in a decision, regardless of whether they were previously "announced" by the legislator or not. Owing to the different relations between the normative act and the judicial decision, and in particular due to the possibility of basing the decision only on the previous decisions (without referring to the act),[33] the discriminant of legality related to locating a reference in the provision is omitted.

The effect of the above properties is a "looser" definition of the basis for referring to an extra-legal criterion in the form of either the borrowing of the criterion or its jurisprudence.

We should relate the borrowing of a reference predominantly to a precedent decision, and in the context of the features of such a reference, it is a typical decision-making procedure based on the use of *ratio* in conditions of similarity of facts, which is even an element of the paradigm of applying the law in this culture.[34] Also, the "additional creation" of references (referring to a criterion that was not mentioned in legal texts at all) should be perceived differently, mainly due to the natural reference in the decision to social values, especially in the absence of statutory regulation or precedent. One of the basic theories of precedent – the so-called declarative theory makes such revocation a fundamental argument, since, by protecting against treating the court's decision as an act

31 Cf., J.M. Marshall, "Examining," pp. 55 ff., J.M. Marshall, M.D. Kmetz, G.A. Otstott, "Stare Decisis," pp. 59 ff.

32 Cf.. S. Pomorski, *American*, pp. 45–70.

33 Cf. S. Pomorski, *American*, pp. 71 ff., 90 ff., R. Tokarczyk, *Prawo,* pp. 24–26, A.M. Ludwikowska, *System*, pp. 49 ff.

34 According to the theses of the so-called realists that "actual law" is what the courts decide while what is only regulated by statutes should be treated as "probable law" (cf. J. Frank, *Law*, pp. 27, 32–35, 46, K.N. Llewellyn, *Jurisprudence*, p. 22).

creating a norm, it involves making decisions discovering customary and moral rules accepted in the environment in which the said decision is being made.[35]

The functioning of the rule of "overruling the precedent" may be based on various arguments. The participation of extra-legal criteria cannot be excluded therein, even if this context is not put forward as the main factor of such an operation.[36] The use of these criteria as an element of a *leading case* may form a reaction to changes in social axiology and be associated with different assessments, especially moral ones, with regard to the facts of the present case, which is similar to the facts considered in the precedent. This is done in a softer way than in the statutory law order, because it is usually not associated with a general negation of some values (which happens more often in the case of a legislative reaction), but with the declaration of a different individual assessment, "important" in the case under consideration, which will be used as a precedent. It seems to render it easier to justify decisions that do not have to be "axiologically involved" as it is in similar situations in the statutory order.

(2) The issue of creating and applying the law is different in the Japanese legal order, which forms part of the Far Eastern legal culture.[37] To begin with we should state that the reception of the basic structures of German law to this legal order was characterized neither by the adoption of a legalistic attitude nor the practice of creating and applying extra-legal references.[38]

This legal order is based on three basic features of its social culture: belonging to a group (family, work, social, state), hierarchy within this group and the consensual nature of relations within it, clearly separating the internal (*uchi*) and external (*soto*) spheres of the group. It includes at least three different layers of legal rules: traditional norms shaped in the course of the development of Japanese law, with a significant share of rules adopted from the Chinese law, norms adopted under the condition of certain "coercion" from the Western legal orders (European, mainly German at the turn of the nineteenth and the twentieth centuries and the American after World War II) as well as autonomous

35 Cf. S. Pomorski, *American*, pp. 36–38.

36 A.M. Ludwikowska (*System*, p. 65) indicating the reasons for departing from the precedent, developed by the US Supreme Court (ineffectiveness of a legal rule in practice, failure to bind society with a precedent, incorrectness of the factual premises of a precedent, development of law in similar areas in the opposite direction) does not address the issue of changes in the social axiology accepted by the court.

37 More specifically on this, cf. L. Leszczyński, *Gyoseishido*, pp. 31 ff., pp. 233 ff.

38 More on connections between European legal cultures (in their German version) and the Far Eastern ones (in its Japanese version) cf. S. Ehrlich, "Refleksje," pp. 46 ff.

customary and moral rules shaped in various social groups. As a consequence, within its framework, arguments stemming mainly from legal provisions are often treated as official justifications, on the basis of the content of those traditional and autonomous extra-legal rules that play a decisive role, for the actually adopted solutions. Here the written law might be treated as *tatemae* or *omote* (official view) as opposed to the actual regulators (*honne*, *ura*).[39] In its juridical layer, it is admittedly a system of statutory law, with statutes (*horitsu*) as the basic normative acts, nevertheless it is precisely because of the role of extra-legal rules and the openness of judicial interpretation of law,[40] that it constitutes an order open to extra-legal axiology, and that much more broadly than is the case in European legal orders.

What we find there in the system of sources of law, understood as the basis for decisions on the application of the law, apart from normative acts, is custom (*kanshun*) and *jori*. The latter is understood in the doctrine as, among other things, unwritten law, natural rules or social understanding of justice.[41] It is precisely *jori*, that is quoted in Art. 3 of the Japanese Decree on the Application of Law of 1875 as the criterion for adjudication by civil courts. In the absence of clear legal provisions, the judge may apply customary rules or deduce the basis of decision from *jori*. Even if *jori* is, in practice, not generally treated as the sole basis for the content of decisions made, still the impact of this category on the judge's mindset cannot be underestimated.[42]

Besides, the inclusion of extra-legal references in normative texts, extending the basis for the use of extra-legal criteria in legal transactions, follows European tradition. The Japanese Civil Code (of 1896) refers to such criteria of public interest and good faith as a criterion of exercising the private rights,[43] criterion of good faith as a condition of acquiring the fruits from the possessed thing[44] or criterion of custom in interpreting contracts as long as the parties agree to it.[45] The practice of concluding contracts, correcting their content during their validity (depending on changing social circumstances) and withdrawing from them (for

39 Cf. J.O. Haley, "The Role," passim.

40 Cf. H. Itoh, "How Judges," pp. 780 ff.

41 Cf.. M. K. Young, "The Japanese," p. 28 (a similar role is played by the Chinese category of *li* and Korean category of *ye*; cf. C. Choi, "Ancient," pp. 80 ff.).

42 Cf. H. Itoh, "How Judges," pp. 775–804.

43 Art. 1 of this Code: cf. criteria of public interest (公共の福祉 *Kokyo no Hukushi*) and of good faith (信義に従い誠実に *Singi ni Shitagai Seijitu*).

44 Art. 189 of this Code.

45 Art. 92 of this Code.

the same reasons)[46] clearly indicates that importance is attached to the role of this extra-legal criterion.

One must also notice the institution of conciliation, which evolved for several centuries and which is also conducive to departing from formal arguments. It undoubtedly both influences the attitude of "settling" disputes within the group, and in turn is related to the lack of tendency to submit disputes to courts.[47] This is the clearest example of a "reference" that is as broad as possible both in terms of its content and grounds for application. Therefore, the functioning of the entire Japanese law includes the processes of applying norms expressed in regulations, but also decision-making processes (e.g. administrative recommendations in the form of *gyoseishido*),[48] for which it would be difficult to find a formal normative basis in the meaning of the legalistic legal culture.

2. Type of social and political environment of law

We will present the comparison of the impact of the social environment of law on the use of extra-legal references in this chapter collectively in the form of a summary of the earlier, often quite extensively analysed, features of the judicial practice of courts. Within this framework, we will define the aspects of "measuring" the impact of two main components of this environment: the type of political system (autocratic and democratic ones) and the state of stability confronted with a situation of profound social change.

2.1. The autocratic and democratic political system

When we assume a simplified character of the distinction between types of political systems and the possibility of further nuance of features within them[49] (leading, for example, to distinguishing authoritarian and totalitarian systems

46 Cf. T. Kawashima, "The Legal," pp. 1–20.

47 Cf. S. Ehrlich, "Refleksje," 47, J. O. Haley, "The Role," p. 18, T. Ohta, T. Hozumi, "Compromise," pp. 97–99, M. Yokota, "Japanese," pp. 121 ff., T. Tanese, "The Urbanization," pp. 20–38.

48 Cf. L. Leszczyński, *Gyoseishido*, pp. 81 ff.

49 For example, in the jurisprudence of the European Court of Human Rights, the features of a democratic system are associated with democratic pluralism and tolerance, which were indicated in the interpretation of the "necessity in a democratic society" clause by the said Court (cf. ECtHR Judgment of 7 XII 1976 Handyside v. UK, A.24).

within the autocratic systems[50]), we should state that the extra-legal references are found in both of these two basic types.

As a signal of their characteristics, we can indicate that the democratic type of political system is characterized, among others, by the functioning of the rule of law, an operating system for protection of human rights, being bound by the principles of international law, as well as by social acceptance of the law and the system of power in the state, activity that constitutes a civic society, and, particularly in case of the extra-legal references, recognition of individualism and pluralism of axiological preferences weighed against the social and political dimensions of axiology. In a way, *a rebours*, in autocratic systems we can speak about the lack, or only limited scope, of operation of all the above features.

Since the model constructed in previous Chapters, referred mainly to democratic systems, here, for comparative purposes, we can indicate the most important components of the practice of applying references in an autocratic system (which, moreover, are easy to "reverse" in order to indicate its relationship with the features of a democratic system). Although various features of the political system affect the use of extra-legal references in a different way and to a different extent, they are all related to the dependence or independence of courts from political power.

The relatively greatest influence of these features is related to the determination of the content of extra-legal criteria. The practice of preferring political axiology (both in its ideological and instrumentalized form, sometimes related to completely current political activities, as long as it falls within the framework of the official ideology), independent of the name of the criterion and the form of reference, is the most visible effect of such influence. It leads to the reading of the content of moral criteria in the context of its "fitting" in the official political axiology. This is accompanied by a reluctance to bind the content of moral criteria with the legal principles resulting from the legal tradition in favour of making the content of these criteria dependent on systemic (political) principles, expressed in the normative acts established in this system (and disclosed, for example, in political documents). It manifests itself in the form of the functioning of specific "safety valves" or "meta-clauses" (principles of political system, state objectives) that define the way all other criteria should be interpreted in.

---

50 M.C. Vernon (*Authoritarian*, p. 38) says: "Supreme political authority of one person or a group of persons without being responsible to people under control. No. legal or orderly method of terminating functions short of forceful overthrow." See also A. Gryniuk, *Przymus*, pp. 73 ff

The impact of political axiology also causes that the determination of the moral content itself realizes the preference of the general social dimension of this axiology in relation to individual or group values. The attempts to precise "reading" of the social moral axiology are hampered here, as the autonomous social values seem to remain concealed. For the society in this system is neither active in the expression of its values (since it does not matter much) nor, even if it manifested such a will, can it effectively articulate its preferences under the conditions of the axiological monopoly of official ideology.

Since authoritarianism in the sphere of politics is most often associated with a centrally planned economic system, the influence of political axiology extends to determining the content of economic criteria. Moreover, the very lack or limited role of private economic (commercial) law and its administrative or "quasi-judicial" application thereof,[51] "force" the way the content of economic criteria is determined. The decisive factor here is the perspective of generalizing this content in the form of favouring the interests of the national economy or its planning tasks at the expense of the requirements of rational management or the criteria of fair trade, linking economic and moral content. Only in certain, specific situations of "loosening the regime" are these proportions subject to a certain correction, strengthening the economy of production or trade.

Therefore, there is no doubt that determining the content of extra-legal criteria is the field in which the politicization of the legal order can take place most profoundly, which autocratic systems make use of, regardless of the form of verbal references specified in normative acts. It is a stable trend because autocratic systems usually plan their "development" and even its phases, which does not allow for departing from their assumptions even in situations when they become unequivocally dysfunctional or simply ineffective.

The role of norms reconstructed from extra-legal criteria in building the content of a single norm reconstructed from a provision containing a reference, and in combining these contents with legal criteria as part of building a normative basis of a decision to apply the law is just a derivative of the aforesaid characteristic. In particular, this refers to the politically conditioned influence on the interpretation of legal provisions (which is sometimes a component of the official interpretative rule[52]), to reduction of the role of strictly legal arguments as components of such a norm and such a basis, or to the use of such content-related criteria to adjudge conflicts between legal criteria (between norms reconstructed

51 Cf. Art. 1 of PAG

52 As it occurred in art. 1 of POPC of 1950 or in Art. 4 (derogated in 1990) of KC.

from regulations or even between legal principles). All of them are associated with a greater role of the teleological and functional interpretative rules, which indicate the political arguments contained in them, in the process of interpretation. What is important is that it is not the very essence of these operations but the features of the autocratic system that prove their widespread and deep politicization of the axiology used in carrying them out (as in democratic systems they are associated with the use of moral axiology).

Constructing a normative basis for a decision in this way influences the result of its decisive reduction. This refers to the influence of the politicized content of the extra-legal criteria both on the qualification of facts and on the determination of their normative consequences (which is particularly dangerous when making criminal law decisions[53]).

The influence of the features of the political system on the basis of the application of the reference is relatively more modest, although a certain "validation relaxation" related to the presence of non-traditional components of the functioning of the legal order can be observed. This may be associated with a politically justified invocation of a criterion that is not expressed in regulations or the extension of the scope for borrowing criteria from other parts of the regulatory system. Again, it is not these actions themselves but their political entanglement that determine their relationship to the autocratic system, In addition, the latter is certainly not conducive to referring to international law or foreign law, unless in the latter case it is referring to criteria of a related, and in particular of the "leading" autocratic system.

The characteristics of the autocratic system may, on the other hand, influence the dependence of the basis for the application of the provisions on the content of politicized extra-legal criteria. Despite the overall uniqueness of this procedure, it may still be significant, especially in the first period after the establishment of the autocratic system (constituting a filter for applying the provisions taken over from the previous legal system).

Obviously, when it comes to the above-mentioned elements of the judicial practice of applying the extra-legal references in an authoritarian system, they should be relativized due to degree of dependence of the judiciary on political power. Strong versions of such dependence strengthens all features. On the other hand, each manifestation of independence of judiciary, clearly visible in

---

53 Cf. art. 50 of KK of 1969, indicating criterion of "social danger of the act" (e.g. SN Judgment of 19 IX 1978, VI KRN 238/78, OSNKW 1979, item 9 or SN Judgment of 30 IX 1982, Rw 843/82, OSNKW 1983, item 8)

softer authoritarianisms (such as in the Polish People's Republic), creates a certain margin for weakening the scale of the above effects. The use of referrals by administrative bodies is far more sensitive to the type of political system, even if the autocratic system creates the seeds for judicial control of their activities.[54]

2.2. References in a situation of social change

(1) The distinction between the democratic and autocratic political regime and the centrally planned and market-based economic system related to it does not exhaust all situations of the influence of the social environment on the use of extra-legal references. It is equally important to distinguish between a stable and changing social and legal order. Also in this case, as the model presented in previous Chapters, concerned the condition of relative stability of this order, it is now necessary to indicate the most important differences resulting from the situation of profound change.

Obviously, the depth of social change is gradual in its scope as well as in speed or intensity. It might go in general to autocratic and to democratic direction.[55]

Both directions of change generate different processes, both in terms of creating, and applying extra-legal references. Broadly speaking, they consist in gradually taking on the characteristics of the "target" system. The process of "maturation" may, however, be subject to a certain correction, related to "modification" changes, which can, in a sense, slow down or even halt this process (usually for some time).[56]

The impact of each component of the social environment of the law on the functioning of extra-legal references is a resultant of the legislative policy of

---

54 As it happened in 1980 in Poland, when the limited system of the judicial control of carefully selected administrative activities has been created, in that the review has been exercised by Supreme Administrative Court, acting as the one-instance court (cf. Polish Law of 31 I 1980 on the Supreme Administrative Court).

55 If we applied the model of such a change within the twentieth-century Polish social and legal reality, we may observe the strict autocratic change after World War II, on the one hand, and democratic change after 1989 that relates to the system functioning before World War II.

56 Such a situation of corrective change in communist Poland took place in the mid-1950s (the so-called post-Stalinist thaw) and in 1980–81 (the "Solidarity" period). To some extent, the same type of change (corrective) in relation to being permanently shaped democratic system jas been initiated in Poland in 2015 and is further deepened, but as for now the judiciary, in spite of many legislative interventions remains essentially in its previous (democratic and rule of law) position.

creating reference clauses[57] and their judicial application, nevertheless, in a situation of social change, this relationship is the most sensitive and essential for the legal order. For a change, and a profound change in particular, opens this legal order to extra-legal criteria, and the legislator itself, despite a delayed reaction to some extent, wants to "sanitize" the direction of these changes as quickly as possible and define them in terms of content. In this light, the judiciary openly "weighs" taking into account also the axiology related to the previous order (in the case of a profound change) or the modified order (in the case of a correction change). It does this more clearly, especially in the case of an autocratic change (at least as long as it remains independent), which results from the divergence of the objectives and principles of operation of the legislator and the judiciary. Democratic change, on the other hand, results in a faster and more harmonious change of attitude and openness to a new axiology of both main actors.

(2) The main effects, when the application of references is considered, are caused by profound (deep) social change, which entails transformations of the political, economic and legal system in both possible directions.

The change leading to an autocratic system is usually more abrupt and faster to reach the "planned" (target) effects corresponding to the features of this system also in terms of the use of extra-legal references. Admittedly, one can distinguish between situations in which the intensity and depth of this change makes the judicature quickly and decisively dependent, even if the previous political system was not a democratic one, but only a little less authoritarian[58] and situations where it is not so violent and leads to a certain degree of independence and preservation of the jurisprudence traditions of the previous (democratic) system.[59]

The latter situation took place, among others, in the Polish People's Republic between 1944 and mid-1950s (when the fundamental phase of transformation has ended) could be characterized by such features as:

- use (albeit careful) the formula of making the application of the provisions taken over from the previous system dependent on their compliance with the principles of the political system and the objectives of the state
- the application (for the truth – incidental) of the criterion (the principle of social coexistence) not yet established in the new regulations but already functioning in the USSR system,

57 Cf. I.

58 E.g. in Soviet Russia after 1917, where the new autocratic system (later transformed into the Soviet Union) has replaced the old autocracy (Tsarist' Russia).

59 E.g. in Poland after World War II.

- stronger use of the above open criteria for the interpretation of regulations, both those adopted from the previous, and formed already in the current system,
- abandoning the use of old references in favour of new references that are consistent with the official axiology of the new system,
- a change in axiological preferences, firstly, favouring political values, grounded in the official ideology in any collision with other types of values, secondly, imposing the political context when determining the content of economic and moral criteria, and thirdly, favouring the general social perspective over the individual one, when reading the content of social criteria referring to moral values.

The effects of democratic change are more complex, also because of its usually accompanying "gentleness" and the intention to maintain the requirements of legality in the transition to new forms of jurisprudence.[60]

This also applies to the functioning of extra-legal references, which already at the stage of creating clauses in normative acts often referred to the European nomenclature and construction, resigning (although not always consistently and universally[61]) from the references sourced from the previous formation, albeit not in the form of a "validation filter" in relation to the adopted (old) regulations. To a large extent, therefore, they were the "reverse" of the autocratic change and of the more permanent practices shaped in the autocratic system. Its most important and gradually shaped trends with regard to the use of references include:

- strengthening of the practice of using statutory references (including pre-WWII laws) and (especially after the adoption of the new Constitution of 1997) – constitutional references, at the expense of references contained in sub-statutory and internally binding acts,

60 This is well illustrated by the example of a profound change in the Polish system that has been taking place since 1989, the specific characteristic of which is the "return" to judicial practices from the interwar period (1918–1939), that were "inherited" from the period of German and Austrian partitions (1795–1918) as well as the French law, adopted in 1807. This undoubtedly influenced the jurisdictional "efficiency" of incorporating practices rooted in the cultural tradition of continental Europe. One of the marks of that process is the citing judgments of the foreign courts by Polish courts, mostly the courts of the highest instances (cf. SN Judgment of 26 I 2018, II CSK 191/17, LEX 2455728 referring to judgments of German Supreme Court).

61 Cf. discussion in Poland in the decade of the 1990s of the twentieth century (e.g. A. Tomaszek, "Dobre," passim, L. Leszczyński, "Dobre," passim).

- no attitude of negation with regard to the use of old (but not repealed) references, especially if the way they are applied in the frames of the stable jurisdiction and the content of the criteria themselves might be compatible with the new axiology,
- breaking, if necessary, the continuity when determining the content of old references in the form of a reference to a new axiology shaped on the basis of new references, connected with the European cultural tradition and the principles of international law,
- resignation from politicizing the content of economic and moral criteria and restoring balance in the proportions of the general and individual dimensions when determining the content of moral criteria and taking into account the role of rational management criteria,
- applying the new axiology to interpretation of legal provisions, both with and without a reference,
- combining extra-legal axiology with the classic principles of law of the European legal tradition and with new legal principles, formed both in normative and by judicial practice,
- using the references and principles of the law to correct the judgments of the "old" modified order, that were based on an axiology inconsistent with the democratic and rule of law order,[62]
- expanding the sphere of controllability of the axiological decision-making discretion that appears when applying references, also as part of judicial control of administrative activities,[63]
- reinforcement of the belief that it is necessary to combine the use of a reference with a careful explanation of the facts of the case,
- the dissemination of precedent practice in the context of the use of the methods of functioning of references and the content of extra-legal criteria established in the case law,

---

62 Cf. SN Judgment of 20 IX 1991, II KRN 154/91, OSNKW 1992, item 3 and SN Judgment of 17 X 1991, II KRN 274/91, OSNKW 1992, item 19 (where Court evaluated the former SN decision sentencing strikers against Martial law in Poland introduced in 1981). Cf. also more general statement: "In judgments relating to persons repressed for political reasons, it is possible to recognise that action which is an attempt to oppose the totalitarian system (...) although formally falling within the scope of the criminal law, is not a criminal offence because of the absence of social danger in such action". (SN Provision of 25 IV 1991, WRN 45/91, OSNKW 1991, item 49, p. 20).

63 Cf. (for the judicial control of the implementation of Art. of KPA by administration) SN Judgment of 18 XI 1993, III ARN 49/93, OSNIC 1994, item 181.

- a gradual change in the style of justifying decisions made with the use of references, strengthening the openness and depth of axiological argumentation.

(3) Change of the corrective type within a respective type of political system produces effects that are far less relevant to the use of references. It can also be observed more clearly as part of the correction in the autocratic system, because the very "development plan" of the system is subjected to a certain disturbance, which may lead, for the reasons indicated above, also to changes in the judicial use of references. The democratic system changes in this context much more "gently" or "more difficult" since the autonomy of the judiciary is essentially preserved and consists in the thoroughness of the requirements of a democratic rule of law state. The effects of a correction aimed at restoring certain autocratic features are more complex, as they depend both on its intensity (which may lead to an autocratic profound change) and on the maturity and scope of independence of judicial practice, within which also the use of extra-legal references may be based on lines of case-law based in the legal order thus modified.

The effects of the corrective change, taking into account the above-mentioned situation of the judiciary and the scale of the changes, actually boil down to a correction in determining the content of extra-legal criteria. The other elements of the practice of using references no longer have such significance in the context of corrective changes, even if some differences could be discerned in the opening or closing of the basis for the use of a reference (e.g. the application of a new criterion, contained in a provision not yet in force[64]). Changes in determination of the content of the criteria basically duplicate the changes from the situation of profound change, albeit reaching a clearly smaller scale. This applies both to the impact (depending on the direction of the change) either on the politicization of the content or on the greater content autonomy of moral and economic values, as well as on the correction of the relationship between the dimensions for reading moral axiology. The latter leads either to the preference of the general (public) perspective or to the weighting of the general and individual dimensions in determining the content of these criteria. They can also lead to establishing the relationship between these criteria as well as the relationship between the extra-legal axiology and the axiology of legal principles.

---

64 Cf. SN Judgment of 22 I 1991, WR 420/90, OSNKW 1991, item 44.

3. Place of the references in the structure of the legal system

3.1. Systematics of a legal act

(1) From the point of view of the function of references in the process of applying the law, very important role plays the location of references in the systematics of the act. It might be related to their placement: (a) in the basic "procedural" institution of normative act or in regulations determining the type of reasoning,[65] (b) in general provisions of a substantive law, especially in its initial provisions,[66] (c) in institutions of substantive law that are significant enough to affect other legal relations regulated by this act[67] (d) in the basic provisions for a specific section of a given branch of law (e.g. contract law[68]); (e) in numerous detailed provisions, but in such a repetitive way that it makes a given reference a basic criterion, potentially taken into account in all decision-making processes in a given branch of law,[69] (f) in specific legal institutions, but of such a basic importance for a given branch that the reference criteria are "necessarily" transferred to other institutions, based in some sense on that basic one[70] (g) in such detailed legal provisions that they can be applied mainly in relation to this matter.[71]

(2) The place of the reference in the systematics of a normative act affects the reasoning of the operative interpretation primarily with regard to the determination of the basis for the application of the reference (its direct application, borrowing of a reference either from a general provision, or *per analogiam legis*). It also influences the frequency of application of references in decision-making processes. The latter will decrease as we move from version (a) to version (g), because using the reference will involve more and more specific legal institutions. As we move from (a) to (g), the very basis of the reference also becomes concretized. Variants (a), (b) and (c), and in a sense (d) allow the use of the references

---

65 E.g. derogated provisions of Art. 417 and Art. 421 of KPC or provisions of Art. 7 of KPA and Art. 53 KK of 1997.

66 E.g. Art. 5 of KC, art. 1 of KK of 1997.

67 E.g. Art. 56, Art. 58 or Art. 65 of KC.

68 E.g. Art. 354 of KC (for the law of obligations) or (derogated) Art. 386 of KC for the law of commercial transactions in centrally planned economy.

69 E.g. regulations of Art. 23, 39, 56 or 125 of KRiO where characteristic for this branch of law criteria of "good of child" and "good of the family" appear.

70 E.g. criteria defining the content of the property right in the Art 140 and Art. 144 of KC

71 E.g. the criterion of the scope and use of real easement in Art. 287 of KC or at the criteria of responsibility of the state for the actions of their officials in Art. 417^2 of KC.

referred to therein also in regulations that do not refer to extra-legal criteria themselves (a kind of borrowing references from supplementary provisions). Variants (e) and (f), and to a certain extent (g), in turn, indicate the possibility of analogous use of extra-legal references, based on the similarity between the regulated conditions and legal institutions.

The location of references is also important for determining the content of extra-legal criteria . References in variants (a), (b) and (c) play the most significant role. They also contain references typical for the respective legal system, pointing to the basic values for this system. They define, as a kind of meta-clause, the framework for content of the remaining criteria They trigger the practice of generalizing the content ascribed to them, as long as it is favoured by official axiology. These also more strongly correct the content of the *stricti iuris* criteria, doing it in a general manner, and may also trigger the practice of cataloguing the criteria included in the respective reference, thus confirming their place on the scale significance for the legal order. Finally, they cause the states of axiological "entanglement" of decisions, because the "universality" of their role in decision-making processes requires broader axiological considerations when making decisions. These tendencies play a decreasing role up the moment, when variant (g) of locating references is reached.

As regards the role of references in the process of interpreting legal provisions, the location of the reference in variant (a) may define it as a criterion forming a basis for refusing to apply a provision or as a component of an official interpretative directive,[72] which does not mean that any other location does not increase the overall role of open axiology rules in an operative interpretation.

3.2. Type of normative act

Another element of the systemic analysis of the functioning of general reference clauses in legal transactions is the context of the type of legal act, in which the references are formulated, which is primarily related to their different legal force. Taking into account the fact that the model functions of references, as analysed in the previous chapters, are related to their statutory location (and their location in codes in particular), certain differences in their application should be related to the presence of references in the constitutional regulation, as well as in executive acts and internal acts.

72 Cf. Art. 1 of POPC of 1950 or Art. 4 (derogated) of KC.

(1) As for the effects of the localization of the constitutional extra-legal references with regard to the basis for their application, they focus, among other things, on:

- the width of the scope of application, covering the entire legal order, resulting from treating these references as the most general in the scale of the entire system,
- the use of these references by variety of courts – from the constitutional court to regular and administrative courts (in various scopes of their jurisdiction, generating various detailed dependencies),
- the limited role of references as a criterion for the constitutionality of statutes, not acting independently, but as an additional argument to use in this role constitutional provisions or previous decisions of the constitutional court,[73]
- the possibility of common courts and administrative courts to apply either only a constitutional reference (based on the principle of direct applicability of constitutional norms) or a constitutional reference together with a statutory reference.

When it comes to determining the content of constitutional references, the following are of the greatest importance for judicial practice:

- emphasizing the public dimension of axiology, with the possibility of a greater preference for political values than in private law (what depends on the type of political system),
- the impact of the content of constitutional references on the content of statutory references through supplementing and modifying their specific content,
- weighing the axiological content of constitutional and statutory references, with a model preference for the content of constitutional references in the process of resolving conflicts between these references,
- clear linking of the content of constitutional references with the constitutional principles of law, resulting in the widening of the "axiological margin" between legal and extra-legal axiology.

(2) A completely different perspective on the implementation of references may result from the presence of references in executive acts and internally binding acts. Their presence itself raises some doubts from the point of view of the

73 Cf. TK Judgment of 17 VI 2014, P 6/12, OTK ZU 6/A/2014, item 62 (where criterion of principles of social justice played minor role) and TK Judgment of 12 VII 2012, P 24/10, OTK-A 2012/7/79 (where the content of these principles had been analysed quite precisely and finally compared to the content of the principle of equality).

legislator's "axiological rationality," not to mention the potential effects in the context of the coherence of the legal order. It is important because such acts, forming the domain of administrative law, are mainly used in the administrative type of law application, which, from the point of view of the use of references, cannot be fully controlled within the continental model of judicial review of administrative activity. The latter feature does not relate to the basis of the use of a reference, especially since these references coexist in the decision-making process together with statutory references. On the other hand, it concerns the determination of the content of the referrals that falls outside the scope of judicial review. This is because this does not eliminate the decision-making freedom of administrative bodies justified by the implementation of public objectives, also when judicial control includes the assessment of the compliance of this content with the legal principles, which determine the criterion of such compliance,
Evidently, the detailed arrangements should be relativized in the context of the type of acts of this group. This is because the situation is different with regard to the use of references contained in ordinances as acts directly related to the statute in the form of special delegation, and differently with the use of references contained in internally binding acts, regardless of their nature and the scale of "autonomy." This also applies to managerial actions that "force" the decision-maker to "operating" (discretionary) treatment of the referral criterion (e.g. as means for managing a workplace). The use of correct criteria, regardless of whether they form a component of a reference or simply result from the pragmatics of management, becomes a determinant of the rational and effective management, thus eluding the classic properties of using extra-legal references.

3.3. Type of branch of law

3.3.1. Branches of the domestic law

(1) The type of branch of law is undoubtedly one of the factors that deeply differentiate the use of extra-legal references. This is related in particular to the differences with regard to the subject and methods of normative regulations, which could already be observed when analysing the processes of creating reference clauses.[74] The branch perspective also allows us to notice the genesis of extra-legal references, significant features of the evolution of their forms, and their transition from private law to public law, which significantly affects the processes of their application.

---

74 Cf. I.

The context of the genesis of extra-legal reference in the form of general clauses links our analyses with the use of referrals within the private law[75] as the main point of consideration, supplementing them with comparative threads with the broadly understood public (administrative and criminal) law.

Comparison of the processes of using references in civil law with analogous processes in the application of constitutional law and administrative law should constitute our starting point for the comparative analyses. The issue of applying constitutional references has already been manifested when indicating the impact of the type of a normative act,[76] and moreover, it will be included in this analysis to the extent that it is related to the use of references from other branches of law. On the other hand, the signalling of the distinctness of the application of administrative law references will be presented within the framework of the comparisons based on the type of decision-making practice distinguished in the structure of the present chapter.[77]

(2) The basic component of the comparative analysis at this point is the perception of differences within criminal law, mainly through the prism of their juxtaposition with the features of the application of civil law. Speaking in the most general manner, however, references in criminal law do not play a role that would comparable to that of private law, mainly due to the greater dimension of legalism and the operation of *nullum crimen* and *nulla poena* principles.

In criminal law, there is practically one reference in the form of social danger or social harmfulness of an act, which, having the feature of gradation (significant or negligible degree), may play an important role both in the qualification of the facts and in determining the criminal sanction. Even if it is not possible to base a positive qualification decision solely on this extra-legal criterion, it may play a practical role of a criterion excluding liability or constituting the basis for discontinuation of the proceedings. These criteria, on the other hand, may play the role of one of the components (and therefore not acting independently) of the directive on the selection and on size of a criminal sanction, and it is here that the above-mentioned gradation is of paramount importance.

The basis for the application of this criterion, which is a model related to the implementation of a legal provision, usually located in the general part of criminal codification (so that it can be applied in all regulated cases), does not

75 Cf. e.g. S. Grzybowski, "Struktura," passim, E. Łętowska, "Funkcjonowanie," passim; A. Stelmachowski, "Klauzule," passim; M. Safjan, "Klauzule," passim.

76 Cf. above: 3.2.

77 Cf. below: 4.

change substantially. On the other hand, it is characteristic to determine the content of such a criterion, which by pointing to social axiology does not exclude it from being associated with political interests and goals (or politically justified economic interests), which is made possible especially by the term "danger" (and which in practice of the autocratic order also applies to qualifying acts as crimes[78]). Against this background, the term "harmfulness" is less exposed (although it cannot be entirely excluded) to such associations because of the greater "measurability of the effect." We can observe it, among others in practice to indicate the factual circumstances, which then lead to the derivation of such and not another assessment.[79]

Nevertheless, this does not mean that the above criteria cannot coexist ("overlap" in terms of their content) with other references containing separate extra-legal criteria.[80] It is noticeable when combining them with the criteria of political and economic interests of the state or social good, which turn out to be easier to "operationalize."[81] Moreover, criminal courts may also apply the criterion of the principles of coexistence[82] and the criterion of public interest[83] as auxiliary criteria for assessing behaviour, and the considerations of equity may be important as a criterion of the scope of penalty.[84]

(3) Another component of our comparative signalling must recognize the specific features of the use of references in branches directly related to civil law, which concerns family law, commercial law and labour law. It must also be stated right away that there will be more similarities to the general model based on classical civil law than distinctiveness, especially since these branches are not completely separated from civil law in every legal system (this applies, in particular, to family law). This results in interchangeability of references at the level of legislation and application of law in all these branches.

---

78 Cf. SN Judgment of 18 XI 1993, III ARN 49/93, OSNIC 1994, item 181.

79 Cf. (on the social danger) SN Resolution of 25 VI 1980, VII KZP 47/78, OSNKW 1980, item 65 and (on the social harmfulness) SN Judgment of 13 VIII 1979, Rw 267/79, OSPiKA 1981, item 54.

80 E.g. Art. 130, 132, 135, 179, 194, 195, 246, 271 of KK of 1969.

81 C.f. SN Judgment of 17 V 1979, Rw 146/79, OSNKW 1979, item 93 and SN Judgment of 21 IX 1981, I KR 171/81, OSNKW 1981, item 65.

82 Cf. SN Judgment of 14 I 1953, KO 221/52, PiP 1953 No. 7, pp. 138–9 or SN Resolution of 18 X 1973, VI KZP 37/73, OSPiKA 1974, item 34.

83 Cf. SN Provision of 4 XII 1951, I K 202/51, PiP 1952 No. 2, pp. 350–51.

84 Cf. SN Provision of 21 X 1953, II KO 43/53, PiP 1953 No. 12, pp. 913–14.

With regard to the basis for the application of reference, an important feature that connects these branches of law is the referring, in decision-making practice, to the most extensive references of the classical civil law. This happens regardless of whether or not an explicit provision indicating the appropriate application of civil law "allows" it, or whether there is no such authorization, and regardless of whether identical or similar references are included in the regulations of these branches or not.

We can observe certain differences in determining the content of references and differentiating the role of individual types of axiology.

The distinctness of family law relations connects its content primarily with moral axiology. There is no spontaneous reference to political and economic axiology here,[85] although in an autocratic system it is possible to give some political context to extra-legal criteria.[86] Nevertheless it remains characteristic that the typical references in family law (good of child[87] and good of the family), often find "support" in constitutional principles, especially in the context of revising the *stricti iuris*[88] criteria. However, this has no implication on determining the special meaning of the references. Neither does it change the general model of the impact of references on individual arguments of the operative interpretation.[89] The application of the references in family law is therefore much more uniform than in other branches of law. All this seems to stem from the limited effects of legal regulation in such an autonomous area of social relations as family relations.

The above remarks are generally valid with regard to the application of commercial law, which is in fact private economic law. This is especially true of the basis for the use of references and the use of the criteria of classical civil law. However, what plays the role of moral axiology in determining the content of extra-legal criteria in this branch is the economic axiology pointing to the market dimension, the clearest manifestation of which is, for example, using the criterion of the company's interest.[90] It can also be combined with moral axiology,

85 In the PRL in relation to the socialist system, this practice was additionally reinforced by the argument that the importance of the property factor was lost in this sphere of social relations.

86 Cf. SN Resolution of 30 IX 1976, III CZP 97/75, OSNCP 1977, item 83.

87 Cf. K. Hanas, "Interpretative," pp. 187 ff.

88 Cf. SN Resolution of 24 II 1978, III CZP 4/78, OSPiKA 1979, item 3.

89 Albeit the completely unique possibility, at least in our legal practice, of departing from establishing the objective truth when negating motherhood or fatherhood due to child welfare criterion (cf. SN Judgment of 14 II 1969, I CR 570/68, OSNCP 1969, item 186).

90 Cf. E. Rott-Pietrzyk, "Interes," pp. 6 ff.

which is revealed in the criterion of the principles of social coexistence and good customs in commercial law.[91]

Relatively the greatest number of differences occurs in the application of references in labour law.[92] This is mainly due to the "quasi-hybrid" nature of this branch, which is located on the border between private and public law. Hence, despite the duplication of certain constructions of civil law (e.g. as to the role of references in establishing the fact of abuse of law) and indicating the appropriate application of civil law, there is a more public, and certainly more general social dimension to the references of labour law.[93]

Among the functions that the general clauses play in labour law, one can distinguish, among others, determining the scope of exercising rights in labour relations, determining the manner of fulfilling obligations in the said relations, shaping the content of legal action and limiting the operation of *stricti iuris*[94] norms. Therefore, these functions are extensive and qualitatively significant, resembling those that we encounter in civil law. Only in insurance relations, for example within the framework of disability insurance relations, a stricter implementation of the letter of the law is usually required, which limits the determination of their content on the basis of inherently unmeasurable criteria.[95]

3.3.2. International law

(1) Signalling the specific characteristics of the use of references should also include international law. The presence of extra-legal criteria in Art. 31–33 of the Vienna Convention on the Law of Treaties, formulating interpretative directives, assume their wide application in the interpretation of this law, both in the case law of international courts and domestic courts applying this law.[96] This is particularly so, since their role is enhanced by the role of universally recognized principles of international law, which, on a much larger scale than in the case of state law, are located outside the normative text, thus broadening the dimension of the "axiological margin" that connects both types of axiology.

---

91 Cf. K. Kopaczyńska-Pieczniak, "Dobre obyczaje," pp. 93 ff.

92 Cf. A. Kosut, "Dbałość," pp. 107 ff.

93 What was a characteristic clause was the referral to the good of the workplace from art. 12 (derogated in 1996) of KP.

94 Cf. T. Zieliński, "Klauzule generalne w prawie," pp. 141 ff.

95 Cf. SN Judgment of 5 V 1981, I PR 38/81, OSNCP 1981, item 224.

96 Art. 31 of VCLT .

(2) The case law of the ECtHR offers us a good field for the observation of specific features of the role of references. It applies the references contained in the ECHR relating to the interests of national and public security, legitimate public interest, public order, the country's economic welfare or morality, as well as to the criterion of "necessity in a democratic society," which is the most characteristic of this system.[97] It is characteristic that all of them constitute a criterion for Court's consideration of Member-State actions limiting the fundamental standard for protection of the right to respect for private and family life (Art. 8), freedom of thought, conscience and religion (Art. 9), freedom of expression (Art. 10), the right to assembly and association (Art. 11), as well as the right to respect for property (Art. 1 of Protocol I) and the freedom of movement and choice of place of residence (Art. 2 of Protocol IV).

These criteria are applied (either alone or in conjunction with relevant references to domestic law) both by the ECtHR and by courts of the parties to the Convention, adjudicating under domestic law on the violation of these rights by the organs of that state. This extends the scope and basis for the application of these references, both in the subjective and objective context (their relation to references in domestic law concerning the protection of human rights), even though the Court maintains a certain distance from the domestic legal order of the states that are parties to the Convention, as regards reaching to referrals from their law.

The most important features of the ECtHR's jurisprudence practice are related to determining the content of the extra-legal criteria indicated in the Convention. These include:

- prudence in determining the universal content of the above-mentioned criteria,[98] connected with the belief that the authorities of the states-parties always have better possibilities to decide on their content in the conditions of

97 Cf. B. Liżewski, "Klauzule," pp. 191 ff.

98 This does not mean a complete lack of formulation of repeating criteria that all constitute the notion of public interest. This criterion is very broad, and its components in jurisprudence include various goods, from e.g. care for the economic development of the state (ECtHR Judgment of 9 XII 1994 Stran Greek Refineries v. Greece, A.101-B), socio-economic development of the local community (ECtHR Judgment of 25 IX 1996 Buckley v. UK, RJD 1996), order in the recording of names (ECtHR Judgment of 25 XI 1994 Stjerna v. Finland, A:299-B)) or protection of the freedom of speech (ECtHR Judgment of 24 II 1994 Casado Coca v. Spain, A:285-A) including in particular the activities of the press (ECtHR Judgment of 26 XI 1991, Observer and Guardian v. UK, A-216).

the respective country, and the findings of the Court itself may only be auxiliary or even secondary in their character,[99]

- the lack of practice of generalizing their content, which means the concretization of the basis for assessment by linking the meaning of these concepts with the given factual conditions,
- no practice of politicizing and ideologizing the content of these criteria,
- comparison of the scopes of general and individual (public and private) interest, so as to find a meaning that would properly weigh both interests,[100]
- weighing the axiology of references and the axiology of universally recognized principles of international law,[101]

---

99 This is how the quite recent statement of the ECtHR should be understood, that the national authorities have a certain margin of discretion in determining what is in the public interest and it is up to them to make a preliminary assessment as to the very need to take this criterion into account and how to apply it. This is so because the notion of public interest, extensive in its character, always requires us to consider the political, economic and social questions, and beliefs concerning these may differ, with the state authorities conducting their own policies in this field. Only the lack of *reasonable foundation* in determination of content of this. criterion justifies the interference of the Court (cf. ECtHR Judgment of 25 IX 1996 Buckley v. UK, RJD 1996)

100 E.g. the reference to the protection of the right to privacy (cf. § 44 of ECtHR Judgment of 25 V 1994, Keegan v. Ireland, A.290) and § 31 of ECtHR Judgment of 27 X 1994, Kroon and Others v. Netherlands, 197-C) dealing with protection of an individual against arbitrary action by public authorities). Lack of "*fair balance*" between public and private interests becomes a violation of art. 1 of Protocol no. 1 (respect for the right to property, cf. § 69 of ECtHR Judgment of 23 IX 1982 Sporrong and Lörnoth v. Sweden, A.52). Cf. also the weighing of both these criteria – of public and general interest. In the case of James and others v. UK (ECtHR Judgment of 21 II 1986, A.98) the Court distinguished between the two interests, pointing out that the public interest may affect even a relatively small part of society and yet play a significant role as a criterion for assessing the conduct of state authorities, while the general interest, by its very nature, concerns the impact on the situation of the largest possible number of social groups ("many thousands and millions"), therefore determining its content must be based on taking into account this wide range of impact. The detailed criteria of the general interest in the interference with the respect for the right to property may include, among other things: the method of taking over property by the state, supporting social justice through reasonable compensation to the owner for the acquired property. Cf. also M.A. Nowicki, *Europejska*, pp. 251, 281, 291–298.

101 While discussing art. 1 of Protocol no. 1 of EKPC it is also worth to briefly mention another clause, which, albeit it does not have the character of extra-legal reference, still refers to criteria that are general enough. It is the criterion of "general principles

- associating axiological arguments with estimated references, also in cases when they are not formulated in the text of the Convention (e.g. important and sufficient reasons[102] or reasonable and objective justification[103]).
- the specific axiological involvement of the ECtHR's decisions and their justifications resulting from the above-mentioned characteristics (although also found in adjudication by national courts), which also results from the much stronger axiological dimension of human rights as a juridical structure than in other matters.

What is the most characteristic reference of the Convention is the clause referring to the criterion of "necessity in a democratic society."[104] Although this reference does not take the verbal form of the typical extra-legal reference, as found in national legal orders, it is functionally a general reference clause and a partially a reference to an estimate (as to whether something meets the requirements of "necessity"). This phrase has been the subject of numerous interpretations by the Court. The practice of determining the meaning of this clause is related to both moral, political and economic criteria. Explaining the concept of "necessary in a democratic society" is based on a linguistic analysis of both the word "necessary" (in the context of its juxtaposition with related, but separately understood terms: indispensable, admissible, ordinary, useful, reasonable, desirable[105]), and "democratic society," for which the most important values are pluralism and tolerance.[106] It seems that the Court (and the Human Rights Commission operating until 1998) attach much greater importance to the linguistic interpretation of individual components of the names of the reference than is the case in the application of national legal references. Its jurisprudence defines the word "necessary" with the emergence of a pressing social need, as long as the intervention itself is proportional to the legitimate aim.[107] However, teleological and functional interpretation dominates in determining the content of the entire phrase, taking into

of international law," the fundamental matter about which is the scope of application and relation to the criterion of public interest.

102 Cf. § 88 of ECtHR Judgment of 24 III 1988, Olsson v. Sweden, A.130), § 88 of ECtHR Judgment of 7 VIII 1996 Johansen v. Norway, RJD 1996), § 64 of ECtHR Judgment of 16 XII 1992 TPC-Niemietz v. Germany, 251-B.

103 Cf. ECtHR Judgment of 2 III 1995 McMichael v. UK, A:307-B.

104 Cf. e.g. L. Leszczyński, "Kryterium," pp. 48–53.

105 Cf. § 48 of ECtHR Judgment of 7 XII 1976 Handyside v. UK (A.24).

106 Cf. M.A. Nowicki, *Wokół*, p. 238.

107 § 67 of ECtHR Judgment of 24 III 1988, Olsson v. Sweden, A.130, § 70 of ECtHR Judgment of 29 X 1992, Open Door & Dublin Well Woman v. Ireland, 246-A.

account the objectives of the interference and the necessity and proportionality of the means applied to achieve the objectives.[108] Thus, even in this reference, it cannot be stated that the content of the reference was over-generalized. It is so, since the latter is always determined in the context of a specific facts of the case.

The content of Art. 8–11 of the Convention "sets" the practice in such a way that this criterion is taken into account, whenever assessing whether the state's interference with the above-mentioned rights was justified. Determining the content, therefore, always has a political context (which does not mean the politicization of the content of the criteria), as it is connected with the possible transgression of the sphere of the discretion of state authorities[109] and the protection of the public interest by state authorities. In this way, both of the criteria (necessity in a democratic society and public interest) overlap, which forms the basis for their joint application in the individual decision-making processes. The public interest justifies the state's interference with the rights granted by the Convention, while "necessity in a democratic society" is the criterion for assessing these actions by the authorities on the part of the Commission and the Court of Human Rights. In view of the above-mentioned limited role of the Court in determining the content of the public interest, the factors taken into account by the Court include the importance, objectivity and justification of the interest invoked by the intervening State.[110] It is also in this case that we can notice that the Tribunal recognizes a better position of the state in defining the basis for the actions of its authorities,[111] despite the need for a very strict translation of extra-legal criteria related to the possibility of abuse of references by individual states.[112]

---

108 Cf. § 53 of ECtHR Judgment of 22 X 1981 Dudgeon v. UK, A.45, § 42 of ECtHR Judgment of 6 IX 1978 Klass and Others v. Germany, A.28.

109 The mere fact that the state authorities do not exceed the sphere of recognition is treated by the ECtHR as a condition for observing the rule of law. "It would contradict the rule of law, if the authorization to decide within "free discretion" given to administrative bodies would manifest itself in completely free power" (Cf. ECtHR Judgment of 25 VIII 1984, Malone v. UK, A 82: cf. also M.A. Nowicki, *Wokół*, pp. 230 ff.)

110 Cf. § 53 of ECtHR Judgment of 26 IV 1979, Sunday Times v. UK, A.30, § 35–36 of ECtHR Judgment of 24 V 1988, Müller and Others v. Switzerland, A.133 and § 66 ff. of ECtHR Judgment of 26 XI 1991, Observer and Guardian v. UK, A.216.

111 Cf. § 48 of ECtHR Judgment of 7 XII 1976 Handyside v. UK, A.24.

112 Cf. § 59 of ECtHR Judgment of 26 IV 1979, Sunday Times v. UK, A.30.

4. Type of decision-making practice

The use of extra-legal references also depends on two additional factors related to the characteristics of the decision-making process itself, as well as its result. The first is related to the type of decision-making process, while the second – to the type (subject and instance) of court and the type of court decision.

4.1. Type of law application

Distinguishing between the judicial and extrajudicial type of application of the law, allowing for the administrative type (as the basic one) to be distinguished within the latter,[113] draws our attention to the properties of using extra-legal references by administrative bodies. Overlapping with the influence of the features of administrative law as a kind of public law, it supplements the influence of the structure of the legal system, and especially its branch division, on this process.[114] It also allows us to see the specificity of using references in specific branches or sub-branches (such as tax law and public economic law) of administrative law being the broadest, most diverse and most complex branch of law.

(1) The basis for the use of a extra-legal reference in the activities of an administrative body does not undergo any fundamental change from the point of view of the need to refer to the provision of administrative law containing the clause. The system of sources of this law, however, expands the catalogue of types of normative acts, including executive acts and internally binding acts,[115] thus generating various application relationships of such references with statutory or constitutional references (in its part regulating the structure of the state apparatus). It is of particular importance in the light of the lack of codification of substantive administrative law, which causes the "scattering" of the effects of legislative activity. Due to the width of the subject that this regulation, also the horizontal relations between the provisions of various sub-branches of this law, provide much wider possibilities for joint application of references located in different parts of the regulatory system, despite the limited role of borrowing them *per analogiam legis* (due to the domination of ordering norms in this law). In this context, the basic act authorizing the

---

113 Cf. W. Dawidowicz, "O stosowaniu," passim, J. Zimmermann, *Motywy*, pp. 14 ff., W. Lang, J. Wróblewski, S. Zawadzki, *Teoria*, pp. 411–414.

114 Cf. above: 3.3.

115 Cf. above: 3.2.

use of the reference structure is the Code of Administrative Procedure (KPA). Although it covers all the basic elements of the activities of administrative bodies, it also opens the possibility of loosening the rigors of establishing the grounds for applying the referral clause to the subject of the decision-making process.[116]

We should also remember that a reference in the application of administrative law may be an element of using the construction of administrative recognition (*Verwaltungsermessen*), which, by overlapping two sources and methods of application or decision-making, only from the second half of the twentieth century, is based to some extent on legal criteria.[117]

Moreover, contrary to judicial competences, the competence of far more diverse administrative bodies is not always specified precisely, and may also be general (e.g. resulting from task standards), which significantly broadens the possibilities of these bodies to refer to extra-legal criteria.

Significant differences in the use of the construction of references are related to the determination of their content by the administrative authority.[118] The most important properties in this area, strongly susceptible to the type of political system, include:

- determining the content of extra-legal criteria in the perspective of an axiology appropriate for the implementation of the objectives and tasks of the public administration (depending on the type of political system and the scope of the state's organizational and regulatory activity),
- stronger generalization with less interchangeability of the content of references, reducing the number of criteria to a few of the most important ones (public or social interest and the interest of the citizen or of the party) and allowing for their mutual complementation,
- the practice of weighing the general dimension of the indicated interests by juxtaposing them, depending on the type of political system, in either symmetric or asymmetric manner (with the domination of the general interest in the autocratic system),

116 Cf. KPA containing many references to both of these "interests" (in its Art. 7, 154 or 155) as well as to other criteria (e.g. – to criterion of "important interest of state" in Art. 74 and Art. 161 or to criterion of "public order" in Art. 107).

117 Cf. e.g. G. Schmidt-Eichstaedt, "Ermessen," passim, H. Ehmke, "*Ermessen,*" passim, H. Izdebski, *Historia*, pp. 49 ff., esp. pp. 63–84, M. Mincer, *Uznanie,* esp. pp. 45 ff. Cf. also NSA Judgment of 19 I 2021, I OSK 2310/20, CBOSA.

118 Cf. M. Wyrzykowski, *Pojęcie*, passim.

- the possibility of politicizing the moral (social) and economic axiology, the scale of which will also depend on the scope of the authoritarianism of the political system, and the scope of central management within the economic system.

What we should point out in the context of judicial control of the administrative application of law, is its limited scope, resulting from the control model based on the criterion of legality of the decision-making process and the administrative decision itself. However, the scope of this control is expanding (which is particularly noticeable in the event of a profound democratic change) to gradually cover also discretionary decisions[119] that may grossly violate the law, also if the extra-legal reference was incorrectly applied when issuing them.[120] However, the most important change affecting the understanding of the consequences of the public-law nature of administrative law is the influence of judicial control on establishing the appropriate relationship between the public interest and the individual interest, which is balanced in a democratic and rule of law state, in the form of an indication of the lack of space for the "mechanically and rigidly understood principle of the primacy of the general interest over individual interest."[121] Nevertheless, it is not the control of the determination of the content of the criteria, but the control of the basis and method of application of the reference that is the subject of the administrative court's reaction to the application of references by administrative authorities.

(2) The administrative decision-making type also applies the part of the administrative law (*sensu largo*) that includes tax law.[122] Its certain distinctiveness results from the lesser meaning of extra-legal references than in general administrative law as means of legislative expression, operating essentially with orders. The extra-legal references of this law, focusing on the criteria of public interest, social interest, but also the important interest of the taxpayer, party or addressee, allow for value weighting, the result of which depends on the type of

---

119 Cf. M. Mincer, *Uznanie*, pp. 112 ff; cf. also VI.2.2.

120 Cf. NSA Judgment of 25 XI 1994, SA/Wr 2146/94, ONSA 1995, item 107 and NSA Judgment of 24 II 1995, III SA 767/94, ONSA 1995 item 46.

121 Cf. SN Judgment of 18 XI 1993, III ARN 49/93, OSNIC 1994 item 181 (p. 73).

122 They are subject to procedural regulation in tax ordinance (cf. A. Hanusz, P. Krukowska-Siembida, "Ważny," pp. 181 ff.

political regime. The participation of evaluations in determining the meaning of legal concepts and terms[123] is also visible.

The type of political system also determines the characteristics of the use of references under public economic law.[124] Market mechanisms not only strengthen the dimension of economic rationality as the most general criterion, but also limit the role of the administrative type of law application, shifting it towards judicial application, or at least a wider judicial review of administrative decisions. Economic criteria thus acquire, also in this type of economic law, somewhat similar to commercial law, an ethical dimension, which is implemented in the functioning of the criteria of good customs (morals). However, the decisive factor here is the criterion of public interest,[125] apparently adhering to the matter regulated in this branch of law.

4.2. Type of court and decision of the court

(1) Recognizing the issue of the scope of judicial control of administration in the context of the use of extra-legal references allows us to return to the judicial use of references, which is the fundamental point of reference for their functioning in the legal order.

The basic factor determining the efficiency of this activity is the maturity of judicial practice, which in the culture of statutory law should be understood as the development of sufficiently durable and elaborated ways of applying legal norms. This includes a necessary degree of independence in relation to the legislator in the sense of developing their own methods of reasoning and argumentation. There is no doubt that it remains decisive for the use of references. The degree of this maturity depends on many factors, including the degree of complexity of the decisions made, influencing the acquisition of experience or the type of court and its instance position, the type of composition of the court or the type of court decision.

A mature, strong and independent judicial practice will use the construction of references more boldly, and the general clauses themselves will influence the reasoning in the process of applying the law as an element that actually supplements or corrects the arguments arising from norms reconstructed from

123 Cf. criteria of "public interest" and of "important interest of taxpayer" (Art. 22, 240, 253 of OP) as well as of "social interest" (Art. 234 of OP).
124 Cf. E. Komierzyńska, M. Zdyb, "Klauzula," pp. 161 ff.
125 Cf. e.g. TK Judgment of 8 IV 1998, K 10/97, OTK ZU 1998 No. 55 item 363 or TK Judgment of 14 VI 1999, K 11/09, OTK ZU 1999/5/97.

legal provisions. In this case the axiology of clauses will be a strongly manifested one, clearly declared and effectively competing with *stricti iuris* criteria, not only serving as an argument strengthening the justification, or even more so as an "axiological ornament." In its entirety, such a practice therefore takes into account axiological arguments stemming from the basic principles of the legal system or its main parts and the socially established values, i.e. those that are sufficiently visible, named and defined in the socially dominant hierarchy of values. The conformity of the reading of values and the actual social preferences to which the clauses refer is not a defining feature of the maturity of the practice, although, and in a general nature only, it is conductive to shaping this maturity. This is because it is certainly related to the content of the decision built on the basis of an extra-legal reference.

The self-formed way of applying clauses will be similarly "strong." It may, evidently, be different in various branches or legal institutions, but uniform within these branches or institutions. The specific degree of uniformity in the application of clauses is probably the clearest sign of such maturity, which is associated with not exceeding the scope of the accepted decision-making discretion, both in terms of the content of the decision and the manner in which the references are applied. This does not necessarily conflict with "bold" exploitation of the discretion, wherever it is foreseen and can be rationally justified.

It is evident that this maturity is shaped within the framework of the necessary permanence of the law, especially if it takes place in a democratic system based on the rule of law. Each social change, especially a profound one, requires some time for this maturity to take shape, although also in this matter a democratic change has much better prognosis than an autocratic one.

(2) The practice of applying the construction of extra-legal references demonstrates differentiation in the judicial type of application of law,[126]

126 Outside the scope of this work, therefore, are the differences in decision-making process undertaken by bodies such as, for example, disciplinary commissions, which also adjudicate within the framework of a judicial type of decisional process, without fully fulfilling all the characteristics of a situated subject. Important in this context is the jurisprudence of the ECtHR in connection with Article 6 ECHR, in which the concept of due process of law also refers to decision-making by various other organs of Member-States to the Convention (cf. Cf. ECtHR Judgments: of 23 VI 1981 Le Compte and Others v. Belgium, A.43, of 8 VI 1976 Engel and Others v. Netherlands, A.22 and of 28 VI 1984 Campbell and Fell v. UK, A.80).

depending on the place of the adjudicating court in the hierarchical organization of the judiciary. Even if it is considered that the type of composition of the court is also important, especially the participation of the so-called social factor, its effects are not comparable with those resulting from the use of references by courts of various instances.

Speaking in most general terms, any possibility of instance control, even regardless of the perception of one's own legal knowledge and experience, is an element of self-limitation of this discretion.[127] The decision-making freedom is markedly better visible in the highest instances. Usually, also the content of the justification of the decision also changes there, developing the axiological argumentation. It concerns in particular the issues of determining the content of extra-legal criteria, also dependent on the subjective reading of the extra-legal axiology.

Higher and the highest instances can also "afford" to generalize the content of the criteria. The less general (abstract), and more strictly related to the elements of a specific facts of the case, determination of the content of the respective extra-legal criterion is additional element of this caution of lower instances in this respect,[128] further correlated with the failure to apply a reference where the higher court deems it necessary.[129] The inclusion of referrals in the decisions of lower instances is also more often referred to the *stricti iuris* criteria, and the most common "cautious" search for a common direction of evaluation, where the extra-legal criteria would constitute an additional criterion, supporting legal arguments. This is perceived by these courts as, as it seems, a safer, from the point of view of judicial structure, form of applying references than treating the extra-legal criteria as the sole basis for their decisions. The Supreme Court often indicates that regular courts could more clearly, in the circumstances of a given case, give an advantage to the extra-legal arguments,[130] On the other hand, if the content of the decision "must" be based on an extra-legal criterion, common courts seek at least to strengthen

---

127 Cf. SN Judgment of 9 V 1973, I CR 242/73, OSNCP 1974, item or SN Judgment of 18 V 1978, II CR 130/78, OSNCP 1979, item 101.

128 Cf. e.g. SN Judgment of 22 VIII 1968, II CR 318/68, OSPiKA 1969, item 201.

129 Examples can be given of decision-making processes in which the clauses are not used by the ordinary (lower) court, but are used by the Supreme Court in appeal procedure (cf. SN Judgment of 12 XI 1974, I CR 602/74, OSPiKA 1976, item 143 and SN Judgment of 18 V 1978, II CR 130/78, OSNCP 1979, item 101).

130 Cf. e.g. SN Judgment of 16 I 1969, I PR 434/68, OSPiKA 1969, item 258.

their axiology by supporting the basis of adjudication with other extra-legal arguments, not necessarily referred to by the applicable provision.[131] This does not mean that the Supreme Court cannot assess that the lower instance court incorrectly determined the content of the extra-legal criteria (leading to the indication of different content thereof[132]) or that the use of the reference was incorrectly justified.[133]

(3) Certain decisions of the Supreme Court and the Supreme Administrative Court also shed different light on the application of references. Generally speaking, the form of decisions influences the way in which references are applied, indicating their most modest influence when issuing formal decisions (provisions), greater – when issuing judgments, and the greatest – when issuing resolutions.

Resolutions of the highest court instances, which are adopted in extended panels (7 judges, entire chambers, combined chambers or full court) occupy a special place. This form of "judicial legislation," that becomes binding, to a certain extent, for other courts and other formations of the court, follows requests that may raise questions about the participation of extra-legal referrals in the decision-making process. In principle, this does not apply to open-ended questions concerning the content of the criteria, although it does happen so that they lay out their own understanding of this content in order to obtain confirmation of its correctness.[134] More often the question concerns the role of the criterion in the decision-making process,[135] and the effects that referrals may cause to the disposition of a decision addressed to specific addressees in particular.[136] Questions concerning, for example, the principles of social coexistence relate both to the issue of the possibility of applying this criterion in a given decision-making process (whether something "is subject to assessment" or "can be assessed" from the point of view

---

131 Cf. e.g. SN Judgment of 2 VI 1966, II CR 167/66, OSNCP 1967, item 65.

132 Cf. SN Judgment of 14 XII 1973, II CR 692/73, OSPiKA 1975, item 94 and SN Judgment of 16 I 1971, III PZP 47/72, OSPiKA 1973, item 242 or SN Judgment of 7 I 1972, I CR 12/71, OSNCP 1972, item 135, SNC-231, w. z SN Judgment of 9 V 1973, I CR 242/73, OSNCP 1974, item 91.

133 Cf. SN Judgment of 22 VIII 1968, II CR 318/68, OSPiKA 1969, item 201 or SN Judgment of 6 IV 1978, IV CR 523/77, OSNCP 1979, item 34.

134 Cf. SN Judgment of 8 XII 1951, C 1191/51, PiP 1952 No. 8–9, pp. 364–6.

135 Cf. e.g. SN Judgment of 21 III 1975, I PR 27/75, OSNCP 1976, item 13.

136 Cf. e.g. SN Judgment of 19 V 1981, III CZP 18/81, OSNCP 1981, item 228.

of respective criteria[137]) or the relationship between such a criterion and the established facts.[138]

The Supreme Court often assesses the legitimacy of such questions. For example, it indicates that the question is too general and lacks sufficient description of the situational context of the use of the reference[139] (sometimes the Supreme Court independently determines the most important elements of the actual situation, on which the use of the formulated answer depends[140]). The effect of this state of affairs may be to answer only the part of the question that does not relate to the reference.[141] But also in a situation, where the question is too detailed it may fail to receive an answer with an indication that the question does not formulate a legal issue at all, but a request to resolve a specific case.[142] We also encounter a specific "escape" of the answer from the problem of referral, which is expressed in taking only the legal arguments ("failing to notice" the reference in the question[143]) or a particularly cautious answer, usually expressed in a conditional manner ("could mean," "may lead to") and making the content of the reference dependent on other phenomena.[144] Sometimes a general statement is combined with quoting exceptions that could help the questioning entity in qualifying a given factual state.[145] The most accurate answers are to those questions that contain a proposal (suggestion) for their own solution to the problem, for example in the form of an independent analysis of the elements of individual extra-legal criteria, and which, additionally, discuss the essential elements of the actual state in the context ("in the language") of the proposed extra-legal criteria. This is because they make it possible to provide an answer that will be sufficiently concretized for the needs of the respective decision. This does not mean, however, that sometimes the answers to such formulated questions, may elaborate

137 Cf. e.g. SN Judgment of 7 I 1972, I CR 12/71, OSNCP 1972, item 135.
138 Cf. e.g. SN Resolution of 18 VII 1969, III CZP 44/69, OSNCP 1970, item 4 and SN Judgment of 13 X 1981, I CR 336/81, OSPiKA 1982, item 70 or SN Judgment of 12 XI 1971, III PZP 36/71, OSPiKA 1973, item 4.
139 Cf. e.g. SN Resolution of 30 I 1976, III CZP 95/75, OSNCP 1975, item 158.
140 Cf. e.g. SN Resolution of 2 IX 1977, I PZP 51/77, OSPiKA 1978, item 99.
141 Cf. e.g. SN Resolution of 1–15 XII 1951, C 15/51, PiP 1952 No. 12, pp. 887–91.
142 Cf. e.g. SN Resolution of 20 V 1966, III PZP 6/66, OSNCP 1967, item 5.
143 Cf. e.g. SN Resolution of 15 XI 1968, III CZP 104/68, OSNCP 1969, item 154.
144 Cf. e.g. SN Provision of 3 IV 1969, I CR 171/69, OSPiKA 1970, item 222.
145 Cf. e.g. SN Resolution of 22 IX 1972, III PZP 12/72, OSNCP 1973, item 22.

on axiological issues, which makes it much easier to take decisions in similar cases, not only for the court submitting the question, thus constituting a kind of shaping the jurisdictional line.[146]

146 The analysis of the relationship between different judicial instances should not ignore the no longer existing (since 1990) institution of guidelines on the interpretation of law and judicial practice (until 1985 – guidelines of the administration of justice and judicial practice). They constituted an essential element for unifying the practice of applying the law by the Polish Supreme Court, also in the context of using the structure of extra-legal references. These guidelines, as not being a decision on applying a legal norm, were not of a court type, but of managerial style in applying the law. By relating not to a specific decision-making process, but to the entire practice of applying formally interrelated norms, they expressed the "policy on law application" agreed by the Supreme Court. These were thus the element of the above-mentioned "judicial propriety" in the reality of socialist legal system. Their binding character gave them additional meaning and strengthened the political element (in terms of the policy of applying the law, but also in the sense of taking into account official political values) in the actions of the courts. What was characteristic for them was also the place the extra-legal references held there. One can distinguish two ways in which the references are included in the guidelines. The first one is to gather different extra-legal criteria in the "preface" to guidelines, which was to point the attention to the social importance of the analysed legal question. Sometimes such a "preliminary" reference to extra-legal criteria was enough, because in the further (basic) part, they were not analysed anymore (cf. e.g. SN Resolution of 18 III 1968, III CZP 70/66, OSPiKA 1968, item 151 or SN Resolution of 29–30 IX 1966, III PZP 28/66, OSPiKA 1967, item 1). This was, by far, not the dominant manner. The second and typical way for using extra-legal criteria in the guidelines was a detailed analysis of the entire text of the guidelines of the role and content of the respective extra-legal criteria in the application of a given norm or, which was more often the case, a whole group of norms of a given legal institution (cf. e.g. SN Resolution of 19 XII 1972, III CZP 57/71, OSNCP 1973, item 37 or SN Resolution of 9 VI 1976, III CZP 46/75, OSNCP 1976, item 184). This analysis was carried out from the viewpoint of objectives or functions of the legal institution, and frequently connected with relation to the systemic principles, or even directly to the state policy concerning the respective social relations. The general content of the guidelines sometimes heightened the impression of politicization of legal norms or the politicization of the moral and economic criteria referred to in these norms.

Chapter VI Functions of references and their optimization models

1. Functions of references (the issue of dialogue between legislature and judiciary)

The universality and basic nature of these functions rests in that they appear in the legal order, albeit to a different extent and depth, regardless of the political or economic system and other features of the social environment of the law, as well as regardless of the type of branch of law, of the kind of normative act and of provisions that contain such clauses, of the type of law application and even the type of judicial decision. They also appear irrespective of whether the reference clauses act independently from the *stricti iuris* criteria, or whether they act in conjunction with these criteria, "merely" supplementing, modifying or correcting them.

1.1. Opening ("deformalizing") the content of the law

(1) The most general and perhaps the most fundamental effect of the formulation of reference clauses is the deliberate and explicit opening of the content of the law (the content of legal norms) to values and judgments that are not incorporated into the legal system. It happens regardless of the intentions behind the formulation of clauses in legal texts. By the very fact of referring to these values in the form of a clause, these values do not become *stricte* legal values. Being an element of the legislative policy, they are only an expression of the legislator's intention to include them in the processes of applying the law as an element of decision-making reasoning and argumentation. Without becoming part of a legal norm they still result in application of a legal sanction (sometimes even determined by these criteria).[1] In the context of the evolution of the content of the law as a whole, they may also become an element of the axiological foundations of changes in the content of the law without changing the content of legal provisions.

Observation of the role of judicial and administrative practices renders it possible to unequivocally establish that the law applying authorities are the primary addressees of extra-legal references. The legislator, as the addressee of

1 Cf. J. Wróblewski, "Concepts," passim.

constitutional reference clauses concerning legislative activities, only seems to be an "additional" addressee of these. Such an addressee is neither the legal doctrine, the role of which in determining the meanings and functions of clauses cannot be underestimated, but which, nevertheless, lacks means for exerting direct influence. The so-called ordinary addressee can be given greater significance. For it, reference clauses may become a component of a directly formulated pattern of behaviour (e.g. in a norm indicating that a legal act contrary to the principles of social coexistence is invalid) or of a "indirect" pattern (e.g. from the norm ordering the administrative authority to take into account the legitimate interest of the citizen). Courts (and, to a certain extent, administrative authorities) are the primary addressees here because they establish, in a binding manner (even if only for a specific case), the content of the extra-legal references. As long as they outline decision lines, they decide about the perpetuation of this and no other way of applying referring clauses and the "climate" that will be associated with the use of clauses. It is the courts that are thus authorized to classify the behaviour of ordinary addressees and determine the legal consequences thereof.

(2) Opening the content of the law means the transfer of some responsibility for this content from the legislator to the legal practice, making decisions on the application of the law also on the basis of criteria indicated in reference clauses under the conditions of a decision-making discretion. It is so, because a properly constructed normative basis for the judicial decision, although it only concerns a specific decision-making process, may nevertheless become an element of the decision line, which in turn, also in the absence of the *stare decisis* rule and widespread *per rationem decidendi* reasoning, becomes a component of "soft" precedent practice in the statutory legal order.[2] Since this line will depend on open criteria present in reference clauses, not only does the independence of legal practice increase, but also the degree to which it determines the content of the law and is socially perceived as an essential component of it. The legislator formulating the clauses either directly creates such role of practice or "only" accepts it, but it must agree to it as the least.

This does not necessarily entail recognition of the law-making nature of decisions based on reference clauses. Doubts as to the theoretical and legal qualification of a particular decision-making process from the point of view of granting it law-making features[3] do not favour such qualification on the part of

2 Cf. L. Morawski, M. Zirk-Sadowski, "Precedent," pp. 219 ff.

3 Cf. R. Dworkin, *Law's*, p. 407 (underlying the role of the courts and the judges), M. Zirk-Sadowski, "Tzw. prawotwórcza," pp. 255 ff., A. Stelmachowski, "Prawotwórcza," passim, L. Morawski, *Główne*, pp. 183 ff., 197 ff.

the legal doctrine. Courts (not to mention administrative bodies) also defend themselves against such qualification of their decisions, which can be seen in justifications (motives), cutting themselves off from "judicial law-making." However, the increased role of this case law cannot be overlooked when applying the clauses. There are many intermediate states and situations between creating a new norm in the form of a court decision and the application of the norm, which indicate an increased or diminished role of the decision maker. In this context, recognition of the law-making character is simply not required to functionally define the increased role of the practice of applying the general reference clause in deciding on the content of the legal order (as it is perceived by the addressees of norms).

(3) When we return to the issue of the legislator's liability in this context, we can speak of a shift to legal practice only of a part of it. This is because the legislator, by creating reference clauses, does not and cannot shed all responsibility from it. It is so because the use of clauses is an element of legislative policy, with specific particular substantive objectives behind it. Therefore, the legislator's responsibility consists, firstly, in the ability to predict the effects to which the practice of creating clauses in the given social and legal reality will lead to, and secondly, on the proper binding of these effects as means for achievement of the said substantive objectives (independently from the fact that these objectives may also be the subject of evaluation and liability).

The most general requirement for the legislator is to attempt to limit the negative consequences of the application of reference clauses already at the stage of creating the law. No. contemporary legislator is able to achieve it on its own. Hence, the transfer of a part of the responsibility related to the functioning of reference clauses to legal practice should also be understood in the way that a mature legal practice (including administrative) should contribute to an efficient, rational, and also free from dysfunctional factors and socially acceptable operation of the law containing extra-legal references. The manner and frequency the clauses are applied, determination of their content, the style of justifying their application, etc., then become an essential part of the practical legal discourse.

1.2. Extending the decision-making discretion in applying the law

(1) The widening of the discretion in the processes of applying the law is related to the extra-legal and general nature of the reference. This contributes to the achievement of the flexibility of the law application processes assumed by the legislator when resorting to the use the construction of reference clauses. In the consequence, legal transactions, and then the entire legal order, are subject to a

specific "deformalization" in the sense of weakening the role of intra-legal values and loosening the rigorism in applying *stricte* legal requirements.[4]

The use of the term "extending" and not "creating" the decisional discretion is accompanied by the belief that it may arise naturally or intentionally (consciously). Its inevitability results from the very nature of the process of applying the law, i.e. making a specific and individual decision based on a general norm, from the vagueness of legal language terms and the asymmetry of the static moment of the provision's creation and the dynamics of changes in the social environment. The effects of intentional construction can its scope "only" extend further.

The scope of this extension depends, among other things, on the degree of vagueness of the direction of evaluative choices, as signalled in the general clause. The name of extra-legal criteria contained therein does not trigger the interpretative task of establishing such precise linguistic meanings as it is in the case of other legal terms. However, the very fact that the legislator names various extra-legal criteria in different ways in different acts and branches of law, makes treating their names at least as a guideline towards the axiological choices. It cannot, of course, be targeting a specific assessment. On the other hand, it is an orientation towards the type of value as the basis of choice, which in relation to a specific act of evaluation plays the role of either moral, political or economic criterion (the same applies to the reference to customs, except that it does not refer to values). However, the legislator wants to attach some importance to the name of the referring clause, even though the boundaries between the types of values are not strict, and the division itself is not separable and exhaustive. After all, it does not formulate one reference for the entire legal system, which of course would extend the scope of the discretion even further. Nor does it formulate even a single reference solely for a given branch or legal institution. It wants to differentiate the references themselves, although not in every case we can consider such a terminological differentiation justified. It is clear, however, that this way of formulating clauses, having the features of a general reference, without prejudging specific assessments, expands (in a controlled manner) the decision-making freedom in applying the law based on other sources.

(2) The fact that the attention of all addressees of legal norms is drawn to extra-legal criteria causes a specific "climate" for weakening the role of intra-legal

---

4 What creates the problem of relations between judicial activism and passivism (cf. L. Morawski, "Stressing," pp. 47 ff.) as well as possible misuse of discretion (cf. L. Leszczyński, "Open," pp. 52–55).

values. This applies to both the value of legalism in the creation of legal norms and the value of legalism, certainty and uniformity in the application of legal norms, especially those containing reference clauses.

The most general consequence of extending the decision-making discretion by referring to extra-legal criteria is making the decision-making process of applying the law more flexible. Flexibility is the value most closely related to the functioning of reference clauses. It must be assumed by the legislator if it is guided by the elementary requirements of rationality and foresees the effects of its actions. At the same time, the flexibility of law application, being a procedural value, does not in any way prejudge the specific objectives of using clauses in law-making practice. Therefore, it is very "convenient" for the legislator, who may thus and with the same justification for creating references associate them with various substantive content (and even influence their realization). The flexibility of law application, corresponding to the individualization of decision-making processes, results in the flexibility of the law itself, understood as a uniform system of organization and control. Flexibility simply weakens this uniformity of legal content. However, it may contribute to strengthening the adequacy of the law and its application to social needs, which is a highly desirable effect.

Taking into account the classification of aspects of judicial discretion proposed by B. Hoffmaster,[5] the use of the construction of extra-legal references in the judicial decision-making process should be connected with the obligation of the judge to consider the use (but not the mere use) of extra-legal criteria in every case where the applied legal provision contains a general referral clause. It is valid even if the parties do not invoke it (although such invocation reinforces this obligation). This means that in each such case the judge must consider referring to them when constructing the content of the decision and using them as arguments to justify the decision, especially if they were applied. However, this should be done with the awareness of the need to always link this content and extra-legal argumentation with the assumption of the existence of legal standards (e.g. intra-legal axiology in the form of principles of law). It is they that define the scope of judicial discretion in the use of extra-legal references, without actually eliminating it (if only because they are also subject to interpretation), shaping together with the doctrine and judicial practice (expressed by precedents and lines of case law) the feasible uniformity of judicial reasoning. Although the use of extra-legal references makes it significantly more difficult (if not impossible) to assume the existence of only a correct and just judicial decision and the reality

5 Cf. B. Hoffmaster, "Understanding," pp. 26 ff.

of the pursuit of such a decision in the light of the established facts of the case in a given process of applying the law, the reality of this pursuit (despite the lack of grounds for denying the need for the efforts themselves in this regard) with the use of extra-legal references can only be considered in the context of "fitting" within these standards, prevailing doctrine and sustained jurisdictional practice.[6]

(3) The "deformalization" and liberalization of the application of the law are visible in the individual reasoning and argumentation in the decision-making process and the operative interpretation of law. The decision-making discretion extended in this manners concerns actions in the phases of validation, of reconstruction arrangements and of the construction of a normative basis for judicial decision, and even, to a certain extent, as part of establishing facts of the case. This also affects the style of justifying decisions, in which the proportions of use of arguments resulting from legal provisions and from the extra-legal arguments provided in the reference are changed.

What is important, is that the explicit, deliberate and targeted decision-making discretion, caused by the very structure of reference clauses, simultaneously becomes both controllable and realistically controlled phenomenon in the course of judicial practice as a whole. This creates not only the likelihood of standardizing the practice of applying references, but also a non-accidental and balanced "measuring" the desired scope of the decisional discretion in applying the law.

1.3. "Axiologization" of the process of applying the law

(1) The decisional discretion, flexibility and individualization of the clause application processes, deformalization of the law and its application, as well as the extra-legality and generality of referencing are related to saturation of the law application process with values determined by the content of extra-legal criteria. This axiological entanglement is presupposed and manifests itself in every action

---

6 The discretion thus defined in the case of the use of extra-legal referrals approaches (although does not always equate to) the "measurements" of that discretion established in B. Hoffmaster's classification as the situations indicated in Ic, IIb, IIIc, IVb, Vc, VIb, VIIa, VIIIb, IXb, Xb, XIb, XIIa, XIIIa, and as a negative response to the thesis in XIV (cf. "Understanding," pp. 28–30). As for comparison, the typology of decision-making situations developed by M. Król (cf. "Pojęcie," pp. 69 ff.) based on the nature and degree of decision-making discretion allows to treat the discretion connected with the use of reference clauses as an essentially undetermined decision-making situation, the essence of which is closest to weakly bound discretion.

in the process of applying norms. It is then fully visible in the justification of the decision, in which the axiological arguments stemming directly or indirectly from the reference clause may play a leading role in "relaxation" of *stricti iuris* rigors.

First, however (i.e. before the given facts become the subject of a decision of the application of the law), the criteria of extra-legal references axiologize the grounds for the behaviour of the so-called ordinary addressee of a legal norm. The presence of a reference in the norm, which formulates a pattern of behaviour, primarily affects those behaviours that are related to the implementation of the rights granted to the addressee or the scope of the addressee's obligation resulting from conclusion of legal acts (i.e. where the addressee "has time to think" about the consequences of its behaviour). However, this has no direct impact on those activities in which compliance with the norm is not the result of a direct "tactics" (e.g. when committing an unintentional offense)

Reference clauses, becoming a criterion for granting rights or determining a given scope of a legal obligation in legal transactions, affect the addressee's behaviour either directly (e.g. if it considers whether the concluded legal act is consistent with the principles of social coexistence) or indirectly, by anticipating the reading of references by a court or administrative body that later decides to apply the law. In the latter case, it may be a referral addressed to both ordinary and qualified addressees, as well as one referring solely to the manner of making decisions by a state authority.

(2) The axiologization of the process of applying the law is most visible in determining the content of the reference and the extra-legal criteria contained therein. The wording of the referring clause, regardless of its name and the type of criteria invoked, always triggers the statement of the assessment (with one exception though – provided it is not a reference to custom). It may be an assessment of a specific nature, related to a specific facts of the case (this is especially the case when the clause is combined with an estimate, by nature directly related to these facts), but it may also be an assessment abstract in its nature, detached from the immediate grounds and premises of preferring certain phenomena and states of affairs (e.g. when the subject applying the law attempts to determine the basic proportions or types of values with which the respective clause is associated). While in the former case, the decision-making entity will usually try to verify the assessment, in the latter case – paying attention to actual social preferences does not have to come to the fore. The context of generalization may also be different. Sometimes an individual point of reference will be more significant, another time – a supra-individual perspective, linked with some understanding of the social interest, either group or maximally generalized

collective interest. It depends on many additional factors which vary these detailed functions decisively.

The saturation of the process of applying norms with axiology in the case of the use of reference clauses is a feature so common that it takes place virtually regardless of the actual name of the general clause itself and the type of value to which the said clause refers. It cannot be determined with certainty that referring to the principles of coexistence or good manners triggers a greater saturation of the decision-making process, and the very decision, with evaluations than referring to good faith or social interest. The axiology of reference can be measured on a general scale (of some typical type of value) and on a specific scale, not always coinciding with the general scale, which further enhances the axiological "instability." Hence, the organs do not always try to establish the specific content of the criteria.

It also remains uncertain (although the scale of uncertainty is slightly smaller here) what kind of criteria will be applied in the act of applying the given reference clause. If we were to stick to the generally vague and non-disjunctive division of these criteria into moral, political and economic ones, then they would be among those clauses which refer beyond all doubts to political criteria (e.g. objectives of the state) or to economic criteria (e.g. interest of company), but with most names of criteria, interchangeability and overlapping types of values are still possible. For example, the principles of social coexistence or good manners are associated in their "basic content" with moral criteria, but this does not lead to the conclusion that it is impossible to read them "politically" (determine their content in accordance with the dominant political assumptions) or apply them in qualification of states arising in the course of trade (e.g. in good commercial practices). It is in particular the possibility of using political judgments to determine the content of moral and economic criteria that seems obvious because of their strongest nature (which can be seen in the case of a conflict of values). As regards the type of criteria, the name of the referring clause only "orientates" axiologically as to the indication of their type. It is by no means an infallible indicator as to the specific content of the reference.

Regardless of the above properties, it must be stated that the type of value with which the referencing clauses most often associate are moral values. This is not contradicted by the fact of the construction of clauses in public law, which also refers to the basic political criteria, or the fact of the politicized use of clauses in all branches in autocratic legal systems. The corrective function of clauses in relation to the content of the law is most strongly associated with moral values. This is evidenced by, for example, the traditional relationship between the processes of applying reference clauses and *equity* jurisprudence, which is, in a way, a method that is competitive for the traditional decision-making. Equity as the most general extra-legal criterion, is the value with which the use of clauses is most directly related in spite of fact, that except for a few cases, lawmakers do not often refer directly to equity as a separate criterion. It can be said that it "works" in the process of applying clauses through other, more directly indicated criteria, constituting the "ultimate" basic point of reference.

(3) The axiologization of the legal order in the form of extra-legal references causes a conflict of values to be inscribed in the essence of the decision-making process. Regardless of how closely the legislator tries to specify a given reference, the assessment derived from the respective criterion will form a specific combination of individual preferences of the decision-maker (in collective decisions this additionally overlaps with the interactions of these preferences), of group preferences (e.g. a "model judge" acting under given conditions) and of an intuitive reading of social preferences, which are juxtaposed (often in a collision convention) with the intra-legal axiology. It is characteristic that as we move from individual to general social preferences, regardless of the difficulties in grasping preferences that would be genuinely preferred by the entire society, the "certainty" of reading even only partially objectified values will clearly decrease.

The axiological complexity of the judicial decision taking into account the extra-legal reference, and particularly the freedom in determining the specific content of the reference, does not mean, however, that the general "line of assessment" and decision-making resulting from the use of clauses becomes unpredictable. We can even state that the maturity of the practice of applying the law causes greater predictability of the application of references and the determination of their content. It becomes further enhanced, when it is accompanied by a democratic social and political environment and minimum of a legalistic approach of state bodies and society to the role of law as a means of control. This is because it is a guarantee that the axiology of extra-legal references will, in its essential content, be still consistent with the basic legal axiology. General meta-clauses acting as a general framework of axiological choices, or rather as specific "safety flaps" protecting the legal order from troublesome "deviations" in individual decision-making processes, that would otherwise make it difficult to keep its unity, work more efficiently in such situations. These roles are partially played by the guiding legal principles, formulated especially in the initial parts of the constitutions, codes and basic laws from the point of view of the construction of the state legal system. It is also impossible, especially in contemporary conditions, to negate the role of the basic regulations of international law, the axiology of which probably most closely corresponds to the axiology that democratic legislators would like to observe, in referring to the classical principles of law and the values contained therein.

This last thread transferred our considerations, perhaps quite unexpectedly, to the internal axiology of law. We are dealing with a situation in which the construction of a clause, which by definition refers to extra-legal criteria, reduces the meaning of these criteria to the most fundamental values of the legal order. In other words, it is a situation where the structure referring to extra-legal criteria results not only from the widening of the discretion, but also, paradoxically in part, may result in its limitation ("controlled" extension). There is probably nothing surprising in this, as it meets the requirements of an axiologically rational and effective legal order. The legislator expects to base the decision on the application of reference clauses on the fundamental legal axiology, assuming that the practice of applying the law will not "break" the unity of the legal order or render it dysfunctional. This is also expected by the "self-limiting" practice of law application concerning the use of discretionary power, which assumes that not so much the legal system (regulation system) as the legal order (rules taken into account in decisions on the application of law) is rational, e.g. means that there are axiological assumptions at its foundations, at least in terms of their basic content, which are also important for determining the content of extra-legal criteria. Finally, this is also expected by the addressees of the law, who may perceive the extra-legal references as a forecast of use, in the judicial decisions, of evaluations that were shaped in the social life independently from the lawmaker, but at the same time they also expect uniformity of such evaluations. The latter has the greater chance of realization if the basic core of evaluation choices in the decision-making processes of applying the law is closer to the basic legal values.

1.4. Review of detailed interpretative functions of extra-legal references

One may gather detailed functions of reference clauses in relation to the process of application of law, specifying the above-discussed general functions of extending the decisional discretion and its axiological dimension. They relate to all reasoning and actions at the individual stages of operational (mostly judicial) interpretation and constitute a summary of the findings presented in the previous chapters.[7]

In this context, we should not forget that the open criteria may, to some extent, influence the fact-finding process,[8] located essentially outside the operative

7 Cf. II–IV.

8 Cf. II.1.1.

interpretation. These criteria may become: (a) a component of evaluative reference clauses, requiring also its assessment to fully establish the fact (e.g. the reason is to be valid, the diligence is due or special, etc.), (b) a component of the free assessment of evidence, especially when it requires a certain axiological interference to determine their decision-making role, and (c) which, however, is very rare, a component of the general clause that makes it impossible to reach the procedural truth (as is the case with the best interests of the child in relation to the determination of parentage).

The essential functions of references can be related, first of all, to the reasoning undertaken at particular stages of the operative interpretation.

Within the framework of the findings of the orientation phase,[9] the referral criteria, without playing a basic role, may, however, contribute (together with the legal axiology criteria) to the initial assessment of the respective case as deserving legal protection ("worth initiating a trial").

The problem of establishing the basis for the application[10] of a reference is far more complex. It includes: (a) the general relationship between the basis for the application of a reference and its presence in a directly applicable specific legal provision, located at least at the statutory level or in an executive act based on a statute, (b) – the possibility of indirect use of a reference contained in the applicable general provision of a given act, branch of law or even the entire legal system (e.g. in a constitutional provision) or international law (e.g. ECHR) and the supranational one (e.g. EU law), c) – the possibility of "borrowing" a reference *per analogiam* from another specific provision, related in content to the applicable provision, (d) the possibility (careful and requiring good justification) of detaching the test of the applicability of the reference and the legal provision in the form of the application of the reference from provisions not in force (already or yet) as well as provisions of non-binding foreign law, (e) no possibility of "additionally creating" the reference (extra-legal criterion) by means of court decisions.

Reference clauses may also, to some extent, affect the basis for the application of other carriers of law, including legal provisions, including those that contain references.[11] It may consist of: (a) indication of a criterion causing the refusal to apply, in the respective decision-making process, an applicable (not repealed) legal provision (with or without a reference) which applies usually to provisions

9 Cf. IV.2.
10 Cf. II.
11 Cf. IV.3.

adopted from the previous (i.e. preceding deep social change) legal order, (b) the role of (solely) modifying the basis for the application of "old" principles of law or earlier decisions on the application of law.

The wording of the reference in the legal provision necessitates the establishment of the content of the open (extra-legal) criteria contained therein and the reconstruction of the pattern of behaviour expressed therein.[12] It consists in: (a) identification of facts (e.g. customs) and values (e.g. common good, good of child) and norms having an axiological justification (e.g. rules of equity, principles of coexistence, principles of justice), (b) introducing extra-legal axiology to the process of operative interpretation by assigning political, economic or, in the broadest scope, moral content to the axiological criteria, (c) determination of the human-general, general-social, group or individual perspective for the "dimension" of values and moral norms associated with the particular criteria, (d) inclusion, in the process of determining the content of the relationship between the values of one and different kinds, or mutually supporting ones (also "against" the *stricti iuris* criteria), which leads to establishing their total content or content conflicts between them, that require resolution, (e) juxtaposing the content of extra-legal criteria with legal axiology expressed by principles of law, also potentially leading to a joint content of both types of axiology, or resolution of collisions in their content, (f) normativization of the content of extra-legal criteria in the form of specifying the scope of rule and the scope of application of the rule included in the extra-legal criterion (e.g. in the principle of social coexistence) or protecting the axiological content of this criterion (e.g. good of family) (g) concretization of the general content of this behaviour pattern, consisting in comparing it with the properties of the facts established simultaneously in order to verify its suitability for the subsequent qualification of facts.

The content of a reference formulated in this way, containing an axiologically defined pattern of behaviour, should be compiled into a normative pattern reconstructed from the "juridical part" of this legal provision.[13] This juxtaposition may lead to: (a) joint use of the content of the legal and extra-legal criteria, which may result in the cooperation of both types of criteria in determining the pattern of behaviour reconstructed from the entire provision, or (b) modification of the legal content by extra-legal criteria, aiming, in the extreme version, at refusal to include them in the content of the behaviour pattern reconstructed from such a provision for the needs of a given decision-making process.

---

12 Cf. III.
13 Cf. IV.4.

Such a cumulative pattern of behaviour from a provision containing a reference, irrespective of the version highlighted directly above, enters into various relationships with other patterns, reconstructed in an analogous manner from other relevant legal provisions in order to construct a normative basis for a decision on the application of the law (applicable norms).[14] The functions of references in the construction phase of this basis, regardless of whether it is the basis of partial decisions or the final decision of the process, can be identified as: (a) the impact of references on the content of the normative basis of a decision jointly with norms reconstructed from legal provisions (detailed or general) and other decisions on the application of law, which does not mean that it is precisely the open criteria that will not play an decisive role in the interpretation process, determining its result, (b) differentiating the role of referrals in the construction of the competence base (minimum share), procedural bases (indirect share) and substantive legal bases (relatively largest share in both parts – that define the criteria for qualifying the facts and for establishing its consequences), (c) the possibility of supplementing this fragment of the basis of the decision, which included behaviour patterns reconstructed from legal provisions or other decisions by the participation of open criteria in inferential reasoning (e.g. supporting *reasoning per analogiam iuris*, *per analogiam legis* or *a fortiori*), (d) the participation of open criteria as additional (relatively weakest) components of rules for resolving conflicts between legal provisions or between provisions and other court decisions.

The reduction of the normative basis of a decision to a singular (individual and specific) content of the decision of the application of law may also include the participation of open criteria,[15] both in terms of building a decision qualifying the established facts, and a decision determining the consequences of this qualification. The most important manifestations of this participation are: (a) influencing the qualification of facts together with the *stricti iuris* criteria or independently of them, both as part of the interaction of one open criterion and several such criteria, which may additionally be appearing in a single or different provisions, (b) – the possibility (rather an exceptional one) of influence of the extra-legal criterion on the resignation to qualify facts normatively (this concerns, among others, the criterion of good of child), (c) – the potential status of a component of the choice directive and the dimension of legal consequences (including criminal penalties) generating the possibility of a decisive, and even

14 Cf. IV.5.
15 Cf. IV.6.

in certain situations exclusive, impact of open criteria on both these "consequential findings," (d) the possibility of influencing the resignation from the application of legal criteria when determining the consequences (including the grounds for criminal liability).

The above mentioned aspects of the participation of open criteria in individual reasoning and activities of the process of operative interpretation of law are reflected and rationalized in the justification of the decision. Assuming that the justification refrains from concealing the axiological argumentation resulting from the applied extra-legal references (which, of course, cannot be excluded at all), it consists primarily in: (a) noticing the potential of axiological argumentation in convincing both to the correctness of the decision-making process and to the accuracy of partial and final decisions, which results in granting this argumentation the position of the dominant element of the justification or the non-foreground component of the "deeper structure," that is not directly visible in the text of the justification, (b) a possible axiological "entanglement" of the decision's justification, causing not only a radical strengthening of its axiological arguments, but also such "accumulation" of them in its text that it becomes difficult to precisely identify the role of their particular types and actual preferences.

2. Outline of optimization models

Our attempt to construct, in the present subsection, and based on previous detailed premises, an optimal model for the functioning of reference clauses in a democratic rule of law state relates separately to the optimization of creation and application of the extra-legal references.

2.1. Optimizing model for creating extra-legal references

Optimal practice of creating general reference clauses should take into account certain initial conditions which, on the one hand, enhance the rationality of the legislative process itself, and, on the other hand, create opportunities for their efficient use in law application processes.

They include social trust in the law as a regulator and means of social control, as well as its efficient and lawful creation, which further enhances the scale of this trust. This applies in particular to the presence of elements of the negotiating model of law-making in defining the role of organized interests. This corresponds to the assumptions concerning the need to limit the scope of legal interference in autonomous social processes, where efficient autonomous rules are created (e.g. ones concerning economic phenomena and processes).

The legislator acts in a specific social situation and under certain conditions of legal culture that determine the initial conditions for creating general reference clauses. The direct influence of the legislator on shaping this situation is limited, although it may also be accomplished, to a certain extent, by creating such and not other general reference clauses, not otherwise located in the system. This may favour the realization, in the form of a "delayed effect" (depending on the actual processes of clause application), of specific legislative objectives. Hence, in the end, especially with a construction such as a general reference clause, everything in this regard depends on the "arrangement of relations" between the processes of creating and applying the law.

When determining the components of the optimization model for creating reference clauses, it is necessary to repeat the thesis that was stated here several times, saying that the legislator, by creating clauses, deprives itself of a decisive influence on the content of the decision to apply the law. The independence of entities applying the law then has a much greater degree than it is in the case of other, "ordinary" normative constructions. The legislator thus "gets off" itself a part of the responsibility for the content of the legal order, that was created and is functioning with use of reference clauses, transferring it to courts and administrative authorities. However, it cannot be concluded that the legislator cannot implement a specific law-making policy as regards the creation of clauses, or that its activity in this field cannot be qualified from the point of view of meeting certain requirements of legislative technique.

The implementation of such a policy implies at least two assumptions: that the desired model of applying the law is acceptable, and that there is "connectivity" between the two processes. Under such circumstances, the legislator, when creating general clauses, should take into account all the current properties of the processes of applying the law and those phenomena of the social environment of the law that may affect the functions of references. Trying to predict the actual effects of the presence of clauses in provisions, should formulate the clauses in such a manner, include them in the respective fragments of the legal system, and finally should define their roles in the decision-making process in such a manner, that all elements of the optimal model of using references can be implemented. The legislator's influence on the behaviour of ordinary addressees, who construct patterns of their own specific behaviour based on clauses formulated in legal texts, but also on the basis of references used in decision-making processes, will constitute a reflection of these dependencies.

(1) The first two components of the optimal model are related to the nomenclature of open criteria included in the reference clauses.

The current practice of differentiating the names of criteria should be continued. Even if we recognize that the impact achieved in this way on the actual determination of the content of references in the law application processes is limited, there are no grounds for postulating the resignation from such a differentiation. It is related to the concept of the legislator influencing of various reasoning in the decision-making process, in which the most important thing is to direct the determination of the content of the extra-legal reference. Nevertheless, in order to organize the nomenclature, it could be postulated to limit the number of clauses, indicating quite distinct types of criteria characteristic for the entirety of a given law (e.g. principles of equity, good customs, social interest, public interest, social and economic objectives) and for individual branches of law (e.g. social harmfulness of an act, good of child or good of family, the interest of the taxpayer, the interest of the company, the interest of the party, etc.). It is so that these criteria are the ones that determine the "shape" of the extra-legal references in the entire legal system and its individual parts. The other clauses, although they do not express any diametrically different values, may cause a specific "axiological instability" at the stage of applying the law (that is why reference to the rules of social coexistence in the post-communist legal orders should be step by step replaced by the classic references to rules of equity and good customs). They may also contribute to the popularization of an attitude of not attaching importance to the name of a clause, and, consequently, to the type of criterion referred to in it, which, under favourable circumstances, may lead to even greater judicial discretion.

The maximally explicit indication of social axiology, and refraining from structures that politicize it, should constitute an indispensable element of legislative practice concerning the creation of references. This applies in particular to clauses of public law, especially administrative law, where politicization usually leads to linking the content of references with current interests or political programs. Whenever such practice is accompanied by a real weakness of the rules of democracy and the institutions implementing it, the effects of not meeting social preferences will be reinforced. To some extent, such effects also apply to criminal law, despite the limited application of clauses in it. The scale of politicization may affect civil law, even if it is relatively most independent of these trends. In general, connecting the content of criteria with a political as well as a politicized social or economic axiology (e.g. interests of the national economy) should be subject to particular restraint in a democratic rule of law state.

(2) Three further components of the optimization model are related to the location of the references in the regulation system. Placing clauses in such and not other parts of a normative act, in an act of a specific type or in a specific

branch of law is of such an importance that in some aspects it is even decisive for the effects of the functioning of references in legal order.

There is no doubt that formulating the extra-legal references anticipates their place in the regulations of the detailed parts. The subject of discussion may be the type of legal institutions in which the clauses should appear or the way in which the reference is to influence the reasoning, actions and decisions related to the application of these specific provisions. However, the question where there is need to construct norms included in general provisions (especially the initial ones) of a given normative act, potentially influencing all activities related to the application of all specific norms of such an act (or even more broadly – the entire branch of law, if such a structure were included in a code) remains open. In other words – do we need a structure of the type expressed in § 7 of ABGB, Art. 4 of ZGB or Art. 5 of KC? The question seems to be accurate, since in each of these acts, references are formulated also in other general (not initial) provisions, covering certain aspects of the application of all provisions of a given act. Regardless of the complex systemic relationships created by such references,[16] such a practice cannot be accused of being unreasonable, although undoubtedly carefully consideration of such a structure, especially if it concerns the establishment of the same extra-legal criteria, would meet the requirement of legislative rationality to a higher degree.

The position of references in the so-called vertical division of the legal system seems to constitute a more unambiguous element of the optimal model. Undoubtedly, references should not be formulated in executive acts, and in particular in the field of public law. And this covers both the form of repeating clauses that have already appeared in acts of statutory rank, and even more so, the form of creating new "executive clauses" with names that do not appear in the acts or that are changed in relation to the statutory clauses. The places where clauses may be formulated are the provisions of statutes and, as long as we remember about their different function (e.g. influencing ordinary legislation), the constitutional provisions. From the point of view of technical and legal conditions, their most desirable location is a code, which through clauses has a unified axiological effect on the entire branch it (usually) creates.

---

16 In the case of the Polish KC, this is valid in relation to Art. 58 concerning the validity of a legal transaction or Art. 65 concerning the interpretation of a declaration of intent. Moreover, in this Code, irrespective of these references for implementation of civil law in general in Book One ("General Part"), identical criteria are indicated in the criteria of the general part of Book Three ("Obligations") in Art. 354 of KC applied to all contract law).

General clauses appear in various branches of law and today, apart from criminal law, they do not arise major emotions. However, legislators should be aware of the differences between the various branches, also in the context of the characteristics of the formulation of reference clauses. The catalogue of "classic" references and, in a sense, ones that are fundamental to the entire legal system, was constructed on the basis of private law (civil law in the broad sense). On the one hand, it would require supplements in specific branches of this law (e.g. family law), and on the other – supplements in the field of public law. It is so, because the features of this division of the legal system have the greatest impact on the practice of creating references. Additions in the field of public law would entail the presence of clause of public interest, which would be counterbalanced by a referral to the (legitimate) interest of the citizens. The principles of equity under private law have an equivalent here in the form of the most general, constitutional reference to the principles of justice (social justice). The clause of necessity in a democratic society (or possibly – a democratic state, although this is a slightly different aspect of the issue) as received from the ECHR should play an important role in the protection of human rights and the rights of a citizens also in domestic law. In criminal law, despite the different function of references, a certain role could be played by the clause of social harmfulness of an act, but it should be absolutely avoided to formulate clauses in specific provisions that define the grounds for qualifying the behaviour as a crime. As long the references stay within the afore described circle, they will meet the postulate of numerical limitation of various forms of clauses and, as it seems, introduce a fairly clear axiological orientation, although the latter can never be conclusively decided at the level of legislation.

(3) The elements of the optimal creation of references are also attempts to define the type and scope of the decisional discretion that they should induce and the type of assessments they should be associated with in the process of applying the law. More generally, the legislator should formulate reference clauses in regulations in such a way that the resulting discretion does not lead to the creation of dysfunctional elements in relation to its legislative concept. This is favoured by both consistency in nomenclature and limiting the form of clauses, precise differentiation of the roles of clauses appearing in general and specific parts, or due attention to the postulate of only including references in acts with the rank of statute.

The discretion created in the result of creating references is explicit, deliberate (intentional), directed and controllable. However, the degree to which particular properties are achieved depends, apart from the transparency, which is created by the very fact of formulating a clause in a legal text, on specific legislative assumptions. We may most generally state that it is optimal to achieve these qualities to the highest degree. Due to the fact that controllability is a property that is the result of procedural solutions regarding the control of the application of clauses and the practice formed on the basis of the actions of the authorities applying the law, it must be assumed that it relates primarily to the intended nature and direction of the discretion, because here the legislator has the greatest "freedom to act." The discretion should be intentional in the sense, first of all, of predicting the fields of its operation and its scope in individual decisions of the law application process. The gap should also be directed. That should be understood as diligence in distinguishing extra-legal criteria, leading to the legislator not depriving itself of the possibility of at least general influence on the type of values, on the essential content of the extra-legal criterion, and on the relationship between this content and the fundamental values of the legal order.

The latter property leads us to have a closer look at the possibility of the legislator's determining the content of extra-legal criteria in such a way that, despite the programmatic openness of reference clauses and a significant weakening of the degree of influence on legal practice, a certain concept of influencing the content of the decision on the application of the law is achieved. That, in other words, there is a relationship between the axiology of creation and the axiology of applying references. In particular, the legislator should, however, try to direct judicial choices explicitly, avoid invoking axiomatized criteria that have no reference to socially verifiable assessments, and formulate references so that the politicization of the content of the criteria is at least hindered. Perhaps the most important substantive indication would be the postulate of a proper "balancing," in the entire legal system, of arguments in favour of the protection of individual interests and general interests (public, social), so that it would be impossible to automatically prefer the latter, leading to axiomatization, politicization or "ideologization" of the content of references. It is also important that the legal framework for evaluative choices is precisely formulated, as the basic values of the entire legal system cannot be negated by the extra-legal references.

The legislative authorization of entities applying the law to use the structure of references in specific decision-making situations should also form a component of the optimization model in the field of shaping the scope of decision-making discretion. Each specification of the scope for the application of references limits the scope of this discretion as a model, and certainly imposes – on the entity applying the law – the obligation to make the referral "fit" within the scope of the legislative authorization. This applies to linking the use of clauses with the absence or ambiguity of legal provisions, the lack of legal principles or with specific activities and reasoning (validity of a legal action or interpretation of a declaration of will).

(4) An optimal model for creating reference clauses should also include appropriate influencing on the reasoning and argumentation in particular phases of the law application process, based, of course in particular, on the principle of independence of judiciary.

What should be correctly delineated is primarily the basis for the use of an extra-legal reference, understood as the authorization of such action, including the obligation to consider basing the decision-making process and decisions on such a criterion. Here the influence of the legislator takes place primarily by means of clear wording of the referring clause in legal provisions and its placement in a normative act in such a way that there is no doubt as to when it may be applied.

Legislative caution should be associated with formulating extra-legal criteria in the structures constituting the basis for the derogation of applicable provisions, although the use of such structures, e.g. in a constitutional regulation by a constitutional court, will no longer depend on the legislator (hence the required caution when including clauses in constitutions). This also applies to the grounds for creating structures that make it possible to refuse to apply a provision, especially based on political criteria.

When the general impact of formulating references to extra-legal axiology on the processes of interpreting regulations is considered, the postulate of legislative caution is an argument of limited power, as it is precisely in this field that the essence of judicial discretion is based. The point is rather not to create structures that would allow the politicization of such an impact.

While clauses should not be constructed with the intention of affecting the determination of the facts (although such an indirect impact takes place, both in the context of estimated and general extra-legal references), the construction of the impact of extra-legal criteria on the qualification of facts (outside criminal law) is their basic function in the context of the reduction of the normative basis for decisions. A more cautious, especially in terms of the independent (and certainly – politicized) operation of such a criterion, should consist in the inclusion of extra-legal criteria in the directives determining the type and size of consequences, with the specific determinants depending on the type of branch of law and applicable legal provisions.

2.2. Optimizing model for applying extra-legal references

An attempt to outline the optimal model for the functioning of extra-legal references in the practice of applying the law must refer to the findings contained in previous parts of the work. There, based on the observation of the processes of applying general clauses, the possible ways of determining the content of reference clauses, the grounds for applying the clause in the process and the impact of the presence of clauses in the decision-making process on the validation and interpretation arrangements, as well as the determination and qualification of the facts were all described.

The model presented below refers to the practice of applying the law in general, but it is based on the recognition of the judicial type of law application as the basic one, under which the use of extra-legal references can be linked with the implementation of the concept of the rule of law and a rational decision on the application of law. This model is based on the distinction between postulates, first, as to the content of the criteria of the extra-legal reference, secondly, as to the basis for the use of reference, thirdly, as to the determination of the optimal role of references in the process of operative interpretation (building a normative decision to apply the law), and fourthly as to the qualification of facts and determination of the final content of the decision on the application of the law.

(1) The determination of the content of extra-legal criteria expressed in reference clauses is the most sensitive, and at the same time the most indefinite and unstable element of this model, bringing about a real dimension of the decision-making discretion. The optimization model should, however, define the method for determining the content of the references sufficiently to exclude such methods of interpreting the references that would make this discretion dependent on the predefined methods of evaluation or which would lead to the decision-making process that would not meet the requirements of rationality of action in this field. This model includes several basic constituents.

The content of the referrals should be so objectivized that it is neither an expression of only the subjective preferences of a particular subject making the decision (although their participation cannot be fully eliminated) nor a direct expression of some values and objectives assumed by the dominant ideology. It should therefore be a specific product of the preferences of an organ applying the law and socially accepted moral preferences (as the basic criteria), public interest (connected with the state perspective) or relevant economic criteria (that in market conditions are focusing on, generally speaking, economic rationality).

The content framework of such an interpretation of extra-legal references should be dominant and sufficiently relate the social values and the main values of the legal order. The role of socially rooted moral values, which is the canon of contemporary democratic systems, results from the fact that it is moral values that are the main direction of axiological verification of legal norms in general and the basic point of reference for extra-legal references. On the other hand, the need to "fit into" the axiological choices defined by basic legal values (principles of law) results from the need to maintain the axiological unity of the entire legal order, also when specific normative grounds for decisions embrace extra-legal content. Moreover, what is becoming increasingly important, the content of clauses established in the processes of applying national law should correspond to the content of clauses established in the processes of applying international law (also based on generally recognized principles of international law) and the content of references in developed national legal orders of the same circle of legal culture (e.g. in the circle of continental European culture).

The most important in the application of law, both public and private, is to moderate the content of referring clauses in terms of public (social) and individual interests. This is a fragment of the issue concerning the way of expressing judgments in the decision-making process, in which the manifestation and not hiding the axiological conflicts occurring in this process promotes the openness of their solutions, which is the first, but very important, premise of the procedural correctness of decisions taken in the conditions of possible axiological conflicts. However, establishing the overall relationship between these interests is also, if not more important. When we assume that the law itself is, by definition, an element of caring for both these interests and the appropriate relations between them, it should be even more so that the resignation from overt and prudent "moderating" both of these interests in the processes of applying clauses, favouring "ideologization" and axiomatization, cannot fulfil the conditions of correctness and rationality of the process. This seems to be the primary task of decision-makers (and courts in particular).

The content of the references and extra-legal criteria should be set as specifically as possible so that it is possible to identify the assessment expressed by the organ applying the law and possibly confront it with the values that constitute its starting points or point of reference. The specificity of evaluation, which should in no way be confused with the usually negatively assessed cataloguing of evaluations and norms fulfilling the content of specific reference clauses, means expressing the assessment in the context of a specific facts, subject to current qualification, and formulating a specific value (principle) that becomes a component of the basis of the decision. This enhances the possibility of social verification of the assessments used in the decision, and secures the decision-making process and the decision itself against excessive generalization, associated in favourable conditions with the politicization or "ideologization" of the basis for expressing such assessment.

In the decision-making process and in the very justification of the judicial decision, the assessments that constitute the content of the extra-legal criterion should be sufficiently separated and possibly detached from each other (in particular when there are multiple references in a single decision-making process). This applies to the relationship between criteria appearing in different parts of the same act of law or related legal acts. Systemic relations between the provisions of the general and specific parts result in assigning them different roles in the process, but do not imply setting different contents of the criteria with the same names. The joint application of differently named criteria from these two parts of an act, on the other hand, may not result in the identification or even partial overlapping of their content, even when they refer to the same kind of values (e.g. moral). The care for semantic distinctiveness does not trigger such "axiological entanglement" of the decision-making process and the content of decisions, which would not only lead to the accumulation of evaluative statements, or support of various extra-legal evaluations, usually "playing together" against legal arguments, but also to mixing meanings and blurring content differences between specific assessments, which would result in difficulties with orientation as to the axiological basis of the very decision-making.

(2) The use of reference clauses takes place in the decision-making process, the formal requirements of which are not abolished by the presence of clauses nor even "softened" so that they do not play a sufficiently important role. This should be particularly apparent in determining the basis for the application of a reference clause in the respective process of law application.

The basis for the use of a reference should be associated with its presence in normative acts, which brings the test of applicability of clauses closer to the test of applicability of provisions related to the formal (thetic) justification for their application. However, this does not mean that the clause must be applied whenever it forms part of the applied provision. Nevertheless the authorization for such use therefore presupposes an obligation to consider such an operation whenever a provision containing a reference is applied. However, some caution or even restraint in the use of references should be the general standard. And more, if a clause is applied, the name of the criteria contained therein should always be clearly formulated in the decision on the application of the law and, in principle, coincide with the name of the clause in the applicable normative act. Both of these properties allow for the identification of the reference itself and the association with a specific clause, in the context of the entire practice, of certain values or expressed evaluations. Although any modification of the nomenclature of clauses does not have to lead to dysfunctionality of the legal order and even to the effects contrary to the intention of the legislator, it nevertheless results in an additional "loosening of the nomenclature of clauses" overlapping with the already existing gap resulting from the very application of reference clauses.

The effects of "additional forming" of the references by the judiciary would depart even further from this model. Even though it would not have to lead to effects that again, are dysfunctional or opposite to the legislative concept, it would still reach beyond the scope of the independent application of law in the culture of statutory law. As long as we accept at least minimal standards of legalism, it proves impossible to accept (unless there is some extraordinary situation) the creation of references "only" in the process of applying the law, referring to the axiological importance of extra-legal criteria that were "not noticed" by the legislator.

As for the type of legal acts, that should form the basis of application of reference clauses by the authorities, these are, in terms of state law, primarily statutes. The requirements related to the proceeding the statutes, as well as their technical and legal features, which are even more apparent in the case of codification, safeguard the minimization of the negative potential effects of the application of the clauses. References appearing in executive acts should not play an independent role in the decision-making process. On the other hand, entities applying the law have a "free hand" in applying the constitutional clauses and clauses of the applicable international law. They may also, to a certain extent, as justified by common features of legal culture, use clauses contained in formally non-binding foreign law, if it is justified by the similar nature of legal institutions and the state of development of judicial practice.

In searching for a normative basis for the application of clauses, a question may arise concerning the limits of "borrowing" such specific references from other legal provisions, that are useful in the opinion of entities applying the law. Of course, the fact that all provisions of the general part of acts are "complementary" makes borrowing clauses from these provisions to construct a complete pattern of behaviour resulting from the provisions of the specific part quite understandable. On the other hand, borrowing clauses contained in other specific provisions is another issue here, and must be subject to the general conditions of argumentation *per analogiam legis*, but applied more restrictively (requiring similarity of not only the facts, but also the legal institutions within which such borrowing takes place). For example, the scale of the systemic and objective "distance" of the provision from which the clause is borrowed should be smaller, mainly due to the already large "instability" of its normative foundations.

Another complex and controversial issue is the possibility of detaching the test of the applicability of the reference and the provision containing the reference, which should always lead to the postulate of careful use of such a procedure. This includes the above-mentioned situation of applying a reference from foreign law, but also the application, within a given decision-making process, of clauses contained in regulations that are not yet in force or have already been repealed. The latter situation is related, *among other things*, to the significant phenomenon of using references from the previous legal system. It is acceptable if the previous legal system met the minimum conditions of the rule of law, and the practice of the previous period, accepted at least in principle, has sufficiently precisely defined the content of the clauses and the manner of their application in the decision-making processes. Taking into account the characteristics of transitional periods, the possibility of a "gentle" transition of practice to new ways of expressing extra-legal axiology in the processes of applying the law should be accepted. It seems all the more actual, when the "old" clauses were based on classic references found in the same legal culture, and the practice referring to them thus wishes to extend and strengthen these classic references.

(3) What we must distinguish from the basis for the application of the reference clause in decision-making processes in general and in specific processes of the application of legal norms, is the impact of extra-legal references on establishing the normative basis of a decision of the application of law. It is also the first element of the impact of general reference clauses on the decision-making process itself, covering the entire process of judicial interpretation as well as determining and qualifying the facts.

When we adopt the assumption that the binding legal provision forms the basis for validation findings in the statutory legal order, it will mean that the role of reference clauses in these findings should be measured basically in terms of supplementing and not negating the basic legal argumentation. This means that in the so-called normal situations, which are not situations of a real axiological breakthrough, a clause can be, albeit with care, applied as a basis for departing from the arguments arising from legal provisions, but cannot decide on declaring a given provision invalid. Nevertheless, it may still affect its applicability in the sense that the non-compliance of the provision with the criteria of the reference clause may result in its non-application, thought it should be used exceptionally in a democratic rule of law state.

The reference clauses may still, to a limited extent, also play the role of a direct participation in the basis of a normative decision, or even an independent basis for a decision on the application of the law. What we assume here is the inadequacy of legal criteria assumed by the legislator or recognized in practice to make a decision on the application of the law, leading to a shift towards the extra-legal criteria. Such action, if it does not become a common method of making decisions, is permissible under certain conditions and in certain branches of law (it certainly cannot be an independent basis for recognizing a given act as a crime, e.g. on the basis of the criterion of social harmfulness of an act that has not been formally prohibited). However, it should have a clear normative basis (as is the case, for example, in § 7 of ABGB, or Art. 1 and 4 of ZGB) or a very strong grounding in legal practice. Moreover, it could be based on the criteria of social axiology and customary norms, but not on the criteria of political axiology. The politicization of the basis for a decision thus determined should be clearly qualified negatively, regardless of the branch of law or the type of its application.

Another object of the influence of the clauses is the interpretative reasoning. The interpretation of provisions can also be made with reference to extra-legal criteria, and in such a case its results usually differ from the result that would have been achieved without the clause being present in the interpreted text. Therefore it is also here that the optimal role of clauses may be associated with the failure to take into account strictly legal criteria of that provision in a given decision-making process or with the determination of the scale of "departing" from the arguments arising from a legal provision.

The basic assumption of the presence of clauses in the processes of operative interpretation of a provision (which is an issue that is separate from the interpretation of the clause itself) should be the assumption that the presence of a clause in the interpreted provision (in the strong version) and that the presence of the clause criterion in the decision-making process in which a provision is interpreted that does not containing a clause (weaker version) results in a more or less clear, but still significant share of axiological argumentation in the said interpretation. This is the case regardless of whether the clause becomes an element of an interpretative directive formulated in the legal text or not.

The impact of the presence of clauses on the interpretation of legal provisions should not lead to resignation from the linguistic interpretation of that legal provision. Neither can it destroy the accepted models of the order of particular interpretative directives, although it does introduce some modifications here. The interpretation with the use of clauses should pass not so much sequentially, but simultaneously through linguistic and extra-linguistic arguments. The inevitability of carrying out axiological (as well as functional) arguments requires considering the role (but not elimination) of the results of linguistic interpretation, if the latter do not raise doubts in terms of legal and common language. The assumed general insufficiency of the linguistic interpretation of the provisions containing the clause should be "confirmed" by the usefulness of non-linguistic interpretative arguments.

The issue of impact of clauses on the solution of conflicts of interpretation is a bit more complex. It should be assumed that the presence of clauses does not have to lead to a preference for interpretative axiological arguments in every case. The inclusion of extra-legal criteria on the basis of the official interpretative directive does not alter this relationship. The caution indicated above concerns not only the collision between extra-legal and legal criteria, but also the participation of references in resolving the conflicts between various legal criteria.

(4) The impact of extra-legal references on the formulation of decisions on the application of law is related to the qualification of the facts and the determination of the normative consequences of such qualification.

This impact is significant as the references should not affect the fact-finding process itself. Of course, nothing prevents the adoption of the postulate that the presence of a reference should strengthen the diligence in explaining the facts, which would facilitate its qualification on the basis of extra-legal values. On the other hand, we should not base the reasons for not establishing certain facts on them. This is especially true of general references. The use of estimates is always accompanied by the qualification of the fact (reason, diligence, breakdown of the marriage) consisting in the estimation of its scale or degree (importance, particularity, lasting). Only the joint expression in one provision to a reference clause and estimate clause may result in the recognition of the determined facts in the context and in the language of the general clause criteria. The optimal model of such use of clauses requires their restrictive application, which would constitute a necessary guarantee of "non-overbalancing" of cognitive elements by axiological elements in the process of establishing facts.

Reference clauses should not be used to change the scope of application of a given legal rule to a specific facts of the case. This general precondition would have to be adhered to in its entirety, both in terms of extending the scope of ordered and prohibited acts, or narrowing the scope of "authorized" action, as well as in terms of extending the subjective and objective scope within which prohibitions and orders are to be implemented (and, accordingly – narrowing the scope within which "rights" are to be executed). Failure to meet this condition would not lead to such inconvenient consequences for the addressees if, on the basis of the significance of the clause criteria, the scope of the "authorized" acts or the subjective and objective scope under which the authorized acts are to materialize was to be extended (and, accordingly, if this was narrowed in relation to acts that are the subject to an obligation). The condition here, however, would be that such changes in the scope of normalization and the scope of application of the rules do not interfere with the "rights" of other their addressees.

The criteria for extra-legal referrals should not also form an argument eliminating the legal criteria from qualifying the facts. They can carefully modify the role of these legal criteria towards taking into account also the extra-legal criteria, which may lead to basing qualifications on arguments "balanced" between legal and extra-legal content (this applies in particular to the social harmfulness of an act in the application of criminal law[17]). It is only in cases where the legal norm makes it possible to "subscribe" a specific facts of the case only under the criteria of reference clauses,[18] the independent role of this criterion may be accepted.

The criteria of reference clauses may play a specific role in the choice of legal consequences. First of all, they can be an element of a directive to choose a specific consequence from a catalogue contained in the law (e.g. type of penalty) or to choose a specific version of a specific sanction (e.g. when imposing a penalty of imprisonment, compensation of damages). On the other hand, clauses should not form a decisive argument supporting the departing of the law applying entity from the legal criteria when determining the consequences (i.e., as a result – from imposing a legal sanction), even when we are dealing with the application of provisions taken over from the "previous" legal order.

References may also, to a limited extent, play the role of an independent substantive criterion for determining the consequences. There is no other option in situations where the norm itself stipulates that the sanction should be determined only on the basis of the clause criteria[19]). On the other hand, one should be more careful with the independent participation of extra-legal criteria in establishing criminal sanctions, where it is optimal to specifically co-define the content of the consequences by both types of criteria.[20]

---

17 Cf. art. 1 KK of 1997.

18 As it is the case when a given behaviour is qualified as an abuse of a right on the basis of exceeding only the principles of social intercourse on the grounds of art. 5 of KC.

19 E.g. the compensation based on rules of equity in the case of damages resulted from the action of state officials (art. 417^2 of KC) or the court's determining the way the obligation should be performed in art. 357^1 of KC.

20 E.g. on the basis of the social harmfulness of the act and other criteria not referring to extra-legal axiology according to Art. 53 of KK of 1997.

2.3. Reference clauses and the axiology of judicial discretion

The listed, detailed elements of the optimization model of using reference clauses in the processes of applying the law lead to the formation of at least a few general features of fundamental importance for the general functioning of reference clauses in the practice of applying the law. They relate to the general issues of the decision-making discretion related to the use of references, the relationship between the value of flexibility and the values of uniformity and certainty in the application of the law, as well as the role of the rule of law in the use of references.

(1) Considering the fact that the decision-making discretion resulting from the reference clauses is "by definition" broad, but moreover an intended, explicit, targeted and controllable one, the latter features, implemented in legal order to a maximum extent, should be associated with an optimal model use of clauses. What will be decisive in terms of the application of the law are the controllability of the use of the discretion created by references and its actual control in specific cases of application of the clause. This should apply to a certain extent to the content of the criteria to be established and, above all, to the way in which the reference is applied in individual activities of the decision-making process. It should be remembered, however, that it is the decisions of the first court instances that have the most real possibilities of determining the meaning of reference clauses in the context of comprehensive finding and explanation of facts of the case. The control of higher instances (regardless of the perceived restraint in interfering with the content of the reference already established by the lower instance) should not arbitrarily "impose" the interpretation of the clause itself, as this could, in the long run, "discourage" lower instances from applying these constructions. However, the very presence of control is important. It creates a chance for a state in which a wide range of discretion will not negate "the minimum axiological unity of the legal order." This does not, of course, eliminate potential "individual acts of insubordination," but nevertheless marks the general line. If this line is also linked to the fundamental trends of legal practice in legal orders belonging to the same legal culture and, moreover, if it is linked to trends in the use of references in international jurisprudence, then the guarantees of not exceeding the reasonable limits of the margin of discretion receive stronger grounds.

(2) The determinant of the scope of the discretion associated with the presence of references in the processes of applying the law should be an appropriately "balanced" relationship between the value of flexibility and the values of uniformity and certainty of law application.[21] For if the flexibility of applying

21 The problem has been noticed in judicial practice (cf. e.g. SN Judgment of 29 XI 2017, II CSK 86/17, LEX 2417587, SN Provision of 26 III 2014, V CSK 344/13, LEX 1460985,

the law justifies the appearance of a gap in the decision-making process, the values of uniformity and certainty lead to the limitation and rationalization of its specific manifestations. The need to "maintain" the role of these properties, emphasized by the legal doctrine, legislation and the judicial practice itself is important insofar as these values are weakened by the mere appearance of clauses in regulations and decision-making practice. It seems that the development of an open and sufficiently strong (deep) precedent practice (obviously within the scope appropriate for the statutory order) could have an important significance for strengthening these values. On the one hand, this would restrict the already wide decision-making discretion, while on the other, it would create a basis for predictability of the content of decisions based on references. This combination would allow them to be more efficiently used by the addressees of norms for the construction of behavioural patterns that would later be qualified in the process of applying the law.

Both of the above elements of the optimal model of using references lead to agreeing on some version of protection of the value of the rule of law, which, due to the flexibility of applying the law related to the use of clauses, may be weakened to some extent (especially if the essence of these values is perceived in connection with value of the legality of the application of the law). This applies especially to the formal and content-related requirements for the application of reference clauses and should be related to the basis for applying the clauses in the decision-making process as well as the course and effects of their impact on individual components of this process. This is an issue that should not raise major doubts, and the specific conditions, supported by the most general condition of not abusing the structure itself, can be determined relatively easily. However, the function of content conditions related to clauses is not so unambiguous, because the extra-legal references cannot directly support the content and role

---

SN Judgment of 22 II 2019, IV CSK 121/18, LEX 2625010 or SN Judgment of 28 I 2016, I CSK 16/15, LEX 1991134. In the latter judgment we can find following opinion: "The assessment of the invalidity of a legal action due to its inconsistency with the rules of social cooperation must be supported by special circumstances. When reviewing legal actions on the basis of article 58 § 2 of the Civil Code, one should keep in mind its double aspect. On one hand, the result of this analysis may cause certain unpredictability of the legal system's functioning, but on the other hand it leads to compensating for it, a fair result of law application. From the necessity of maintaining a balance between these elements arises the postulate to apply the general clause of the principles of social coexistence in exceptional cases, in which it has a strong axiological justification."

of intra-legal values, which, after all, determine what is meant by legality and the rule of law (in formal terms). This dichotomy may, however, lead to a certain postulate, the meaning of which would be to indicate the need to use, within the decision-making process, assessments, that are on the one hand sufficiently important, durable and verifiable in the context of their dominant role in social consciousness, and on the other – related to the values expressed in the fundamental principles of law. The latter would entail remaining within the basic framework of axiological choices determined by the law itself, maintaining the "minimum unity of the axiology of the legal order," without which it would no longer be justified not only to use the notions of "rule of law state," but also to use the notion of "application of law" to denote the decision-making process which applies the structure of the reference clauses.

2.4. Appendix: optimizations and the Polish legal order after 1989

(1) The general optimization model should, of course, and when we take its simplifications into account, be treated as a target for the Polish legal order functioning after 1989. The scope of socio-legal changes that are taking place in this period means that some of its components are already visible, while others are only starting to emerge. It seems, however, that the negation of the practice of the legal order before 1989 should be clear. Despite some "meanders," the main components slowly construct the fundamental trend of the evolution of the model, which largely reflects the previously indicated factors relativizing the creation and use of references in the light of occurrence of deep, democratic social change,[22] within which also the legal system, and with it the "system" of general reference clauses, are changing.

Not only is the creation of these clauses changing, but also their application. Despite the fact that, to a large extent, these processes occur in a transitional form (as the results of social changes have not been firmly established in every sphere of social reality yet), these models are constructed for a democratic social system based on a market economy with a certain scale of state interventionism, which is at the same time a system with relatively solid legal and institutional foundations. Although it is impossible not to notice the existence of some fluctuations in this context, related to specific programs and political activities starting in 2015, which, however, by manifesting themselves mainly in the framework of law-making, did not significantly change (at least so far) the

22 Cf. V.2.

fundamental trend in the judicial processes of applying the law (which in the context of the present work constitute the primary point of reference).

(2) Certain components of the optimization model should be emphasized precisely in the face of the process of shaping a new social and legal reality, referring both to the practice of creating and applying extra-legal references.

In terms of creating references, the most important postulates, covering either the continuation of an already outlined trend or the initiation of a new practice, include:

- resignation, in the new normative regulations, from quoting the references characteristic for the old legal order, especially those that would facilitate the politicization of their content
- referring to the nomenclature of references formed in the developed orders of the European culture of statutory law,
- caution in formulating references in the field of public law, especially those that extend the scope of state interference in civil rights and freedoms (with the simultaneous legitimacy of references limiting the scope of such interference),
- careful placement of references in the systematics of a normative act, considering the possibility of further analogous implementations of clauses,
- constructing more efficient appeal procedures enabling control of the decisional discretion related to the application of referrals, including setting the content of the criteria (e.g. as part of judicial control of the administration's activities).

The most important components of optimizing the current Polish judicial practice of application of extra-legal references consist in indicating the strong need to continue the trends shaped within it during the period of over 30 years of systemic transformation even if some legislative actions weaken its effects. The most important of them include:

- non-politicization of the content of extra-legal criteria, both old and new, aimed at maximally faithful reflection of the well-established social axiology and economic rationality
- weighing (and balancing) the general (public) and individual dimensions of extra-legal criteria, also in the context of the application of public law and judicial control of the activities of the administration,
- weighing various dimensions of moral values, also within their individual dimension, by, *among other things*, avoiding their axiomatization
- combining the extra-legal axiology of references with the axiology of fundamental principles of law (on an appropriate system scale, also including

international law) in order to achieve axiological coherence of the legal order and with the axiology of references functioning in the European legal culture,
- linking the test of the applicability of the reference with the test of the applicability of the legal provisions containing it, with careful use of the indirect application of references from general provisions and the use of the reference from a specific provision *per analogiam legis*,
- striving to develop permanent lines of jurisprudence unifying the method of determining the content of references and the methods of their application and impact on the entire process of legal interpretation,
- gradual dissemination of the discursive style of justifying court decisions, revealing and deepening the axiological argumentation regarding the participation of extra-legal criteria in the decision-making process and the content of decisions.

Bibliography

- Ajdukiewicz K., *Logika pragmatyczna*, Warszawa 1974
- Aldisert R. J., *The Judicial Process. Readings, Material, Cases*, St. Paul 1976
- Alexy R., *A Theory of Constitutional Rights*, Oxford 2002
- Alexy R., "Ermessensfehler," *Juristische Zeitung* 1986, No. 15/16
- Alexy R.. "On the Structure of Legal Principles," *Ratio Iuris* 2000, No. 3
- Allen C.K., *Law in the Making*, Oxford 1964
- Alvares A., Cheibub J.A., Limongi F., Przeworski A., "Classifying Political Regimes," *Studies in Comparative International Development* 1996, Vol. 31
- Andrejew I., *Zarys prawa karnego państw socjalistycznych*, Warszawa 1975
- Atienza M., *Curso de argumentacion juiridica*, Madrit 2015
- Atienza M., Manero J. R., *A Theory of Legal Sentences*, Dordrecht 1999
- Avila H., *Theory of Legal Principles*, Dordrecht 2007
- Bartel W.M., "Z dziejów angielskiej equity," *Czasopismo Prawno-Historyczne* 1964, Vol. XVI, No. 1
- Bator A., *Użycie normy prawnej w regulacji stosunków gospodarczych*, Wrocław 2000
- Bauer H., "Informelles Verwaltungshandeln im öffentlichen Wirtschaftsrecht," *Verwaltungs Archiv* 1987, No. 3
- Bäcker C., "Rules, Principles and Defeasibility," *Archiv für Rechts- und Sozialphilosophie* 2010, Vol. 119
- Berlin M., Metivier L., "Le droit international humanitaire comme source interpretative de la Charte Canadienne des Droits et Libertes: l'incidence de la Convention Europeeenne des Droits de l'Homme," *Revue de Droit International et de Droit Compare* 1987, Vol. LXIV
- *Besondere Verwaltungsakt,* (ed. U. Steiner), Heidelberg 1988
- *Besonderes Verwalungsrecht* (ed. I. von Munch, E. Schmidt-Assmann), Berlin 1992
- Biernat T., "On the Lawmaking Policy, Discretion, and Importance of the Rule of Law Standards," *Studia Iuridica Lublinensia* 2020, Vol. XXIX, No. 3
- Biernat T., Zirk-Sadowski M., "Politics of Law and Legal Policy. Introduction," in: *Politics of Law and*
- *Legal Policy* (ed. T. Biernat, M. Zirk-Sadowski), Warszawa 2008

- Brohm W., "Rechtstaatliche Vorgaben für informelles Verwaltungshandeln," *Deutches Verwaltungsblatt* 1994, No. 3
- Bröstl A., "Jigsaw Puzzle for Rainy Days – How to Put Together the Pieces: Sources of Law, Forms of Law, Principles, Standards, Rules and Norms – to Get a Consistent Picture of Law?," *Studia Iuridica Lublinensia* 2020, Vol. XXIX, No. 3
- Brown E.G., *British Statutes in American Law*, London 1964
- Brown L.N., Kennedy T., *The Court of Justice of the European Communities*, London 2000
- *Bürgeliches Gesetzbuch mit Gesetz zür Regelung des Rechts der Allgemeinen Geschaftsbendingungen* (ed. O. Jauernig), München 1990
- Choi C., "Ancient and New Sources of Law: An East Asian Perspective," in: *Challenges to Law at the End of the 20th Century*, Vol. II (ed. E. Pattaro), Bologna 1995
- Cross R., *Precedent in English Law*, Oxford 1968
- Czapliński W., Wyrozumska A., "Ogólne zasady prawa jako źródło prawa międzynarodowego," *Edukacja prawnicza* 1999, No. 3
- Daniel K., "Kontrowersje wokół wprowadzenia wartości chrześcijańskich do prawa," (in:) *Dynamika wartości w prawie*, (ed. K. Pałecki), Kraków 1997
- David R., *Le grands systemes de droit contemporains*, Paris 1966
- Dawidowicz W., "O stosowaniu prawa przez organy administracji państwowej," *Zeszyty Nauowe Wydziału Prawa i Administracji Uniwersytetu Gdańskiego*, Prawo 1981, No. 9
- Drobnig U., Erp S.V., *The Use of Comparative Law by Courts*, Dortrecht 1998
- Dworkin R., "Hard Cases," *Harvard Law Review* 1975, Vol. 88
- Dworkin R., *Law's Empire*, London 1990
- Dworkin R., *Taking Rights Seriously*, London 1978
- Dworkin R.. "The Model of Rules," *University of Chicago Law Review* 1967, Vol. 35
- Dziedziak W., *O prawie słusznym (perspektywa systemu prawa stanowionego)*, Lublin 2015
- Dżorbenadze S.M., "O kształtowaniu się radzieckiego ustawodawstwa i radzieckiej nauki prawa," *Państwo i Prawo* 1978, No. 12
- Ehmke H., *"Ermessen" und "unbestimmter Rechtsbegriff" im Verwaltungsrecht*, Tübingen 1960
- Ehrlich S., "Refleksje o dwóch prawniczych kulturach: europejskiej i japońskiej," *Państwo i Prawo* 1987, No. 6

- Engisch K., *Einführung in das juristische Denken*, Stuttgart 1975
- Eyermann E., Frohler L., Kormann. J., *Verwaltungsrechtsordnung*, München 1988
- Forsthoff E., *Lehrbuch des Verwaltungsrechts, 1. Band. Allgemeiner Teil*, München-Berlin 1961
- Frank J., *Law and the Modern Mind*, London 1949
- Fujita T., "Die Rechtsprobleme der informelles Handlungsformen der Verwaltung in Japan im Vergleich zum Stand der Diskussion in der Bundesrepublik Deutchland," *Annales Universitatis Mariae Curie-Skłodowska*, Sectio G, Ius, 1991, Vol. XXXXVIII
- *Fundamentals of Legislation of the USSR and the Union Republics*, Moscow 1974
- Galanter M., *Law and Society in Modern India*, Oxford 1989
- Gizbert-Studnicki T., Grabowski A., "Normy programowe w konstytucji," in: *Charakter i struktura norm konstytucji* (ed. J. Trzciński), Warszawa 1997
- *Główne kultury prawne współczesnego świata*, (ed. H. Rot), Warszawa 1995
- Gromski W., *Autonomia i instrumentalny charakter prawa*, Wrocław 2000
- Gryniuk A., *Przymus prawny. Studium socjologiczno-prawne*, Toruń 1994
- Gruchmann L., "Rechtssystem und nationalistische Justizpolitik," in: *Das Dritte Reich. Herrchaftsstruktur und Geschichte* (ed. M. Broszat, H. Moller), München 1983
- Górski J., "Aksjologiczne przesłanki decyzji sądowych w sprawach gospodarczych," in: *Dynamika wartości w prawie* (ed. K. Pałecki), Kraków 1997
- Grzybowski S., "Struktura i treść przepisów prawa cywilnego odsyłających do zasad współżycia społecznego," *Studia Cywilistyczne* 1965, Vol. VI
- Grzybowski S., "Wypowiedź normatywna oraz jej struktura formalna," *Zeszyty Naukowe Uniwersytetu Jagiellońskiego* 1961, Vol. XXXIX
- Guść J., "O pojęciu 'właściwość' (natura) stosunku prawnego" (art. 353 k.c.), in: *Filozoficzno-teoretyczne problemy sądowego stosowania prawa* (ed. M. Zirk-Sadowski), Łódź 1997
- Haft F., "Generalklauseln und unbestimmte Begriffe im Strafrecht," *Juristische Schulung* 1975, No. 8
- Haftl B., *Das nationalistische WillenStrafrecht*, Berlin 2000
- Haley O., "The Role of Law in Japan: An Historical Perspective," *Law in Japan. An Annual* 1982, Vol. 15
- Hanas K., "Interpretative Discretion of Judiciary and the Well–Being of the Child" *Studia Iuridica Lublinensia* 2020, Vol. XXIX, No. 3

- Hanusz A., Krukowska-Siembida P., "Ważny interes podatnika i interes publiczny w klauzulach generalnych Ordynacji podatkowej," *Annales Universitatis Mariae Curie-Skłodowska*, Sectio G, Ius 2016, Vol. LXIII, No. 2
- Harris D. J., O'Boyle M., Warbrick C., *Law of the European Convention on Human Rights*, London 1995
- Hart H.L.A., *The Concept of Law*, London 1965
- Hedemann J.W., *Die Flucht in die Generalklauseln, Eine Gefahr für Recht und Staat*, Tübingen 1933
- Hedemann J.W., *Einführung in die Rechtswissenschaft*, Berlin 1927
- Henf F., *Biligkeit und zivilrechtliche Argumentation*, Kiel 1978
- Hoffmaster B., "Understanding Judicial Discretion", *Law and Philosophy* 1982, No. 1
- Itoh H., "How Judges Think in Japan," *The American Journal of Comparative Law* 1970, Vol. 18
- Izdebski H., *Historia administracji*, Warszawa 1984
- Jones H.W., "An Invitation to Jurisprudence," *Harvard Law Review* 1974, Vol. 74
- Kalisz A., "Klauzule generalne w wykładni prawa UE," in: *Wykladnia prawa Unii Europejskiej* (ed. L. Leszczyński), Vol 3: System prawa Unii Europejskiej (ed. A. Wróbel), Warszawa 2019
- Kalisz A., Zienkiewicz A., *Mediacja sądowa i pozasądowa. Zarys wykładu*, Warszawa 2009
- Kalisz-Prakopik A., Leszczyński L., "Zasady prawa w stosowaniu prawa wspólnotowego," *Europejski Przegląd Sądowy* 2005, No. 1
- Kamiński I.C., *Słuszność i prawo. Szkic prawnoporównawczy*, Warszawa 2005
- Kanowitz L., *Alternative Dispute Resolution. Cases and Materials*, St. Paul 1986
- Kawashima T., "The Legal Consciousness of Contract in Japan," *Law in Japan. An Annual* 1974, Vol. 7
- Kitagawa Z., "Theory Reception – One Aspect of the Development of the Japanese Civil Law Science," *Law in Japan. An Annual* 1970, Vol. 4
- Klima J., *Prawa Hammurabiego*, Warszawa 1957
- Kmieciak Z., *Mediacja i koncyliacja w prawie administracyjnym*, Kraków 2004.
- Kopaczyńska-Pieczniak K., "Dobre obyczaje i zasady współżycia społecznego w prawie spółek handlowych," *Annales Universitatis Mariae Curie-Skłodowska*, Sectio G, Ius, 2016, vol. LXIII, No. 2.

- Komierzyńska E., Zdyb M., "Klauzula interesu publicznego w działaniach administracji publicznej," *Annales Universitatis Mariae Curie-Skłodowska*, Sectio G, Ius, 2016, vol. LXIII, No. 2
- Kopaliński W., *Słownik wyrazów obcych i zwrotów obcojęzycznych*, Warszawa 1983
- Kopp F.O., *Verwaltungsrechtsordnung*, München 1992
- Koranyi K., *Powszechna historia państwa i prawa*, Vol. IV, Warszawa 1967
- Kordela M., "Inter- and Extra- Legal Axiology," *Studia Iuridica Lublinensia* 2020, Vol. XXIX, No. 3
- Kordela M., *Zasady prawa. Zagadnienia podstawowe*, Poznań 2012
- Korybski A., *Alternatywne rozwiązywanie sporów w USA*, Lublin 1993
- Korybski A., "Analogy as a Basis of Precedential Reasoning," in: *Potential of Precedent in the Statutory Legal Order* (ed. L. Leszczyński, B. Liżewski, A. Szot), Berlin 2019
- Kosut A., "Dbałość o dobro zakładu pracy jako źródło obowiązku lojalności pracownika wobec pracodawcy, *Annales Universitatis Mariae Curie-Skłodowska*, Sectio G, Ius, 2018, Vol. LXV No. 2
- Kotarbiński T., *Traktat o dobrej robocie*, Wrocław 1975
- Król M., "Pojęcie luzu normatywnego stosowania prawa," *Państwo i Prawo* 1979 No. 6
- Kupiszewski H., *Prawo rzymskie*, Warszawa 1988,
- Kupiszewski H., Wołodkiewicz W., *Le droit romain et sa reception en Europe*, Varsovie 1978
- Kuryłowicz M., *Prawo i obyczaje w starożytnym Rzymie*, Lublin 1994
- Lande J., "Nauka o normie prawnej," in: J. Lande, *Studia z filozofii prawa*, Warszawa 1959
- Lang W., "Instrumentalne pojmowanie prawa a państwo prawa," *Państwo i Prawo* 1991, No. 12
- Lang W., Wróblewski J., Zawadzki S., *Teoria państwa i prawa*, Warszawa 1979
- Larenz K., *Lehrbuch des Schuldrechts*, München 1976
- Larenz K., *Methodenlehre der Rechtswissenschaft*, Berlin 1975
- Lee H.K., "Die Rezeption des europäischen Zivilrechts in Ostasien," *Zeitschrift für Vergleichende Rechtswissenschaft* 1987, Vol. 86
- Leidig G., *Dominante Werbung. Ziele, Wirkungen, rechtliche Gestaltung*, Frankfurt am Main 1979
- *Leksykon PWN*, Warszawa 1972

- Leszczyński L., "Dobre obyczaje zamiast zasad współżycia społecznego," *Rzeczpospolita* 30 I 1998
- Leszczyński L., "Extra-Legal Values un Judicial Interpretation of Law: A Model Reasoning and Few Examples," *International Journal for the Semiotics of Law / Revue international de Semiotique juridique* 2020, Vol. 33, No. 4,
- Leszczyński L., *Gyoseishido w japońskiej kulturze prawnej. Nieformalne działania administracji a prawo*, Lublin 1996
- Leszczyński L., "Implementing Prior Judicial Decisions as Precedents: The Context of Application and Justification," *International Journal for the Semiotics of Law / Revue international de Semiotique juridique* 2019, Vol. 33, No. 1
- Leszczyński L., *Klauzule generalne w stosowaniu prawa*, Lublin 1986
- Leszczyński L., "Wykładnia operatywna (podstawowe właściwości)", *Państwo i Prawo* 2009, No. 6
- Leszczyński L., "Kryterium 'konieczności w demokratycznym społeczeństwie' w Europejskiej Konwencji Praw człowieka – studium teoretycznoprawne," *Europejski Przegląd Sądowy* 2014, No. 1
- Leszczyński L., "Open Axiology in Judicial Interpretation of Law and Possible Misuse of Discretion," *Studia Iuridica Lublinensia* 2020, Vol. 29, No. 3
- Leszczyński L., "Precedent as an Argument of Judicial Interpretation," in: *Potential of Precedent in the Statutory Legal Order*, ed. L. Leszczyński, B. Liżewski, A. Szot, Berlin 2019
- Leszczyński L., *Tworzenie generalnych klauzul odsyłających*, Lublin 2000
- Levin J., *How Judges Reason. The Logic of Adjudication*, New York 1992
- Levy E., "The Reception of Highly Developed Legal Systems by Peoples of Different Cultures," *Washington Law Review* 1950, Vol. 25, No. 3
- Lizer-Klatka A., "Pojęcie orzekania na zasadach słuszności w międzynarodowym arbitrażu handlowym," *Państwo i Prawo* 2000, No. 1
- Liżewski B., "Klauzule generalne i ich funkcje w Europejskiej Konwencji Praw Człowieka," *Annales Universitatis Mariae Curie-Skłodowska*, Sectio G, Ius, 2016, Vol. LXIII, No. 2
- Liżewski B., *System prawa a porządek prawny. Między konstrukcją normatywną a prawem w działaniu*, Warszawa 2021
- Lllewellyn K.N., *Jurisprudence*, Chicago 1962
- Ludwikowska A.M., *System prawa Stanów Zjednoczonych*, Toruń 1999

- Ławnikowicz G., Pilipiec S., "Nieskazitelność charakteru i nieposzlakowana opinia w prawie prawniczych samorządów zawodowych," "*Annales Universitatis Mariae Curie-Skłodowska*, Sectio G, Ius, 2016, Vol. VXIII, No. 2
- Łętowska E., "Funkcjonowanie prawa cywilnego (Uwagi z perspektywy czterdziestolecia)," *Państwo i Prawo* 1984 No. 4
- Łopatka A., Ziembiński Z., "Próba systematyzacji zasad współżycia społecznego według orzecznictwa Sądu Najwyższego," *Państwo i Prawo* 1957, No. 4–5
- Łyda Z., "Funkcjonowanie klauzuli 'społeczno-gospodarczego przeznaczenia prawa," *Studia Iuridica Silesiana*, 1984, No. 9
- MacCormick D.N., Summers R.S., "Further General Reflections and Conclusions," in: *Interpreting Precedent. A Comparative Study* (ed. D.N. MacCormick, R.S. Summers), Dartmouth 1997
- MacCormick D.N., Summers R.S., "Introduction," in: *Interpreting Precedent. A Comparative Study* (ed. D.N. MacCormick, R.S. Summers), Dartmouth 1997
- Majer D., *Grundlagen der nationalistichen Rechtssystems: Führerprinzip, Sonderrecht, Einheitspartei*, Stuttgart 1987
- Malinowski B.,"Zwyczaj i zbrodnia w społeczności dzikich," in: B. Malinowski, *Dzieła*, Vol. 2, Warszawa 1984
- Maroń G., *Integralność religijna sędziego oraz argumentacja religijna w amerykańskim procesie orzeczniczym*, Rzeszów 2018,
- Marshall J.M., "Examining Judicial Decision-making: an Axiological Analytical Tool," *Studia Iuridica Lublinensia* 2020, Vol. XXIX, No. 3
- Marshall J.M., Kmetz M.D., Otstott G.A., "Stare decisis and Common sense in American Civil and Criminal Jurisprudence," *Studia Iuridica Lublinensia* 2018, Vol. XXVII, No. 1
- Martin J.E., Hanbury H.G., *Modern Equity*, London 1993
- Maskins G.L., "A Problem in the Reception of the Common Law in the Colonial Period," *University of Pennsylvania Law Review* 1949, Vol. XCVII
- Maurer H., *Allgemeines Verwaltungsrecht*, München 1985
- McDougal M.S., Lasswell H.D., Miller J.C., *The interpretation of International Agreements and World Public Order. Principles of Content and Procedure*, New Haven 1994
- Mincer M., *Uznanie administracyjne*, Toruń 1983
- Morawski L., *Główne problemy współczesnej filozofii prawa. Prawo w toku przemian*, Warszawa 1999

- Morawski L., "Instrumentalizacja prawa (zarys problemu)," *Państwo i Prawo* 1996, No. 6
- Morawski L., "Stressing – The Controversy between Judicial Pasivism and Activism," in: *Stressing Legal Decisions* (ed. T. Biernat, K.Pałecki, A. Peczenik, C.Wong, M. Zirk-Sadowski), Cracow 2004
- Morawski L., Zirk-Sadowski M.: "Precedent in Poland," in: *Interpreting Precedents. A Comparative Study* (ed. D.N. MacCormick, R.S. Summers), Dartmouth 1997,
- Mossbauer H., *Staatsaufsicht über die Wirtschafts*, Köln 1990
- Myślińska M., *Mediator w polskim porządku prawnym*, Warszawa 2018
- Nowacki J., *Analogia legis*, Warszawa 1966
- Nowacki J., "Niektóre zagadnienia zasad wspóżycia społecznego," *Państwo i Prawo* 1957, No. 7–8
- Nowacki J., *Prawo publiczne – prawo prywatne*, Katowice 1992
- Nowak L., *Interpretacja prawnicza. Studium z metodologii prawoznawstwa*, Warszawa 1973
- Nowicki M.A., *Europejska Konwencja Praw Człowieka. Wybór orzecznictwa*, Warszawa 1998
- Nowicki M.A., *Wokół Konwencji Europejskiej*, Kraków 2000
- Ohanowicz A., "Gloss to GKA decision of 17 VI 1968 r.," OSPiKA 1969 No. 6
- Ohta T., Hozumi T., "Compromise in the Course of Litigation," *Law in Japan. An Annual* 1973, Vol. 6
- Opałek K., Wróblewski J., *Zagadnienia teorii prawa*, Warszawa 1969
- Pałecki K., "Społeczne opinie o prawie i jego stosowaniu w dziedzinie stosunków rodzinnych," in: *Poglądy sołeczeństwa polskiego na stosowanie prawa* (ed. M. Borucka- Arctowa), Wrocław 1978
- Pałecki K., "Warianty oddziaływania prawem na stosunki rodzinne," in: *Prawo w społeczeństwie*, (ed. J. Kurczewski), Warszawa 1975
- Paszukanis J.B., *Ogólna teoria prawa a marksizm*, Warszawa 1985
- Pawełczyk M., "Uwagi o 'odsyłającym' charakterze klauzul generalnych," *Studia Iuridica Silesiana* 1984, Vol. 9
- Perelman C., *Logika prawnicza. Nowa retoryka*, Warszawa 1984
- Petrażycki L., *Wstęp do nauki polityki prawa*, Warszawa 1968
- Petrażycki L., *Wstęp do nauki prawa i moralności*, Warszawa 1959
- Podgórecki A., *Założenia polityki prawa*, Warszawa 1957

- Pomorski S., *American Common Law and the Principle Nullum Crimen Sine Lege*, Warszawa-Hague 1975
- Pound R., "A Survey of Social Interests," *Harvard Law Review* 1953, Vol. 57
- Pound R., "Common Law and Legislation," *Harvard Law Review* 1908, Vol. 21
- Pound R., *The Formative Era of American Law*, New Haven 1960
- Puttner G., *Wirtschaftsverwaltungsrecht*, Stuttgart 1989
- Radbruch G., "Statutory Lawfulness and Supra-Statutory Law (1946)," *Oxford Journal of Legal Studies* 2006, Vol. 26, No. 1
- Reve A., Ware A., "Interests in Political Theory," *British Journal of Political Science* 1983, Vol. 13, No. 4
- Redelbach A., Wronkowska S., Ziembiński Z.: *Zarys teorii państwa i prawa*, Warszawa 1992
- Rott-Pietrzyk E., "Interes spółki jako klauzula generalna," *Kwartalnik Prawa Prywatnego* 2005, No. 3
- Rümelin M., *Die Billigkeit im Recht*, Tübingen 1921
- Rzucidło-Grochowska I., "Argumenty interpretacyjne w pytaniach prejudycjalnych sądow polskich," in: *Wykładnia prawa Unii Europejskiej* (ed. L. Leszczyński), Vol. 3: System prawa Unii Europejskiej (ed. A. Wróbel), Warszawa 2019.
- Sadurski W., "Wartości chrześcijanskie, Trybunał i tolerancja," *Rzeczpospolita* 25 VIII 1994
- Safjan M., "Klauzule generalne w prawie cywilnym (przyczynek do dyskusji)," *Państwo i Prawo* 1990 No. 11
- Sartorius R.,"The Justification of the Judicial Decision," *Ethics* 1968, Vol. 78,
- Sawczuk M., "Uwagi o europejskim prawie sądowym cywilnym i o odrębnościach krajowego prawa sądowego," in: *Jednolitość prawa sadowego cywilnego a jego odrębności krajowe* (ed. M. Sawczuk), Lublin 1997
- Schmidt-Eichstaedt G., "Ermessen Beurteilungspielraum und eigenerantwortliche Handeln der Verwaltung," *Archiv des öffentlichen Rechts* 1973, No. 2
- Schmidt R., *Offentliches Recht. Allgemeine Teil*, Berlin 1990
- Schmidt R., "Wirtschaftspolitik, Wirtschaftsverwaltungsorganisation, Wirtschaftsforderung," in: *Besonderes Verwaltungsrecht. Ein Lehrbuch,* (ed. N. Achtenberg, G. Puttner), Heidelberg 1990
- Seidler G.L., *Z zagadnień filozofii prawa*, Lublin 1978
- Shaw J., *Law of the European Union*, New York 2000

- Skubiszewski K., "Prawa jednostki, umowy międzynarodowe i porządek prawny PRL," *Państwo i Prawo* 1981, No. 7
- *Słownik Języka Polskiego*, ed. M. Szymczak, Vol. I, Warszawa 1978
- *Słownik Języka Polskiego*, ed. W. Doroszewski, Vol. III, Warszawa 1961. Sołtys A., "Wykładnia prawa UE w orzecznictwie TK," in: *Wykładnia prawa Unii Europejskiej* (ed. L. Leszczyński), Vol. 3: System prawa Unii Europejskiej (ed. A. Wróbel), Warszawa 2019
- Starościak J., *Studia z teorii prawa administracyjnego*, Wrocław 1967
- Stelmachowski A., "Gloss to the SN Judgment of 28 V 1968, III CZP 23/69," OSPiKA 1970 No. 10
- Stelmachowski A., "Klauzule generalne w kodeksie cywilnym," *Państwo i Prawo* 1965 No. 1
- Stelmachowski A., "Prawotwórcza rola sądów," *Państwo i Prawo* 1967 No. 4–5
- Stelmachowski A., *Wstęp do teorii prawa cywilnego*, Warszawa 1984
- Stubenrauch M., *Commentar zür österreiche allgemeinen bürgerlichen Gesetzbuch*, Vol. I and II, Wien 1898
- Studnicki F., *Działanie zwyczaju handlowego w zakresie zobowiązań z umowy*, Kraków 1949
- Stober R., *Wirtschaftsverwaltungsrecht*, Stuttgart 1991
- Szabo I., "Pojęcie słuszności w różnych systemach prawnych," *Państwo i Prawo* 1971, No. 5
- Szot A., *Judicial Review of Admnistrative Discretion. The Influence of Court Decisions on Administrative Actions*, Berlin 2019
- Szot A., "Wykładnia prawa Unii Europejskiej w orzecznictwie WSA i NSA," in: *Wykładnia prawa Unii Europejskiej* (ed. L. Leszczyński), Vol. 3: System prawa Unii Europejskiej (ed. A. Wróbel), Warszawa 2019
- Takanayagi K., "Contact of the Common Law with the Civil Law in Japan," *The Japan Annual of Law and Politics* 1955, No. 3
- Tanese T., "The Urbanization of Lawyers and Its Functional Significance," *Law in Japan. An Annual* 1980, Vol. 13
- Taubenschlag R., *Rzymskie prawo prywatne*, Warszawa 1969
- Tkacz S., *Rozumienie sprawiedliwości w orzecznictwie Trybunału Konstytucyjnego*, Katowice 2003
- Tokarczyk R., *Komparatystyka prawnicza*, Kraków 1999
- Tokarczyk R., *Prawo amerykańskie*, Kraków 1999

- Tomaszek A., "Dobre obyczaje czy zasady współżycia społecznego," *Rzeczpospolita* 21 XI 1997
- Tuor P., *Das Schweizerische Zivilgesetzbuch*, Zürich 1934
- Van Hoecke M., *Law as Communication*, Oxford 2002
- Vernon M.C., "Authoritarian," in: *Dictionary of Political science* (ed. J. Dunner), Totowa 1970
- Wąsek A., *Kodeks karny. Komentarz*, Vol. I, Gdańsk 1999
- Wąsek A., "Prawo karne – minimum moralności?" *Annales Universitatis Mariae Curie-Skłodowska*, Sectio G, Ius, 1984, Vol. XXXI
- Wieacker F., *Das Römische Recht und das deutsche Rechtsbewusstsein*, Stuttgart 1944
- Wiedemann H., "Glos to the judgment of the BundesVerwassungsGericht of 19 X 1993 (1BvR 567 u.1044.89)," *Juristen Zeitung* 1994, No. 8
- Winiarz J., *Prawo rodzinne*, Warszawa 1980
- *Wirtschafts- und Aussenwirtschaftsrecht für ökonomen*, ed. G. Pflicke, Berlin 1977
- Wochelski J., "Zasady współżycia społecznego w projekcie kodeksu karnego PRL," *Ruch Prawniczy, Ekonomiczny i Socjologiczny* 1964, No. 1
- Wolff H. J., *Verwaltungsrecht I*, München 1961
- Wolter A., *Prawo cywilne. Zarys części ogólnej*, Warszawa 1977
- Wolter W., "W sprawie społecznego niebezpieczeństwa czynu i bezprawności," *Nowe Prawo* 1956, No. 2
- Wronkowska S., *Problemy racjonalnego tworzenia prawa*, Poznań 1982
- Wronkowska S., Zieliński M., *Problemy i zasady redagowania tekstów prawnych*, Warszawa 1993
- Wronkowska S., Zieliński M., Ziembiński Z., *Zasady prawa. Zagadnienia podstawowe*, Warszawa 1974
- Wronkowska S., Ziembiński Z., *Zarys teorii prawa*, Poznań 1997
- Wróblewski J., "Concepts of Legal System and Conceptions of Validity," *Acta Universitatis Lodziensis, Folia Iuridica* 1986, Vol. 24
- Wróblewski J., "Gloss to the SN Judgment of 19.01.1972. III CRN 471/71," OSPiKA 1973 No. 2
- Wróblewski J., "Prawo obowiązujące a 'ogólne zasady prawa, " *Zeszyty Naukowe Uniwersytetu Łódzkiego* Seria I, 1965, No. 42
- Wróblewski J., *Sądowe stosowanie prawa*, Warszawa 1988
- Wróblewski J., *Teoria racjonalnego tworzenia prawa*, Warszawa 1985

- Wróblewski J., *Wartości a decyzja sądowa*, Wrocław 1973
- Wróblewski J., *Zagadnienia teorii wykładni prawa ludowego*, Warszawa 1959
- Wyrzykowski M., *Pojęcie interesu społecznego w prawie administracyjnym*, Warszawa 1986
- Yamanaka K., "Kritische Betrachtungen über die Lehre von rechtsfreien Raum," *Kansai University Review of Law and Politics* 1984, No. 5
- Yntema H.E., "Equity in Civil and Common Law," *American Journal of Comparative Law* 1967 Vol. 16, No. 1–2
- Yokota M., "Japanese Judicial System in the New Constitution," *The Japan Annual of Law and Politics* 1959, No. 7
- Young M. K., "The Japanese Legal System, History and Structure," in: *Doing Business in Japan* (ed. Z. Kitagawa), New York 1986
- Zajadło J., *Formuła Radbrucha. Filozofia prawa na granicy pozytywizmu prawniczego i prawa natury*, Gdańsk 2001
- Zawłocki R., *Pojęcie i funkcje społecznej szkodliwości czynu w prawie karnym*, Warszawa 2007
- Zieliński M., *Poznanie sądowe – poznanie naukowe*, Poznań 1979
- Zieliński M., "Współczesne problemy wykładni prawa," *Państwo i Prawo* 1996, No. 8–9
- Zieliński M., *Wykładnia prawa. zasady, reguły, wskazówki*, Warszawa 2006
- Zieliński T., *Gloss to SN Judgment of 7 II 1967, III PRN 86/66*, OSPiKA 1968, No. 11
- Zieliński T., "Klauzule generalne w nowym porządku konstytucyjnym," *Państwo i Prawo* 1997, No. 12
- Zieliński T., *Klauzule generalne w prawie pracy*, Warszawa 1988
- Ziembiński Z., "Argumentacje moralne stosowane przez prawników," *Etyka* 1967, No. 2
- Ziembiński Z., *Etyczne problemy prawoznawstwa*, Wrocław 1972
- Ziembiński Z., *Logiczne podstawy prawoznawstwa*, Warszawa 1966
- Ziembiński Z., *Logika praktyczna*, Warszawa 1994
- Ziembiński Z., "Moralność jako czynnik kształtujący stosowanie prawa," *Etyka* 1969, No. 5
- Ziembiński Z., *Problemy podstawowe prawoznawstwa*, Warszawa 1980
- Ziembiński Z., "Stan dyskusji nad problematyką klauzul generalnych," *Państwo i Prawo* 1989, No. 3
- Ziembiński Z., *Teoria prawa*, Warszawa 1978

- Zimmermann J., *Motywy decyzji administracyjnej i jej uzasadnienie*, Warszawa 1981
- Zirk-Sadowski M., "Precedens a tzw. decyzja prawotwórcza," *Państwo i Prawo* 1980, No. 6
- Zirk-Sadowski M., *Rozumienie ocen w języku prawnym*, Łódź 1984
- Zirk-Sadowski M., "Tzw. prawotwórcza decyzja sądowego stosowania prawa," *Studia Prawnicze* 1980, No. 1–2
- Zweigert K., Kötz H., *An Introduction to Comparative Law*, Amsterdam 1977

List of abbreviations

- ABGB – Allgemeine bürgerliches Gesetzbuch (Austrian Civil Code of 1 VI 1811)
- BGB – Bürgelisches Gesetzbuch (German Civil Code of 18 VIII 1896)
- CBOSA – Centralna Baza Orzecznictwa Sądów Administracyjnych (Central Database of Judgments of Administrative Courts) – www.orzeczenia.nsa.gov.pl
- CJEU – Court of Justice of European Union
- CN – Code Napoleon (Code civil de Francais, French Civil Code of 21 III 1804)
- ECHR – European Convention for the Protection of Human Rights and Fundamental Freedoms
- ECtHR – European Court of Human Rights
- GKA – Główna Komisja Arbitrażowa (Polish Central Arbitration Commission)
- KC – Kodeks cywilny (Polish Civil Code of 23 IV 1964)
- KH – Kodeks handlowy (Polish Commercial Code of 27 VI 1934)
- KSH – Kodeks spólek handlowych (Polish Code of Commercial Companies of 15 IX 2000)
- KK of 1969 – Kodeks karny (Polish Penal Code of 19 IV 1969)
- KK of 1997 – Kodeks karny (Polish Penal Code of 6 VI 1997)
- KP – Kokeks pracy (Polish Labour Code of 26 VI 1974)
- KPA – Kodeks postępowania administracyjnego (Polish Code of Administrative Procedure of 14 VI 1960)
- KPC – Kodeks postepowania Ccywilnego (Polish Code of Civil Procedure of 17 XI 1964)
- KPK – Kodeks postępowania karnego (Polish Code of Criminal Procedure of 6 VI 1997)
- KRiO – Kodeks rodzinny i opiekuńczy (Polish Family and Guardianship Code of 25 II 1964)
- KZ – Kodeks zobowiązań (Polish Code of Obligations of 27 X 1933)
- NSA – Naczelny Sąd Administracyjny (Polish Supreme Administrative Court)
- ONSA – "Orzecznictwo Naczelnego Sądu Administracyjnego" (Jurisdiction of the Polish Supreme Administrative Court)

- ONSAiwsa – "Orzecznictwo Naczelnego Sądu Administracyjnego i wojewódzkich sądów administracyjnych" (Jurisdiction of the Polish Supreme Administrative Court and regional] administrative courts)
- OP – Ordynacja podatkowa (Polish Tax ordinance of 29 VIII 1997)
- OSNCP – "Orzecznictwo Sądu Najwyższego – Izba Cywilna, Pracy i Ubezpieczeń Społecznych"
- (Jurisdiction of the Polish Supreme Court – Civil, Labour and Social Insurance Chamber)
- OSNIC – "Orzecznictwo Sądu Najwyższego – Izba Cywilna" (Jurisdiction of the Polish Supreme Court – Civil Chamber)
- OSNKW – "Orzecznictwo Sądu Najwyższego – Izba Karna i Wojskowa " (Jurisdiction of the Polish Supreme Court – Penal and Military Chamber)
- OSP – "Orzecznictwo Sądów Polskich" (Jurisdiction of the Polish Courts)
- OSPiKA – "Orzeczncitwo Sądów Polskich i Komisji Arbitrażowych" (Jurisdiction of the Polish Courts and Arbitration Commissions)
- OTK – "Orzecznictwo Trybunału Konstytucyjnego" (Jurisdiction of the Polish Constitutional Tribunal)
- OTK ZU – "Orzecznictwo Trybunału Konstytucyjnego. Zbiór Urzędowy" (Jurisdiction of the Polish Constitutional Tribunal. Official Collection)
- PAG – ustawa o Państwowym Arbitrażu Gospodarcznym (Polish statute on the State Economic Arbitration of 23 X 1975)
- POPC of 1946 – Przepisy ogólne prawa cywilnego (Polish decree on general provisions of civil law of 12 XI 1946)
- POPC of 1950 – Przepisy ogólne prawa cywilnego (Polish statute on general provisions of civil law of 18 VII 1950)
- PPM – Prawo prywatne międzynarodowe (Polish statute on private international law of 12 XI 1965)
- PPSA – Prawo o postępowaniu przed sądami administracyjnymi (Polish Law on the proceedings before administrative courts of 30 VIII 2002)
- PRL Constitution – Konstytucja Polskiej Rzeczypospolitej Ludowej (Constitution of Polish Peoples' Republic of 22 VII 1952)
- PUSA – Prawo o ustroju sądów administracyjnych (Polish Law on the system of administrative courts of 25 VII 2002)
- RP Constitution – Konstytucja Rzeczypospolitej Polskiej (Constitution of the Republic of Poland of 2 IV 1997)
- SN – Sąd Najwyższy (Polish Supreme Court)
- TK – Trybunał Konstytucyjny (Polish Constitutional Tribunal)
- VCLT – Vienna Convention on the Law of Treaties of 22 V 1969
- ZGB – Zivil Gesetzbuch (Swiss Civil Code of 10 XII 1907)

Lex et Res Publica

Polish Legal and Political Studies

Edited by

Anna Jaroń

Vol. 1 Anna Jaroń: Socio-Economic Constitutional Rights in Democratisation Processes. An Account of the Constitutional Dialogue Theory. 2012.

Vol. 2 Stanisław Filipowicz: Democracy – The Power of Illusion. 2013.

Vol. 3 Teresa Dukiet-Nagórska (ed.): The Postulates of Restorative Justice and the Continental Model of Criminal Law. As Illustrated by Polish Criminal Law 2014.

Vol. 4 Agnieszka Kupzok: Enforcement of Patents on Geographically Divisible Inventions. An Inquiry into the Standard of Substantive Patent Law Infringement in Cross-Border Constellations. 2015.

Vol. 5 Alicja Jagielska-Burduk / Wojciech Szafrański: Legal Issues in Cultural Heritage Management. A Polish Perspective. 2016.

Vol. 6 Maciej Mataczyński (ed.): The Takeover of Public Companies as a Mode of Exercising EU Treaty Freedoms. 2017.

Vol. 7 Maciej Barczewski (ed.): Value of Information. Intellectual Property, Privacy and Big Data. 2018.

Vol. 8 Pawel Smoleń, Marcin Burzec: Introduction to Polish Tax Law. 2018.

Vol. 9 Łukasz Pohl, Konrad Burdziak: Judicial Interpretation of the 1997 Criminal Code Provisions on Self-Defence. 2019.

Vol. 10 Adam Szot: Judicial Review of Administrative Discretion. The Influence of Court Decisions on Administrative Actions. 2019.

Vol. 11 Michał Peno / Konrad Burdziak (eds.): The Concept of Modern Law. Polish and Central European Tradition. 2019.

Vol. 12 Leszek Leszczyński / Bartosz Liżewski / Adam Szot (eds.): Potential of Precedent in the Statutory Legal Order. 2019.

Vol. 13 Łukasz Bolesta: In Search of a Model for the Legal Protection of a Whistleblower in the Workplace in Poland. A legal and comparative study. 2020.

Vol. 14 Paweł Chmielnicki / Adam Sulikowski (eds.): New Perspectives on Legislation. A Comparative Approach. 2020.

Vol. 15 Marcin Burzec / Beata Kucia-Guściora / Paweł Smoleń: Agricultural Activity in Poland: A Fiscal and Legal Study. 2020.

Vol. 16 Magdalena Półtorak / Ilona Topa (eds.): Women, Children and (Other) Vulnerable Groups. Standards of Protection and Challenges for International Law. 2021.

Vol. 17 Josef Albert Fox: Die polnische Verfassung vom 3. Mai 1791. Hintergründe der Entstehung und der Außerkraftsetzung. Stellung Polens im Zeitalter der Aufklärung. 2021.

Vol. 18 Barbara Janusz-Pohl (ed.): Juvenile Justice Systems: Poland-Brazil-Portugal. 2021.

Vol. 19 Leszek Leszczyński: General Reference Clauses in the Judicial Process. Context of Legislative Intentions and Interpretative Discretion. 2021.

www.peterlang.com

www.ingramcontent.com/pod-product-compliance
Ingram Content Group UK Ltd.
Pitfield, Milton Keynes, MK11 3LW, UK
UKHW041825031026
15587UKWH00002B/557

9 783631 857892